DATE		

DISCARDED

D1236682

The Myth of the Fall

HAYDEN HUMANITIES SERIES

F. PARVIN SHARPLESS, *Series Editor*
Chairman, English Department
Germantown Friends School
Philadelphia, Pennsylvania

The Myth of the Fall

Literature of Innocence and Experience

F. PARVIN SHARPLESS

HAYDEN BOOK COMPANY, INC.
Rochelle Park, New Jersey

Library of Congress Cataloging in Publication Data

Sharpless, F   Parvin, comp.
   The myth of the fall.

  (Hayden humanities series)
  Includes bibliographical references.
   1. Fall of man—Literary collections.
2. English literature (Selections: Extracts, etc.)
3. American literature (Selections: Extracts, etc.)
I. Title.
PR1111.F27S5   820′.8   73-15830
ISBN 0-8104-5072-0

Printed in the United States of America

2   3   4   5   6   7   8   9   PRINTING

75 76 77 78 79 80 81 82   YEAR

Preface

The Hayden Humanities Series uses the term "humanities" in both a narrower and broader sense than in many examples of current curriculum structuring. We see humanities texts neither as conglomerations of stuff from literature, art, music, history, and philosophy purporting to express the spirit of a given time or place, nor as collections of readings supposedly illuminating vaguely suggested themes or subjects. Rather, we see them as focusing on the abiding ideas and values that men have wrestled with and lived by, as reflected through literature (broadly defined) and as informed by a variety of man-centered disciplines: psychology, sociology, anthropology, religion, philosophy, history.

The texts in this series deal with the significant human concerns upon which all human actions, great or small, social or individual, are based, whether we know it and admit it or not. These concerns are the stuff of all literature, yesterday and today; and they provide a background for recognizing, understanding, and defining the issues of the moment that claim our attention and wonder.

The approach in these texts is thematic, since such a structure has proved useful in traditional teaching units and in newer elective programs. But again there is a difference. The weakness of the thematic approach has been its tendency to yield units which are impossibly vague or impossibly broad, or both. What we have tried to do is declare and define an idea or issue thoughtfully and deeply so that others may test that declaration and definition through what they read and know, and find dealing with it a cumulative, organic experience, allowing growth and change.

In contrast to most thematically arranged anthologies, these texts do not pretend a faceless editor or the illusion of authorial objectivity or distance. The compiler has a voice and a point of view, and a conviction that he knows what he is talking about. The introductory essay both introduces and interprets; it defines an idea or issue—in this case *The Myth of the Fall: Literature of Innocence and Experience*—and then tries to see it in the round by explaining its past, asserting its continuing vitality and viability, and suggesting some of the things that can be done with it.

This approach takes us far beyond the usual "knowing about" or "talking about" to which literature is too often reduced. We believe the themes have lasting value as organizing constructs for making sense out of our world and for comprehending how the literary artist makes sense out of it. The themes also have a coherence that such thematic structures as, say, "Man and Society" or "Man and the Environment" or "War and Peace" cannot possibly have. One import of both these observations is that the question of "modern" literature vs. "classical" or "traditional" makes little real sense. Literature, by our lights, is always new and renewable. Forever is now. The idiom and the cultural demands and expectations may be different, but the underlying human concerns that the artist is examining are timeless and universal— and that's what counts.

The reader is not expected to agree with everything in the introduction, but is urged to consider it carefully; a casual reading won't do. The argument needs to be understood, and then questions must be raised about validity, emphasis, application, ramification, relevance to experience, and ultimate usefulness in ordering ideas, feelings, beliefs, and values. The defining essay should be a point of departure and a point of return. Along with the headnotes and questions for each group of selections, it serves as a guide for analysis and discussion, not as a gospel to be ingested, remembered, and regurgitated.

There is no attempt in these texts at coverage of literary periods or schools of writing, but there is a variety of genres, modes, backgrounds, times, and writers. Certain long works have been excerpted; enough has been included from any work to feed the thematic demands and yet not misrepresent the total piece. The aim throughout has been to show how widely diffused in our literature the central concern of each text has been and still is. In the final section, suggestions are made for reading full novels and plays that could not be included in a text of this size.

F. PARVIN SHARPLESS
Series Editor

Contents

The Myth of the Fall

What's hell but a cold heart?
—Theodore Roethke

Introduction

Among the various reasons, verified and hypothetical, which historians of literature and culture give for the existence of myths, we are choosing for our purposes the following explanation: Myths exist because they serve as ways of understanding something important, some issue of permanent and profound philosophic and moral concern. Myths express views about human existence and experience: about the Beginnings of things, of life, of society, about Creation and Destruction, about the Origins of Law, about Man's relationship to the gods or to God, about the lineal descent of Heroes and Warriors, about the origin of Evil figures and of Pain, Destruction, and Hatred. Mythology is not, therefore, an antique function, but rather a kind of metaphysical cement, a moral and psychological ballast, created by all cultures and times, and offering responses to the universal questions of mankind.

Such a view takes mythology seriously in a way somewhat beyond the usual study of the subject, which places it in a narrower literary, historical, or cultural context. The texts in this volume are important not for their connection with any particular historical or cultural period, nor for their place in the whole cultural tradition, nor for their support of modern poets' allusions. Rather, in a more profound sense, these poems, stories, and essays represent concerns of the most grave, universal, and humane sort. Thus, to know ourselves, we must know what these literary structures say.

The Matter of Adam

While such a brief account of our general intent may suffice, we need a more exact account of the reasons for the choice of the Myth of the Fall. What justifies singling out this old story for extended attention?

In an obvious sense, the Myth of the Fall is, both literally and figuratively, the first chapter of the most important literary work of Judeo-Christian culture. With the story of the Nativity and the account of the Crucifixion and Resurrection, it is the most widely known of all Biblical narratives and the most widely diffused into the consciousness of Western Civilization. In the formation of some of the fundamental theological doctrines of the Judeo-Christian tradition, particularly the ideas of the Creation and of Original Sin, the Myth has had at least as great an influence as the accounts of the life of Jesus. Moreover, references to the story of the Fall and its characters and setting and the development of its themes are well-nigh numberless in the works of poets, painters, and sculptors, both secular and sacred, popular and aristocratic. Indeed it can be argued that, considering its simple brevity, the story in chapter three of the Book of Genesis carries more weight per line than any other literary document one can think of.

The reasons for this importance are not hard to find. From a literary point of view the story of the Fall offers a rich variety of dramatic characters, situations, and themes. It offers opportunities to consider questions of the relationship of Man and God, Man and Nature, Man and Woman, Man and Evil, Man and his Past. It allows speculations on the nature of Evil, Guilt, Shame, Innocence, Temptation, Nudity, Erotic Love, and Modesty, as well as Rebellion, Authority, and the relations of Fathers and Sons, Parents and Children. It offers a large cast of characters and roles: Man Alone, Man as Gardener, Husband, Lover, Worker, Namer, Husbandman; it offers the Innocent Female, the Seductress, Woman as representative of Feminine Beauty, Sweetness and Love. It offers a splendid Villain, sometimes a Heroic Villain, and a Tempter, all portrayed with sophistication, urbanity and verbal excellence.

But neither these traditional uses of the Myth of the Fall, nor the dramatic and literary range of the story exhaust the explanations for its appeal. In the last century and a half, indeed, the dramatic and thematic vividness of the Myth has been noticed more and more by a variety of artists and writers. In part this is because the evolution of poetic consciousness in the 19th century produced a new and greater awareness, not only of myth in general, but specifically of the functions of the mythographers of the past and of the relationship between the poet's creative energy, his role as "maker," and the cultural function of mythic material. In particular, the Myth of the Fall has figured largely in modern poets' sense of myth because they have recognized similarities between the psychological and spiritual condition prevailing in modern consciousness and aspects of the story of Adam and Eve.

The consciousness which nineteenth century artists had—and which we still have—of man's alienation from his simpler natural past, of his greater independence of traditional social and moral ideas, created a special interest in the idea of the Adam figure, himself newly free and cast out of his simple Edenic world into a new condition, facing alone and unguarded the necessity of forming principles of action and creating meaning for his life. Other writers perceived parallels between their contemporaries' mass of new knowledge and the condition of the fallen Adam, possessed of sudden knowledge yet uncertain of its consequences. Still other writers noticed parallels between their own era's growing affluence and a decreasing dependence on crude physical labor for survival, and Eden's fruit-filled, self-sufficient garden, requiring no work by its inhabitants.

Each of these perspectives offers many possibilities for elaboration in fiction, drama, and poetry; each offers a basic story, a set of issues and circumstances, a variety of moral and psychological questions, Yet each is open and flexible enough to be adapted by a particular artist to his own time and place and to the insights of his own imagination.

Innocence and Experience

At the heart of this story's vitality and force, whether in ancient or modern versions, is its expression of the most central fact of human experience and the commonest of human discoveries: the experience of growth and change, the recognition that the world is more complicated, ambiguous, and risky, more full of temptations and difficulties than we, as innocent children, had known; the sense, often acquired suddenly and sometimes with shock and pain, that we are not today as we were yesterday. The basic pattern of the story, then, is the Encounter of an innocent person with Knowledge, and the irrevocable change which it causes in him—the permanent alteration of his consciousness and moral perceptions. Finally, and most important, there is the question of how this change is to be lived with, whether it is good or evil, whether its result is positive, resulting in growth, or negative, resulting in bitterness.

Whether we see the story of the Fall as a representation of the growth of individual consciousness and the advent of self-sufficient maturity, or as the account of sinful, childlike disobedience, the story allows us to consider how man grows from child to adult, to understand something of the changes produced by time and experience, and to come to terms with the complexity of good and evil. Since the myth is one of growth, it is *the* myth for the young, for the coming of age; it is the myth of the *rite de passage,* of knowing something today that one did not know yesterday.

Finally, because the story emphasizes youth, because Adam and Eve are in a verdant Virgin Land, without the weight of an historical past, without social forms and traditions, the Adam story and the Myth of the Fall become *the* American story. More than any other, this myth has loomed large in the imaginations of American artists. Hawthorne, Melville, James, Twain, Whitman, Faulkner, Hemingway, Salinger, and many others have dealt with the theme, specifically and repeatedly, as if it represented an essential aspect of their existence as Americans. As R.W.B. Lewis says,

> For what some novelists were to discover was that the story implicit in American experience had to do with an Adamic person, springing from nowhere, outside time, at home only in the presence of nature and God, who is thrust by circumstances into an actual age. American fiction grew out of the attempt to chart the impacts which ensued, both upon Adam and upon the world he is thrust into.

American fiction is the story begotten by the noble but illusory myth of the American Adam.°

In all these ways the Myth of the Fall is a kind of allegory of the basic processes of psychological growth—the construction out of unformed, raw data of patterns and designs, providing the elemental structuring of human experience needed for knowing and learning of the world. Adam is Man, the First Man, but he is also the First Child, the Child of God, the Guilty Child, the Punished Child, the Disillusioned Child. He is the Child Leaving Home, making his painful and courageous way without his Father's protection; he is the first to encounter Deceit, Duplicity, and Evil and to recognize that the words of others may not mean what they seem. He is the first to encounter the idea of Self, to be self-conscious, to know that he is alive and that he must die. He is the first to recognize the difference between Good and Evil and to deal with the choices which such knowledge requires. He is the first to know that life requires him to *know*, but he has yet to learn what Knowledge means.

What Adam Learned: The Encounter with Knowledge

In Latin the word innocent means "uninjured." It is a strange, negative idea—a definition by exclusion. The word implies accidents which are expected and certain to occur. It suggests that injury is the common state and that to be uninjured is to be contrary to the normal state of things. But though the injury of the Fall causes pain, this particular pain is mental, spiritual, or psychological, and the source of the pain is not a physical blow, but an idea—knowledge. Thus Innocence is a state of "unknowledgeability," or simply, of ignorance, lack of awareness, unconsciousness. But ignorance is not the same as stupidity. The Ignorance of the Innocent lies in his not being aware of ideas or experiences which are well within his intellectual range. He *can* know them; he will know them; but he does not know them yet. It is the kind of simplicity associated, both in life and in art, with the child: an innocence and ignorance, and an ignorance that one is ignorant. We do not know that we are innocent; we only discover that we were.

The opposite of innocence is therefore knowledge, a knowledge created by experience. Knowledge is created by something having happened. Knowledge must be preceded by an Encounter, an event which creates complexity in the mind where before there was simplicity. And as-

---

°From R.W.B. Lewis, *The American Adam: Innocence, Tragedy and Tradition in the Nineteenth Century.* Chicago, 1955.

sociated with the Encounter is a distinct and absolute change, for the Experience creates a new condition, a change from the old: the condition of having or being Fallen. With this kind of experience there is a before and an after, and they are radically different because knowledge is the kind of experience which cannot be undone; one cannot learn a fact and then unlearn it, or "unknow" it. One can forget the fact, but that usually means it was unimportant. Important events are permanent; they take possession of a permanent place in our consciousness, and once fixed, become a part of our experience and our view of things.

Thus the Fall is an awareness of irrevocable Change, Growth, and Process, and especially of the passage of Time. Maturity brings an inevitable sense of one's life being lived and one's knowledge being earned along the way, in change, in the midst of the passage of time, as well as an awareness of flow and movement, both in the "stream" of ideas through the mind, and in the movements from youth to age, birth to death. But the Innocent lives in a timeless world where the sunrise is always the same, where each day repeats the events of the day before and consciousness is not changed.

With the closing of the gates of Eden behind the Adam figure, he is transferred from a timeless and unconscious world of animal cycles to one of linear progressive awareness. He now has a past, and is uncertainly setting forth toward a future. Tomorrow will be different. Experience has occurred, and knowledge has changed him permanently and absolutely. He cannot go home again. Thus in mythic fiction we often see the Adam figure on a journey through time, on the road, or the river, or the trail, or a voyage: Huck Finn, Ahab, the frontiersman on his horse, more recently the rider on his motorcycle. Each situation suggests movement, change, and becoming—not being. And the movement is always outward bound, beyond the frontier, into the woods, into the sunset, out of Eden toward a new place, toward a new and unknown experience and its consequences.

The transition period between this Before and this After usually involves a certain amount of pain. The transformation from Innocence to Experience is associated with psychological traumas of one kind or another. Between the child and the man, between the then and now, between ignorance and knowledge there occurs a rearrangement of values, of views of self and the world, which is achieved at a cost. The very term "Fall" indicates this: Falling hurts—whether it causes skinned knees, broken bones, or darker and graver psychological changes in character. Yet why should the process which the Myth of the Fall describes come to be seen as Evil? Why should the gaining of experience and the loss of simplicity, of knowing more today than yesterday, acquire a connection with Sin, Error, and Pain? Is there no choice between ignorance and the Fall into painful experience? Can't the Fall be positive? Suppose we change the metaphor and call the experience a "Rise" instead of a Fall; does this alter the possibilities of the experience for the good?

Such questions are central to the Myth, because in one way or another all versions of the story, especially the modern ones, are more interested in Adam after the Fall than before. Indeed, to some, Adam in the state of Innocence is a bit of a bore. If the Fall is inevitable, one may ask: In what way might it be a positive experience? How can the fruits of knowledge be combined with natural goodness? How can man come to terms with experience and learn to live with the different sense of himself which his new perceptions give him?

What Adam Learned: Some Readings of the Pattern

The answers to the above questions will vary according to the work itself and the attitudes of any given reader. The Genesis version of the story for, example, can be understood in a number of ways. Even the simplest reading suggests that Adam's sin was more than disobedience of God's prohibition against eating forbidden fruit. Implicit in the story is the idea that the damage was done, that the decisive change in human consciousness occurred, not when Adam disobeyed, but when he became conscious of the idea of Disobedience. It is not the act itself, then, that is important, but the idea of the act, the consciousness that an act contrary to God's will is possible; it is the realization by Adam and Eve that they can decide for themselves whether to obey or disobey. In fact, God's prohibition presented no problem at all so long as it remained unquestioned. But when Adam and Eve became aware (how they find out is itself an interesting question) that they have what is called Free Will (though it is not always free), that unlike the beasts in the garden they have an intelligence which offers them behavioral choices, then life acquires new possibilities and new problems. Thus, the Knowledge of Good and Evil is the same as Knowledge itself: an awareness of the difference between two courses of action, and an awareness that man has the powers to choose between them.

This power has a simple biological basis in the difference between the instinctive, unselfconscious mental activity of "lower" forms of animal life, and the self-conscious awareness of human beings. Such distinctions are not absolute and clear, and the "amount" of consciousness possessed by different species and within a species itself varies over a wide range. We notice also that some men are more self-conscious, more fully aware than others. Indeed, the importance of the Myth of the Fall to the creative person may well come from the poet's sense of the difference between his own special degree of awareness and that of lower, less conscious beings around him, whether human or animal. (This is suggested by the relationship of Adam to the birds, beasts, and other forms of life over which he was given dominion.) Also, the feeling of alienation from the simple life, from the uncomplicated round of daily tasks, which the Fall to consciousness describes, is one of the basic characteristics of the artist and provides one of his most important psychological tensions.

Inseparable from the idea of Disobedience is the idea of Guilt, the feeling of hostility toward oneself which arises from an awareness of the difference between the idea of oneself as doing or having done Right, of being Obedient, and the idea of oneself as doing or having done Evil, being Disobedient. Guilt, it should be noted, does not need action to exist; the *idea* of Disobedience, or of the possibility of doing wrong, is sufficient to evoke the feeling. This distinction between thoughts and acts of Evil or disobedience emphasizes the special human quality of imagination—the ability, not possessed by lower forms of life, to consider possibilities of action before performing any act, to think of things one might do without actually doing them. It is this "subjunctive" sense that makes moral choice between Good and Evil possible, and it is the comparison of conflicting courses of action that makes guilt possible. Guilt is experienced when one compares the action taken with an idea of a better action: the Real versus the Ideal. Adam and Eve felt guilt as soon as they remembered that they could have been obedient.

What Adam learned was a simple but important fact about his own character. He learned that he was able to entertain the idea of disobedience of God's prohibition. He came to know that he could give rational consideration to a moral question; he could know Evil in the abstract, apart from action, and afterwards, having acted, he could reflect equally well on the unchosen alternative and compare it with the one chosen. He also had to accept and resolve the new view of his own character which this knowledge implied.

The Origins of Evil: Self, Society, and the Other

The Myth of the Fall represents growth: either a biological and evolutionary change in the human species from less to more conscious psychological capability, or an individual development from childhood to maturity. This process brings men into an encounter with some form of Evil, which may originate either in man's own nature, in his social environment, in the psychological condition in which human beings live, or in some distinct Other, some great Adversary.

The best-known explanation of Evil is that which is usually referred to as the doctrine of Original Sin, elaborated in traditional Christian theology. While a great many complicated (and often obscure) things have been written about this idea, it says essentially that man is Evil, by nature or by definition, which amounts to the same thing. He simply is that way, given to Disobedience, Error, Sin, and a host of violations of specific commandments. Since he *is* evil, he easily and naturally thinks up evil acts. Men do evil because they are evil; they disobey because they are disobedient.

Now it is not difficult to notice a certain circularity to this argument. We can avoid it, however, by supposing a very literal geneology of man's descent from Adam, and by reasoning that Adam fell into evil through some peculiar weakness or error which has been transmitted to all his descendants (all men) by a biological process, through the genes as it were, such as parents might transmit a tendency to nearsightedness or to an overfondness for certain foods and drinks. But even if we can explain satisfactorily the transfer of moral attributes through biological processes, we are left with other difficulties: the unfairness of all subsequent generations' being stuck with an evil they had no choice in, and the question of why God in His Omnipotence should have given poor Adam a moral dilemma he was incapable of coping with, especially if he was to be responsible for all of posterity.

The doctrine of Original Sin makes better sense, however, if we say that the idea of disobedience occurs naturally in the process of human growth, without the requirement of outside assistance. At some point in a child's life, even a happy child in a loving family, the idea of disobedience will occur to him as a function of his relationship with his parents. In a sense this happens because any prescription about behavior requires the idea of its opposite. "Do this" implies the possibility of not doing it. As we have noticed above, the child need not act upon the disobedient idea; but from the moment he conceives it, his life is more complicated, his liability to guilt is increased, and his sense of the world is more mature. According to this view Evil is not so much in man's nature as in his intelligence; and it is more meaningful to say that the doctrine of Original Sin refers to this intellectual capacity rather than to a natural and malicious tendency toward evil which is present in all deceitfully sweet-faced children. If intelligence is a measure of man's humanness, and if it is intelligence which allows or requires him to know what moral choices lie before him, then man's problem *is* Original—i.e., inherent in what he is.

Others see the source of Evil in Society. Evil, the argument runs, is a part of man because of the inevitable conflicts in his natural environment, conflicts which pit one man's interests and welfare and happiness inalterably against another's. Man lives in a world where there is more hunger than food, more work to be done than energy to do it, more aggressive and sexual energy than available satisfactions for it, more insecurity of ego than consolation. Therefore, some people get more of the world's pleasures, some less. Where survival depends upon triumph in a contest for limited resources, there must be losers. To men trying to survive, the thought quickly follows: "If someone has to be a loser, better you than me." Evil, therefore, is not the result of an inherent aspect of human nature, but is caused by instinctive competitive energies brought into play by environmental adversity.

Such an argument has a pleasing simplicity, which accounts perhaps for the popularity of current arguments about territorial imperatives and naturally aggressive behavior, and the value of competition. But this view does not fit the Myth of the Fall, because the action of the Myth takes place in a lush Garden, with plenty of fruit on all sides. Adam and Eve, it seems, lived in an affluent society and could not blame the environment for their trouble. Theirs was the Peaceable Kingdom, where the lion lay down with the lamb, no one ate meat, and nature was not red in tooth and claw.

But the view which is most important in literary treatment of the myth is that which sees Evil originating outside the self, but in a specific human or adversary force rather than in the environment at large. It is this Other who has the idea of Disobedience in his head, who maliciously plots to suggest the idea to the Innocent who would otherwise never have thought of it. This notion has the advantage of allowing individuals to place the blame on others, to find some scapegoat who is responsible for Evil rather than reproaching themselves. It also offers a number of literary and dramatic possibilities: a dramatic Encounter between Innocence and Evil, a Villain who confronts Goodness, and a variety of extended conflicts and modes of contest between the Evil One and the Innocent. This explanation does not, as a rule, directly answer the question of where the Evil One himself came from, but it does allow speculations about his personality, including the possibility that he might at one time have been an Innocent himself.

The Encounter and the Vision of Hell

The psychological and symbolic impact of this Adversary Theory of Evil finds its greatest support in the fact that our knowledge of Evil is usually increased through the influence of someone else. Indeed, though we are quite capable of discovering the idea of Disobedience by ourselves, our awareness of its reality is often verified by the testimony and actions of others; and our own tendency toward the possibility of evil behavior is strengthened and reinforced by others who attest to the same feeling. It is therefore in the social encounter between people that the existence of Evil is verified, so that at one time or another we may all play Satan. It is indeed possible that given the dependency of the child upon others, his sense of the reality of Evil is entirely dependent upon their suggesting it to him.

We come, therefore, to an important point in our understanding of the basic form and meaning of the Myth of the Fall. In its purest and simplest form the Encounter between Innocence and Evil represents an elemental philosophic struggle over the gravest and most consequential moral questions: whether man's nature *is* fallen, morally weak, flawed, degenerate, selfish, aggressive, hostile, fuller of hate than love; and whether the social community in which man lives must reflect this nature. The conflict symbolized by the encounter between Innocence and Evil is a conflict between faith in man's goodness—i.e., in his capacity for love, charity, kindness, and benevolence, and in the degree to which these qualities can and do prevail in human affairs—and doubt about that Goodness.

In this conflict the basic position of the Evil One, of the Satanic Adversary (or the Satan figure), is simply that of doubt, negation, cynicism, lack of faith, and despair of any redemptive view of human beings. The Adversary is the original Nay-sayer and Skeptic. He rejects the existence of all virtues, calling them foolish, sentimental fictions, and he hates and derides those who would uphold them. He has, literally and figuratively, lost his faith.°

To hold such a view is itself a form of punishment, and to hold it is also to recognize the source of the particular pains associated with the Fall. For though one may not doubt all good qualities all the time, as the Adversary does, any Fall is associated with a loss of faith in some positive belief, some affirmation of love, some childish simplicity one used to cling to. To live in a world where *all* such beliefs, all goodness, all honesty, all straightforward professions of virtue are suspect is to suffer psychologically and spiritually in the most agonizing way. In such a world all motives are impure, every action is self-seeking, and every gesture of goodwill conceals a sinister skepticism. In such a world no community of interest is possible, no bonds of truth or understanding, no loyalty, no fidelity to brotherhood or love. To live with a vision of such a world prevailing in one's mind is to live, as Satan does, in Hell.

We may wonder why, cursed with the peculiar vision which makes living a Hell, the Adversary, or any person so extremely Fallen, seeks to destroy the Innocent. Why doesn't he remain in splendid isolation, clutching his own bitterness and disillusionment to his breast; or finding himself alone in a world where there is neither love nor virtue, why not do away with himself and end his misery? There are two obvious reasons why he

---

°There is a three-stage development to this loss of faith. *1.* The individual conceives the idea of Evil out of his own intelligence, but, seeing no verification from others, thinks that it is a mistaken view. *2.* He meets an Evil from outside, a disillusionment which makes his inner sense real. *3.* Since the source of Evil was seen as Good before its true colors were revealed, it is easy to extend the idea that all appearances of Good might be Evil and to proceed as if they are.

does not. First, he sees himself as a participant in a philosophic contest with the Innocent for possession of the Innocent's soul; the outcome will determine whose view of the world will prevail. Thus to a fallen person, to the disbeliever and cynic, any unfallen profession of virtue represents a challenge, because the Innocent, by his innocence, preserves his happiness. This happiness in turn testifies to the existence of a set of values which the Fallen One, try as he might, can no longer believe in, and represents the awful possibility that he may be wrong and his terrible suffering may be unnecessary. In a sense, the Satan figure says that if he must live without love, everyone else must as well. By destroying someone else's faith, by converting the Innocent's Belief to Doubt, he will have proved again that his view is the correct one, that doubt is stronger than faith.°

There is also another view of Satan's motives. Perhaps he is himself looking to be redeemed, hoping that innocence will prevail against him, that his faith will be restored by the strength of the positive assertion which the Innocent makes in the face of the contrary principle. If the faith and love which Satan assails are strong enough, they will not only save the Innocent from falling, they will "deconvert" the Adversary, and he will emerge from the Encounter with his faith restored, his confidence in his previous innocence reinstated. At least, such is the theory.

It has often been observed that from a dramatic point of view, Evil is more interesting than Good; and a number of writers who have handled this theme, especially Milton, have been accused of preferring Satan to Adam or to God's Unfallen Angels. While it is probably not true that Milton's moral sympathy lay with Satan, it is true that he may have recognized that Satan's problem is the most human, and that his difficulties are those which most human beings can understand and sympathize with. For it is Satan's battle, the one which takes place *after* the Fall, rather than the Innocent's struggle, which we undergo from day to day in our lives. Similarly, we recognize that it takes exceptional talent to fall far: the more deeply one loves, the greater the danger of being hurt; the more passionate one's beliefs, the more bitter their loss. This nobility of belief, which leads to an equal depth of suffering, is what the mythology refers to in recounting Satan's history as the first and highest of the angels. Only from such a height can such a depth be reached.

The Fall and the Average Man

The psychological and moral validity of this Myth is clearly reflected in our lives. The kinds of disillusionment and injury which are central to

---

°To identify this Satanic strategy, think of the ways in which embittered adults—parents and teachers—take it upon themselves to disillusion their children.

the Fall Myth are not limited to a few mythical characters undergoing special moral tests, but apply (as good mythology should) to a wide range of human experiences—to various kinds of learning and to the continual interplay in human lives of those forces, situations, circumstances, and experiences which support or cast doubt on belief and faith and love. Nor should it be difficult for anyone to recognize in his own life those events, times, places, and people which strengthened his faith, or, unfortunately, to remember more sharply those which had the opposite effect. Indeed, every man, were he a mythographer, could write his own Fall story, dramatizing the occasions in his life when certain kinds of experience and new knowledge darkened his childish day and made him sadder and wiser.

Since we all undergo this experience, it may be worth our while to look at a few of the rules and principles by which it occurs, and then to turn to some of the specific characteristics of the experience.

The severity of the experiences and the effects they have on the individual vary with a number of factors. One important factor is timing. There seems to be, in the course of human development, a natural progression of the level of consciousness of maturity or experience. If the timing is right, if the experience is somehow properly related to the development of the individual, he can accept almost anything he learns and integrate it into his mind and personality, where it can contribute to growth, without bitterness or trauma. There is a time for everything, and trouble occurs only when one learns too much either too soon or too late. Indeed the *danger* seems to lie not in the particular truths at all, but in the time, level, circumstances and severity of their appearance. Growth occurs when a new truth or experience is confidently faced and learned. Problems that we can solve happily are "good problems." Fear, anxiety, and blocking occur when the experience is too severe or our confidence too weak.

Another general rule seems to be that the danger of being "hurt," of suffering a destructive Fall experience, is greater where our innocence is most exposed. This usually happens where we have made the most extended and perhaps unrealistic leap of faith. Such leaps leave us vulnerable, and the Satan figure is particularly aware of our weakness in that situation. The commonest case is where, usually due to weakness or to fear, we have placed too great faith in the competence or goodness of some authority figure: a parent, a teacher, a national leader, or the Providence of God. Where we have assumed too much unrealistically, we are most susceptible to disillusionment and its pains. Or, we feel most hurt where our good gestures have been taken advantage of; where honesty or directness on our part is used by others against us; when a confidence is betrayed, a promise broken. The degree to which we extend such straightforward policies is the degree to which we are liable to injury if they are not returned in kind. He who trusts no one will rarely be fooled.

Learning through the Fall

Disillusionment begins at home. Indeed, the process of growing up can be defined in terms of the things we do and do not lose faith in. It takes no special intelligence or sensitivity for a young person to undergo an almost daily recognition that things are not as simple as they seemed yesterday, to become aware today that the world is more complex, more subtle, more ambiguous, and perhaps more dangerous than it appeared. We see, looking back, that our simple interpretations of experience, while comforting, were those of a child, and that to retain them is to remain morally and intellectually childish. Yet learning costs—sometimes a little, sometimes a lot—and it is this learning process, the coming of age theme, that figures so largely in literature as a representative of the variety· of patterns of the Fall into knowledge that occur to the child growing up.

The first necessary Fall is from the womb to the squalling, backside-slapping real world. The unborn child grows, surrounded by a warm, sustaining environment, without conflict. From this Eden, the child suffers a birth, a setting out, a traumatic going from the Garden into the World, becoming separate, on his own, experiencing almost immediately conflicts between his needs and the sources of their gratification. This is not a mere metaphor. Many child psychologists feel that one of the distinctive aspects of human development is the suddenness with which the child must adapt to life on his own and to the prolonged period of dependency which learning to survive in the outside world requires. What one must learn is the difference between the self and the mother; and this begins at birth.

It is obvious that the child-parent relationship determines very significantly how much trust the child learns to have in the world, in experiences, and in his relationship to others. The first human bond the newborn, newly isolated infant knows is with the mother. If that relationship produces trust and warmth, if it sets a pattern of reliability and order, the child will be able to view the world as a trustworthy place, where his powers to create order and relationships may themselves be trusted and creatively exerted. If, on the other hand, the mother-child relationship produces suspicion and mistrust, if parents offer rude punishment and disillusionment, then the child's belief in the possibilities of an affirmative relationship with the world of experience and learning, and with other human beings will be severely, and perhaps permanently, damaged.

Another form in which the Fall is experienced occurs with the realization on the part of the child of limitations in the parents' power to protect him from harm. Some events—accidents, sickness, other catastrophes—are beyond human control. Even in happy, well-run, loving homes, the child is required to recognize the dangerous, cruel, random, and irrevocable aspects of such dangers. For many children it is the idea of death—made tangible by the sudden disappearance of a grandparent or schoolmate, with its accompanying solemnities—that demonstrates a range of experience beyond human control. Other events are threatening because of parents' shortcomings. The discovery that a father or mother can make mistakes, become confused, suffer embarrassment, ineptitude or weakness, exhibit tears or anger, just as a child can, may bring about a sudden awareness of a dimension of experience the child has not grasped before.

Related to this experience is the child's sense of his own vulnerability to the same forces. He must, for example, recognize the inevitability of his own death, that his own life is subject to a final, absolute limitation. The discovery of this fact does not require any special experience, no extraordinary traumatic event. Like so many kinds of knowledge, it comes inevitably with time and growing perceptions. Beyond this, the child must come to understand the randomness of human activity, the existence of meaningless bad luck, accidental injury, purposeless misfortune and coincidence: diseases contracted without regard to justice (e.g., colds one catches in spite of overshoes while someone not wearing them remains healthy), right turns when a just-as-easy left turn would have saved the day, the turn of ordinary destiny one meets when, for example, a letter arrives too late or too early. The child must learn lessons of the same kind from history: the fates of millions resting on the eccentricities of a states-man's personality or determined by foolish ignorance and blundering, the wicked who flourish while the good die young. In short, we begin to recognize that to a degree, happiness or misery, success or failure, depend upon silly circumstances wrapped in the fabric of experience which are beyond human control and even beyond understanding. Such knowledge makes it harder to achieve meaning for one's life, and harder to sustain meaningful action; such events encourage doubt and skepticism, making it more difficult to plan and to believe that one's actions can have fore-seeable results.

Then there are the social causes of the Fall. We learn that society is an imperfect, inaccurate mechanism. Instead of simple, natural relation-ships, of mutual order and dependency, we have huge abstract formali-ties, complex organizations and impersonal laws and judges, institutions which make relationships between people formal and cold. Futhermore, society unconsciously imposes forms of behavior, habits and expectations, manners, traditions, and unanalyzed beliefs, and becomes unresponsive to one's personal situation. A nation may make war when its citizens do not wish it and conscript men to fight for causes in which they do not believe in places that would be better off without them. Finally, society encourages special evils—vanity, materialism, technological complexity and excessive ambition—which stifle man's natural goodness and chance at fulfillment. The Fall, then, can be seen as the fall from individual blessedness to the corporate order, from the Garden to the Town or City, where the group's needs take precedence over the individual's.

In many ways, the most important psychological form of the Fall is the Fall of the Self to Consciousness of itself. Time produces knowledge of the necessary errors and frailties of life. We recognize the limitations of our ambitions, our idealism, and our aspirations for goodness, love and happiness. Our own ability to manifest these qualities is imperfect; we make mistakes and act selfishly and badly. And even if we were perfectly able to act in accord with our intentions, others may not always understand our motives; thus our good intentions turn sour, our gestures of love are met with chilliness and rejection. We may come to acknowledge also the force of the Unconscious, which hides our own motives from us, and reveals to us the complexity of motivation in all human beings, and the difficulty of knowing the nature and needs of the Self—either one's own self or that of others.

Such thoughts may lead us to value the *forms* of behavior, to restrain our spontaneity and natural sincerity. We learn that things sometimes do indeed go better when we act in ways that we do not feel, that at times honesty may not be the best policy. We learn that Good and Evil are more often determined by the situation in which we encounter them, by circumstances, than they are by absolute laws, commandments, and precepts. And we learn how difficult moral and ethical behavior become as a result of such knowledge.

Redemption

Does this then mean that we all must fall to Evil Knowledge? Have we no choice but the bitter one between simple innocence—remaining sweet, pure, and virginal, clinging to mother's skirts, untested by life— and a cynical worldly wisdom which sees selfish egocentricity on all sides, and treats every human encounter with suspicion and a calculation of how to take advantage? Or are we not offered a choice? For it may be that Innocence is too fragile to prevail, whether we would have it so or not, even though Evil is unattractive and those who are most convinced of its truth rarely seem very happy about it.

We also need to understand if it is possible somehow to gain knowledge without becoming Evil; to learn about failure, disloyalty, human fallibility, death, time, accident and fate, social impersonality, parental weakness, injustice, complexity of motivation, the difference between ideal and real, illusion and fact—in short, to grow up—without also imbibing bitterness, hostility, alienation, and coldness of heart. Can we become older and wiser without becoming sadder and angrier?

The main thing to realize is that without some confrontation with these facts, no affirmation, opinion, set of beliefs, or attitudes toward life are of much substance or weight. No affirmation of value can be worth much unless it is founded on experience and acknowledges those questions which seem to contradict it. To affirm from the safety and affluence of suburban homes and classrooms or expensive college dormitories that sweetness and goodwill will prevail against poverty is no more convincing than to proclaim the virtues of the simple life from the seat of a sports car. We may see the process of the Fall, therefore, as offering the necessary testing and rigors of growth by which Innocence is tempered to a tougher, more potent and adult condition. The Innocent "rises" to a maturity in which a solid affirmation of the positive qualities of Innocence, now qualified by knowledge, becomes possible.

The story of this rise to knowledge, recounted in different fashions and settings and with the varieties of viewpoint and emphasis which the range of human experience allows, is what the selections in this volume are all about. They offer not only the ordinary stuff of serious art—the experience of knowing how other human beings feel and live—but the way these human beings feel and respond in the face of the painful increase of knowledge. To learn this, and to learn to respond positively to this most common of all human dramas, is the "problem" set by this volume, and the task set by life.

*   *   *

In the Beginning ... Some Opening Considerations

The texts which follow are not designed to offer pat illustrations of the thesis of this book. If the artist has anything new to offer it is the difference between his work and the literary tradition he is using, the unique application of intelligence and sensitivity, and his use of the forces and ideas of his own historical moment. Thus each work should be looked at with the aim of understanding its particularity, the nuances of its own style and point of view; and the reader must bring sympathy and openness to each author's vision.

The explicit questions appended to the texts that follow grow out of the premises of the introductory essay. They do not rule out other, more traditional questions about these works. Considerations of chronology, biography and history, as well as textual analysis, are as appropriate here as elsewhere. What is hoped, however, is that the consistent focus and direction of the works and the suggested questions will offer a clearer idea of the relationship between works of different genres and periods, and identify some of the forces that give these works their power.

The general questions which follow here need not be "answered" or even addressed directly, either before or after reading further. They merely suggest a range of considerations and attitudes, which may be useful to the reader.

QUESTIONS

. What is the content of the "Knowledge" gained through the experience of the Fall? What exactly does the learner learn that he did not know before?

. What is the source of this new Knowledge? Does it come from experience with others or from ideas inculcated by others? Or is the Knowledge a function of experience operating on the self and growing out of the individual's consciousness and intelligence?

. What is the nature of the Encounter with that Knowledge? Is the learner in the Encounter pitted against other human beings, or one other Adversary? Or are the "others" symbolic of Ideas of Evil, or of aspects of society and institutions?

. Does the work admit the possibility of Redemption? Is the Innocent retrievable? Are there any positive consequences of the Fall? Why does the writer occupy himself with the experience at all? Is a long-range view of progress accepted or rejected?

. Is the Fall experience repeatable? Is it a singular affair, more meaningful, more profound, and more moving than other experiences; or does the work imply that the Fall is a series of events? and that similar experiences may occur in the future? If so, how does one event differ from the next?

Are other people involved either in the Experience itself, or in the consequences of it? How does the change in the Protagonist affect his treatment of other people? What effect does the Experience have on the relationships of the Fallen persons with the Innocent Bystanders? What is the proper attitude for them to take toward him?

Consider the various rhetorical modes used by the participants in the Fall story. Why should ironic humor, for example, be a particular aspect of the Satanic character, while the Innocent lacks an awareness of irony? Why do sexual implications or overtones so often appear in the relationship between the Innocent and the Satanic Character?

PART I

The Same Old Story

Adam was but human—this explains it all. He did not want the apple for the apple's sake, but because it was forbidden. The mistake was in not forbidding the serpent; then he would have eaten the serpent.

—*Mark Twain*

The Biblical Roots

It has been said that the following passage from the book of Genesis has had more influence on the thought and attitudes of Western Christian culture than any passage of similar length in its literature. It has been interpreted and discussed in countless commentaries, it has been the subject of innumerable works of religious art, both good and bad, and it has been a favorite topic for sermons, both in the early days of the church and in modern times. It has been either responsible for or expressive of the emphasis in Christian doctrine on Sin, Guilt, and the dangers of Disobedience; in all these respects the story has been invaluable to the organizers and administrators of churches, religious sects, and social institutions.

Such questions, however, are more appropriate to historical than to literary study. What concerns us here is to make sense of the poetry, to find a proper response to the work which does not depend upon explanations drawn from history (e.g., the story supports the patriarchal structure of Hebraic culture), anthropology (primitive people lived in trees and were particularly afraid of snakes) or Revelation (the story is true because it is in the Bible).

We can make poetic sense of the passage by considering it an inspired piece of folk art, a folk poem produced by an ancient culture out of its oral tradition. Such an account does not deny the story's "truth." Quite the contrary, it suggests that it must have a great deal of meaning and psychological force to have survived and to have influenced so many people. Indeed, a useful line of inquiry is to ask about the peculiarities, the oddities, and the artlessness of the story, to try to identify and explain its omissions and inclusions, excisions and ellipses. One can assume, in short, that its form and content are the result of conscious or unconscious choices made by countless tellers which therefore reflect their understanding of the story's "truth."

This short passage contains all the motifs and themes which later accounts take up again and again: the Creation of Adam, Eve, and the Garden; the delights of the pastoral Eden; the Prohibition by the Father; the Naming of the Beasts; the Temptation, the Excuses, the Curses, and the Banishment.

The two versions here are taken from the King James Version of the early 17th century, described as "one of the creative miracles of the English language," and from the recent superb translation, "The New English Bible."

From GENESIS

King James Version

CHAPTER II

4: These are the generations of the heavens and of the earth when they were created, in the day that the LORD God made the earth and the heavens,

5: And every plant of the field before it was in the earth, and every herb of the field before it grew: for the LORD God had not caused it to rain upon the earth, and there was not a man to till the ground.

6: But there went up a mist from the earth, and watered the whole face of the ground.

7: And the LORD God formed man of the dust of the ground, and breathed into his nostrils the breath of life; and man became a living soul.

8: And the LORD God planted a garden eastward in Eden; and there he put the man whom he had formed.

9: And out of the ground made the LORD God to grow every tree that is pleasant to the sight, and good for food; the tree of life also in the midst of the garden, and the tree of knowledge of good and evil. . . .

15: And the LORD God took the man, and put him into the garden of Eden to dress it and to keep it.

16: And the LORD God commanded the man saying, Of every tree of the garden thou mayest freely eat:

17: But of the tree of the knowledge of good and evil, thou shalt not eat of it: for in the day that thou eatest thereof thou shalt surely die.

18: And the LORD God said, it is not good that the man should be alone: I will make him a help meet for him.

19: And out of the ground the LORD God formed every beast of the field, and every fowl of the air; and brought them unto Adam to see what he would call them: and whatsoever Adam called every living creature, that was the name thereof.

20:   And Adam gave names to all cattle, and to the fowl of the air, and to every beast of the field; but for Adam there was not found a help meet for him.

21:   And the LORD God caused a deep sleep to fall upon Adam, and he slept: and he took one of his ribs, and closed up the flesh instead thereof;

22:   And the rib, which the LORD God had taken from man, made he a woman, and brought her unto the man.

23:   And Adam said, This is now bone of my bones, and flesh of my flesh; she shall be called Woman, because she was taken out of Man.

24:   Therefore shall a man leave his father and his mother, and shall cleave unto his wife: and they shall be one flesh.

25:   And they were both naked, the man and his wife, and were not ashamed.

CHAPTER III

1:   Now the serpent was more subtle than any beast of the field which the LORD God had made. And he said unto the woman, Yea, hath God said, Ye shall not eat of every tree of the garden?

2:   And the woman said unto the serpent, We may eat of the fruit of the trees of the garden:

3:   But of the fruit of the tree which is in the midst of the garden, God hath said, Ye shall not eat of it, neither shall ye touch it, lest ye die.

4:   And the serpent said unto the woman, Ye shall not surely die:

5:   For God doth know that in the day ye eat thereof, then your eyes shall be opened, and ye shall be as gods, knowing good and evil.

6:   And when the woman saw that the tree was good for food, and that it was pleasant to the eyes, and a tree to be desired to make one wise, she took of the fruit thereof, and did eat, and gave also unto her husband with her; and he did eat.

7:   And the eyes of them both were opened, and they knew that they were naked: and they sewed fig leaves together, and made themselves aprons.

8:   And they heard the voice of the L<small>ORD</small> God walking in the garden in the cool of the day; and Adam and his wife hid themselves from the presence of the L<small>ORD</small> God amongst the trees of the garden.

9:   And the L<small>ORD</small> God called unto Adam, and said unto him, Where art thou?

10:   And he said, I heard thy voice in the garden, and I was afraid, because I was naked; and I hid myself.

11:   And he said, Who told thee that thou wast naked? Hast thou eaten of the tree, whereof I commanded thee that thou shouldest not eat?

12:   And the man said, The woman whom thou gavest to be with me, she gave me of the tree, and I did eat.

13:   And the L<small>ORD</small> God said unto the woman, What is this that thou hast done? And the woman said, The serpent beguiled me, and I did eat.

14:   And the L<small>ORD</small> God said unto the serpent, Because thou hast done this, thou art cursed above all cattle, and above every beast of the field; upon thy belly shalt thou go, and dust shalt thou eat all the days of thy life:

15:   And I will put enmity between thee and the woman, and between thy seed and her seed; it shall bruise thy head, and thou shalt bruise his heel.

16:   Unto the woman he said, I will greatly multiply thy sorrow and thy conception; in sorrow thou shalt bring forth children; and thy desire shall be to thy husband, and he shall rule over thee.

17:   And unto Adam he said, Because thou hast harkened unto the voice of thy wife, and hast eaten of the tree, of which I commanded thee, saying, thou shalt not eat of it: cursed is the ground for thy sake; in sorrow shalt thou eat of it all the days of thy life:

18:   Thorns also and thistles shall it bring forth to thee; and thou shalt eat the herb of the field;

19:   In the sweat of thy face shalt thou eat bread, till thou return unto the ground; for out of it wast thou taken; for dust thou art, and unto dust shalt thou return.

20:   And Adam called his wife's name Eve, because she was the mother of all living.

21: Unto Adam also and to his wife did the LORD God make coats of skins, and clothed them.

22: And the LORD God said, Behold, the man is become as one of us, to know good and evil; and now, lest he put forth his hand, and take also the tree of life, and eat, and live for ever:

23: Therefore the LORD God sent him forth from the garden of Eden, to till the ground from whence he was taken.

24: So he drove out the man; and he placed at the east of the garden of Eden cherubim, and a flaming sword which turned every way, to keep the way of the tree of life.

From GENESIS

The New English Bible

THE BEGINNINGS OF HISTORY

WHEN THE LORD GOD MADE EARTH AND HEAVEN, there was neither shrub nor plant growing wild upon the earth, because the LORD God had sent no rain on the earth; nor was there any man to till the ground. A flood used to rise out of the earth and water all the surface of the ground. Then the LORD God formed a man from the dust of the ground and breathed into his nostrils the breath of life. Thus the man became a living creature. Then the LORD God planted a garden in Eden away to the east, and there he put the man whom he had formed. The LORD God made trees spring from the ground, all trees pleasant to look at and good for food; and in the middle of the garden he set the tree of life and the tree of the knowledge of good and evil.

The LORD God took the man and put him in the garden of Eden to till it and care for it. He told the man, 'You may eat from every tree in the garden, but not from the tree of the knowledge of good and evil; for on the day that you eat from it, you will certainly die.' Then the LORD God said, 'It is not good for the man to be alone. I will provide a partner for him.' So God formed out of the ground all the wild animals and all the birds of the heaven. He brought them to the man to see what he would call them, and whatever the man called each living creature, that was its name. Thus the man gave names to all cattle, to the birds of heaven, and to every wild animal; but for the man himself no partner had yet been found. And so the LORD God put the man into a trance, and while he slept, he took one of his ribs and closed the flesh over the place. The LORD

God then built up the rib, which he had taken out of the man, into a woman. He brought her to the man, and the man said:

'Now this, at last—
bone from my bones,
flesh from my flesh!—
this shall be called woman,
for from man was this taken.'

That is why a man leaves his father and mother and is united to his wife, and the two become one flesh. Now they were both naked, the man and his wife, but they had no feeling of shame towards one another.

THE SERPENT WAS MORE CRAFTY than any wild creature that the LORD God had made. He said to the woman, 'Is it true that God has forbidden you to eat from any tree in the garden?' The woman answered the serpent, 'We may eat the fruit of any tree in the garden, except for the tree in the middle of the garden; God has forbidden us either to eat or to touch the fruit of that; if we do, we shall die.' The serpent said, 'Of course you will not die. God knows that as soon as you eat it, your eyes will be opened and you will be like gods knowing both good and evil.' When the woman saw that the fruit of the tree was good to eat, and that it was pleasing to the eye and tempting to contemplate, she took some and ate it. She also gave her husband some and he ate it. Then the eyes of both of them were opened and they discovered that they were naked; so they stitched fig-leaves together and made themselves loincloths.

The man and his wife heard the sound of the LORD God walking in the garden at the time of the evening breeze and hid from the LORD God among the trees of the garden. But the LORD God called to the man and said to him, 'Where are you?' He replied, 'I heard the sound as you were walking in the garden, and I was afraid because I was naked, and I hid myself.' God answered, 'Who told you that you were naked? Have you eaten from the tree which I forbade you?' The man said, 'The woman you gave me for a companion, she gave me fruit from the tree and I ate it.' Then the LORD God said to the woman, 'What is this that you have done?' The woman said, 'The serpent tricked me, and I ate.' Then the LORD God said to the serpent:

'Because you have done this you are accursed
more than all cattle and all wild creatures.
On your belly you shall crawl, and dust you shall eat
all the days of your life.
I will put enmity between you and the woman,
between your brood and hers.

They shall strike at your head,
and you shall strike at their heel.'

To the woman he said:

'I will increase your labour and your groaning,
and in labour you shall bear children.
You shall be eager for your husband,
and he shall be your master.'

And to the man he said:

'Because you have listened to your wife
and have eaten from the tree which I forbade you,
accursed shall be the ground on your account.
With labour you shall win your food from it
all the days of your life.
It will grow thorns and thistles for you,
none but wild plants for you to eat.
You shall gain your bread by the sweat of your brow
until you return to the ground;
for from it you were taken.
Dust you are, to dust you shall return.'

The man called his wife Eve because she was the mother of all who
live. The LORD God made tunics of skins for Adam and his wife and
clothed them. He said, 'The man has become like one of us, knowing good
and evil; what if he now reaches out his hand and takes fruit from the
tree of life also, eats it and lives for ever?' So the LORD God drove him out
of the garden of Eden to till the ground from which he had been taken.
He cast him out, and to the east of the garden of Eden he stationed the
cherubim and a sword whirling and flashing to guard the way to the tree
of life.

* * *

Developments in Theology

St. Augustine is one of the two or three most important figures in the history of the Roman Catholic Church; his contribution to the development of its theological positions and doctrines is second only to that of St. Paul. His extensive writings have become the source of numerous Catholic and Protestant beliefs, as well as of disputes about those beliefs. He laid great emphasis on the story of the Fall, and his strict interpretation of it in the doctrine of Original Sin influenced Calvin and both the Catholic and Protestant faiths.

Although Augustine comments on the Genesis account of the Fall in many of his writings, this excerpt from *The City of God* is especially indicative of his interest in the story. He notices, for example, that the Idea of Disobedience must precede the Act, and he therefore makes much of the Sin of Pride, the first of the Seven Deadly Sins, because it is a state of mind necessary to Disobedience. To disobey a legitimate and legal Authority, one must think (proudly) that one is superior to and exempt from the general rules, and feel that one deserves (in Augustine's phrase) "undue exaltation."

Augustine also makes much of the sexual content of the story, and the passage given here suggests some of the reasons why many Christians consider "immorality" and "sinfulness" to refer almost exclusively to sexual activity. One wonders what the history of Western Culture would have been had the Church Fathers emphasized Adam and Eve's excuse-making (which Augustine notices in Section 14) or even limited their complaints to the act of Disobedience itself, rather than concentrating on the sexual aspect of the Fall. Indeed the question of what the marital activities of a naked but innocent and unfallen man and woman might have been has been a subject of interest to a number of celibate monks and scriptural commentators. Augustine's account, however, is as chaste and earnest as an old-fashioned marriage manual.

From THE CITY OF GOD

St. Augustine (354–430)

BOOK XIV: SECTION 10

But it is a fair question, whether our first parent or first parents (for there was a marriage of two), before they sinned, experienced in their animal body such emotions as we shall not experience in the spiritual body when sin has been purged and finally abolished. . . . Their love to God was unclouded, and their mutual affection was that of faithful and sincere marriage; and from this love flowed a wonderful delight, because they always enjoyed what was loved. Their avoidance of sin was tranquil; and, so long as it was maintained, no other ill at all could invade them and bring sorrow. Or did they perhaps desire to touch and eat the forbidden fruit, yet feared to die; and thus both fear and desire already, even in that blissful place, preyed upon those first of mankind? Away with the thought that such could be the case where there was no sin! And, indeed, this is already sin, to desire those things which the Law of God forbids, and to abstain from them through fear of punishment, not through love of righteousness. Away, I say, with the thought, that before there was any sin, there should already have been committed regarding that fruit the very sin which our Lord warns us against regarding a woman: "Whosoever looketh on a woman to lust after her, hath committed adultery with her already in his heart." (Matthew 5: 28) As happy, then, as were these our first parents, who were agitated by no mental perturbations, and annoyed by no bodily discomforts, so happy should the whole human race have been, had they not introduced that evil which they have transmitted to their posterity, and had none of their descendants committed iniquity worthy of damnation; . . .

SECTION 11

. . . But after that proud and therefore envious angel . . . preferring to rule with a kind of pomp of empire rather than to be another's subject, fell from the spiritual Paradise, and essaying to insinuate his persuasive guile into the mind of man, whose unfallen condition provoked him to envy now that himself was fallen, he chose the serpent as his mouthpiece in that bodily Paradise in which it and all the other earthly animals were living with those two human beings, the man and his wife, subject to them, and harmless; and he chose the serpent because, being slippery, and moving in tortuous windings, it was suitable for his purpose. And this animal being subdued to his wicked ends by the presence and superior force of his angelic nature, he abused as his instrument, and first tried his deceit upon the woman, making his assault upon the weaker part of that human alliance, that he might gradually gain the whole, and not supposing that the man would readily give ear to him, or be deceived, but that he might yield to the error of the woman.

SECTION 13

Our first parents fell into open disobedience because already they were secretly corrupted; for the evil act had never been done had not an evil will preceded it. And what is the origin of our evil will but pride? For "pride is the beginning of sin." And what is pride but the craving for undue exaltation? And this is undue exaltation, when the soul abandons Him to whom it ought to cleave as its end, and becomes a kind of end to itself. This happens when it becomes its own satisfaction. And it does so when it falls away from that unchangeable good which ought to satisfy it more than itself. This falling away is spontaneous; for if the will had remained steadfast in the love of that higher and changeless good by which it was illumined to intelligence and kindled into love, it would not have turned away to find satisfaction in itself, and so become frigid and benighted; the woman would not have believed the serpent spoke the truth, nor would the man have preferred the request of his wife to the command of God, nor have supposed that it was a venial transgression to cleave to the partner of his life even in a partnership of sin. The wicked deed, then —that is to say, the transgression of eating the forbidden fruit—was committed by persons who were already wicked. . . .

SECTION 14

But it is a worse and more damnable pride which casts about for the shelter of an excuse even in manifest sins, as these our first parents did, of whom the woman said, "The serpent beguiled me, and I did eat;" and the man said, "The woman whom Thou gavest to be with me, she gave me of the tree, and I did eat." Here there is no word of begging pardon, no word of entreaty for healing. For though they do not, like Cain, deny that they have perpetrated the deed, yet their pride seeks to refer its wickedness to another—the woman's pride to the serpent, the man's to the woman. But where there is a plain transgression of a divine commandment, this is rather to accuse than to excuse oneself. For the fact that the woman sinned on the serpent's persuasion, and the man at the woman's offer, did not make the transgression less, as if there were any one whom we ought rather to believe or yield to than God.

SECTION 15

Therefore, because the sin was a despising of the authority of God— who had created man; who had made him in His own image; who had set him above the other animals, who had placed him in Paradise; who had enriched him with abundance of every kind and of safety; who had laid upon him neither many, nor great, nor difficult commandments, but, in order to make a wholesome obedience easy to him, had given him a single very brief and very light precept by which He reminded that creature whose service was to be free that He was Lord—it was just that condemnation followed, and condemnation such that man, who by keeping the commandments should have been spiritual, even in his flesh, became fleshly even in his spirit; and as in his pride he had sought to be his own satisfaction, God in His justice abandoned him to himself, not to live in the absolute independence he affected, but instead of the liberty he desired, to live dissatisfied with himself in a hard and miserable bondage to him to whom by sinning he had yielded himself, doomed in spite of himself to die in body as he had willingly become dead in spirit, condemned even to eternal death (had not the grace of God delivered him) because he had forsaken eternal life. Whoever thinks such punishment either excessive or unjust shows his inability to measure the great iniquity of sinning where sin might so easily have been avoided.

SECTION 16

Although, therefore, lust may have many objects, yet when no object is specified, the word lust usually suggests to the mind the lustful excitement of the organs of generation. . . . What friend of wisdom and holy joys, who, being married . . . would not prefer, if this were possible, to beget children without this lust, so that in this function of begetting offspring the members created for this purpose should not be stimulated by the heat of lust, but should be actuated by his volition, in the same way as his other members serve him for their respective ends? . . .

SECTION 17

Justly is shame very specially connected with this lust; justly, too, these members themselves being moved and restrained not at our will, but by a certain independent autocracy, so to speak, are called "shameful." Their condition was different before sin. For as it is written, "They were naked and were not ashamed."—not that their nakedness was unknown to them, but because nakedness was not yet shameful, because not yet did lust move those members without the will's consent; not yet did the flesh by its disobedience testify again the disobedience of man. . . . They had no consciousness of their members warring against their will. But when they were stripped of this grace, that their disobedience might be punished by fit retribution, there began in the movement of their bodily members a shameless novelty which made nakedness indecent. . . . And therefore, being ashamed of the disobedience of their own flesh, which witnessed to their disobedience while it punished it, "they sewed fig leaves together, and made themselves aprons," that is, cinctures for their privy parts; . . . Shame modestly covered that which lust disobediently moved in opposition to the will which was thus punished for its own disobedience. Consequently all nations, being propogated from that one stock, have so strong an instinct to cover shameful parts, that some barbarians do not uncover them even in the bath. . . .

In Paradise, then, man lived as he desired so long as he desired what God had commanded. He lived in the enjoyment of God, and was good by God's goodness; he lived without any want, and had it in his power so to live eternally. He had food that he might not hunger, drink that he might not thirst, the tree of life that old age might not waste him. There was in his body no corruption, nor seed of corruption, which could produce in him any unpleasant sensation. He feared no inward disease, no outward accident. Soundest health blessed his body, absolute tranquillity his soul. As in Paradise there was no excessive heat or cold, so its inhabitants were exempt from the vicissitudes of fear and desire. No sadness of any kind was there, nor any foolish joy; true gladness ceaselessly flowed from the presence of God, who was loved "out of a pure heart, and a good conscience, and faith unfeigned." (I Timothy 1:5) The honest love of husband and wife made a sure harmony between them. Body and spirit worked harmoniously together and the commandment was kept without labor. No languor made their leisure wearisome; no sleepiness interrupted their desire to labor. . . .

From COMMENTARY ON THE NEW TESTAMENT

St. Augustine (354–430)

CHAPTER 12 (MATTHEW 5:27-28)

(33) 'You have heard that it was said to the ancients, "Thou shalt not commit adultery." But I say to you that whosoever looks at a woman to lust after her, has already committed adultery with her in his heart.' Therefore, the lesser justice is not to commit adultery by carnal intercourse; the greater justice of the kingdom of God is not to commit adultery in the heart. Whosoever does not commit adultery in his heart guards much more securely against committing adultery in the flesh. Accordingly, He who has given this precept has confirmed the former precept, for He did not come to destroy the Law, but to fulfill it. And of course we must bear in mind that He did not say: 'Whosoever lusts after a woman,' but that He said: *'Whosoever looks at a woman to lust after her.'* That means whosoever fixes his attention on her with the aim and intention of lusting after her. This is not the same as to experience a sensation of carnal pleasure, but it is the giving of such full consent that the aroused desire for it is not repressed, but would be satisfied if opportunity presented itself.

(34) For, there are three steps toward the complete commission of a sin: suggestion, pleasure, and consent. The suggestion is made either

through the memory or through the bodily senses—when we are seeing or hearing or smelling or tasting or touching something. If we take pleasure in the enjoyment of this, it must be repressed if the pleasure is sinful. For example, if the craving of the palate is aroused at the sight of viands while we are observing the law of fasting, it arises only through pleasure; we do not consent to it, we repress it by the law of reason, to which it is subject. But, if consent is given, then a sin is fully committed in the heart, and it is known to God, even though it be not made known to men through the medium of any act. Therefore, these three successive stages are such as if the suggestion were made by a serpent, that is to say, it is made by a slimy and sinuous motion, namely, a transient action of the body. For, if any such images hover within the soul, they have been drawn from without, that is, from the body. And if, in addition to those five senses, any occult operation of a body comes into contact with the soul, it, too, is transient and moving quickly; therefore, the more occultly it glides into contact with thought, so much the more rightly is it compared with a serpent. Therefore, as I was beginning to say, these three successive stages may be likened to the action that is described in Genesis. For the suggestion, as well as a kind of persuasion, is made as though by a serpent; the pleasure is in the carnal desire, as though in Eve; and the consent is in the reason, as though in the man [Adam]. And if a man passes through these three stages, he is, as it were, cast out from Paradise; that is to say, he is expelled from the most blessed light of justice and is cast unto death. And this is most strictly in accordance with justice, for persuasion is not compulsion. While all natures are beautiful in their proper orders and graduations, yet from the higher natures—and the rational mind is one of these—there ought to be no falling down to the lower. No one is forced to do this; consequently, if any one does it, he is punished by the just law of God, because he does not commit this sin unwillingly. Before the habit is acquired, either there is no pleasure whatever or it is so slight that it is scarcely present. But when it is illicit, to consent to it is a grave sin, and whenever anyone consents to it, he commits a sin in his heart. If he then goes so far as to perform the corresponding act, the craving seems to be satisfied and extinguished, but a more intense pleasure is enkindled when the suggestion is repeated afterwards. This pleasure, however, is far less than that which has turned into a habit by continuous acts, for it is very difficult to overcome this habit. Nevertheless, under the leadership of Christ and with His aid, everyone will overcome this habit if he does not debase himself and shrink from the Christian warfare. And in this way, man is subjected to Christ, and the woman is subjected to man—in accordance with the pristine peace and order.°

°Cf. I Corinthians 11:3. "Not by nature, but because of sin, woman was rightly subjected to man. Unless this order is observed, nature will deteriorate and sin will increase."

* * *

Pilgrims and Penitence

In *The Canterbury Tales,* the Parson is one of Chaucer's least interesting Canterbury pilgrims because he has all the virtues except brevity. This passage is a small part of his "Tale," which consists of a lengthy sermon, text, and explication of text, with illustrations, interpretations, and warnings to the faithful. The Parson makes a good deal of "synne" and of lust, which he calls "concupiscense," and emphasizes the commonly held belief that the flesh and the devil are in league with each other. His ideas are representative of the conservative religious doctrine of the late Middle Ages (the poem is dated in the last decade of the 14th century) as it was preached throughout Europe by and to the faithful. If one thinks of this passage doubled and redoubled hundreds upon hundreds of Sundays, in hundreds upon hundreds of parishes, churches, and pulpits, one has some idea of how this and other Biblical stories and characters came to be the common, everyday knowledge of common people throughout Europe.

From THE PARSON'S TALE

Geoffrey Chaucer (ca. 1340-1400)

The seconde partie of Penitence is Confessioun, that is signe of contricioun./ Now shul ye understonde what is Confessioun, and wheither it oghte nedes be doon or noon, and whiche thynges been covenable to verray° Confessioun./

First shaltow understonde that Confessioun is verray shewynge of synnes to the preest./ This is to seyn "verray," for he moste confessen hym of alle the condiciouns that bilongen to his synne, as ferforth° as he kan./ Al moot be seyd, and no thyng excused ne hyd ne forwrapped, and noght avaunte thee of thy goode werkes./ And forther over, it is necessarie to understonde whennes that synnes spryngen, and how they encreessen and whiche they been./

Of the spryngynge of synnes seith Seint Paul in this wise: that "right as by a man synne entred first into this world, and thurgh that synne deeth, right so thilke° deeth entred into alle men that synneden."/ And this man was Adam, by whom synne entred into this world, whan he brak the comaundementz of God./ And therfore, he that first was so myghty that he

320

°*verray:* true   °*ferforth:* far   °*thilke:* that same

sholde nat have dyed, bicam swich oon° that he moste nedes dye, wheither he wolde or noon, and al his progenye in this world, that in thilke man synneden./ Looke that in th'estaat of innocence, whan Adam and Eve naked weren in Paradys, and nothyng ne hadden shame of hir naked-nesse,/ how that the serpent, that was moost wily of alle othere beestes that God hadde maked, seyde to the womman: "Why comaunded God to yow ye sholde nat eten of every tree in Paradys?"/ The womman answerde: "Of the fruyt," quod she, "of the trees in Paradys we feden us, but soothly, of the fruyt of the tree that is in the myddel of Paradys, God forbad us for to ete, ne nat touchen it, lest per aventure we sholde dyen."/ The serpent seyde to the womman: "Nay, nay, ye shul nat dyen of deeth; for sothe, God woot° that what day that ye eten therof, youre eyen shul opene, and ye shul been as goddes, knowynge good and harm."/ The womman thanne saugh that the tree was good to feedyng, and fair to the eyen, and delitable to the sighte. She took of the fruyt of the tree, and eet it, and yaf° to hire housbonde, and he eet, and anoon the eyen of hem bothe openeden./ And whan that they knewe that they were naked, they sowed of fige leves a maner of breches to hiden hire membres./ There may ye seen that deedly synne hath first suggestion of the feend, as shew-eth heere by the naddre°; and afterward, the delit of the flessh, as sheweth heere by Eve; and after that, the consentynge of resoun, as sheweth heere by Adam./ For trust wel, though so were that the feend tempted Eve, that is to seyn, the flessh, and the flessh hadde delit in the beautee of the fruyt defended, yet certes, til that resoun, that is to seyn, Adam, consented to the etynge of the fruyt, yet stood he in th' estaat of innocence./ Of thilke Adam tooke we thilke synne original; for of hym flesshly descended be we alle, and engendred of vile and corrupt mateere./ And whan the soule is put in oure body, right anon is contract original synne; and that that was erst° but oonly peyne of concupiscence, is afterward bothe peyne and synne./ And therfore be we alle born sones of wratthe and of dampna-cioun perdurable, if it nere° baptesme that we receyven, which byny-meth° us the culpe.° But for sothe, the peyne dwelleth with us, as to temptacioun, which peyne highte° concupiscence./ And this concu-piscence, whan it is wrongfully disposed or ordeyned in man, it maketh hym coveite, by coveitise of flessh, flesshly synne, by sighte of his eyen as erthely thynges, and eek° coveitise of hynesse by pride of herte./

Now, as for to speken of the firste coveitise, that is concupiscence, after the lawe of oure membres, that weren lawefulliche ymaked and by rightful juggement of God;/ I seye, forasmuche as man is nat obeisaunt to God, that is his lord, therfore is the flessh to hym disobeisaunt thurgh

---

°*swich oon:* such a one as serpent   °*erst:* at first from   °*culpe:* guilt, sin   °*woot:* knows   °*yaf:* gave   °*naddre:* adder, °*nere:* were not for   °*bynymeth:* takes away °*highte:* is called   °*eek:* also

concupiscence, which yet is cleped° norrissynge° of synne and occasioun of synne./ Therfore, al the while that a man hath in hym the peyne of concupiscence, it is impossible but he be tempted somtime and moeved in his flessh to synne./ And this thyng may nat faille as longe as he lyveth; it may wel wexe fieble and faille by vertu of baptesme, and by the grace of God thurgh penitence;/ but fully ne shal it nevere quenche, that he ne shal som tyme be moeved in hymself, but if he were al refreyded° by siknesse, or by malefice of sorcerie, or colde drynkes./ For lo, what seith Seint Paul: "The flessh coveiteth agayne the spirit, and the spirit agayn the flessh; they been so contrarie and so stryven that a man may nat alway doon as he wolde"/ The same Seint Paul, after his grete penaunce in water and in lond,—in water by nyght and by day in greet peril and in greet peyne; in lond, in famyne and thurst, in coold and cloothlees, and ones stoned almoost to the deeth,/— yet seyde he, "Allas, I caytyf° man! who shal delivere me fro the prisoun of my caytyf body?"/ And Seint Jerome, whan he longe tyme hadde woned° in desert, where as he hadde no compaignye but of wilde beestes, where as he ne hadde no mete but herbes, and water to his drynke, ne no bed but the naked erthe, for which his flessh was blak as an Ethiopeen for heete, and ny destroyed for coold,/ yet seyde he that "the brennynge° of lecherie boyled in al his body."/Wherfore I woot wel sykerly° that they been deceyved that seyn that they ne be nat tempted in hir body./ Witnesse on Seint Jame the Apostel, that seith that "every wight° is tempted in his owene concupiscence"; that is to seyn, that everich of us hath matere and occasioun to be tempted of the norissynge of synne that is in his body./ And therfore seith Seint John the Evaungelist: "If that we seyn that we be withoute synne, we deceyve us selve, and trouthe is not in us."/

Now shal ye understonde in what manere that synne wexeth or encreesseth in man. The firste thyng is thilke norissynge of synne of which I spak biforn, thilke flesshly concupiscence./ And after that comth the subjeccioun of the devel, this is to seyn, the develes bely,° with which he bloweth in man the fir of flesshly concupiscence./ And after that, a man bithynketh hym wheither he wol doon, or no, thilke thing to which he is tempted./ And thanne, if that a man withstonde and weyve the firste entisynge of his flessh and of the feend, thanne is it no synne; and if it so be that he do nat so, thanne feeleth he anoon a flambe° of delit./ And thanne is it good to be war,° and kepen hym wel, or elles he wol falle anon into consentynge of synne; and thanne wol he do it, if he may have tyme and place./ And of this matere seith Moyses by the devel in this manere: "The feend seith, 'I wole chace and pursue the man by wikked sug-

340

345

350

°cleped: called	°norrissynge: nourishment	°refreyded: made cold
°caytyf: wretched	°woned: lived	°brennynge: burning	°sykerly:
surely	°wight: man	°bely: bellows	°flambe: flame	°war: wary

gestioun, and I wole hente° hym by moevynge or stirynge of synne. And I wol departe my prise or my praye by deliberacioun, and my lust shal been acompliced in delit. I wol drawe my swerd in consentynge'—/ for certes, 35 right as a swerd departeth a thyng in two peces, right so consentynge departeth God fro man—'and thanne wol I sleen hym with myn hand in dede of synne'; thus seith the feend."/ For certes, thanne is a man al deed in soule. And thus is synne acompliced by temptacioun, by delit, and by consentynge; and thanne is the synne cleped actueel./

QUESTIONS

1a. Give an interpretation of Genesis that would not be contradicted by a physicist or geologist.

b. Give an interpretation of the story that would not be contradicted by a modern, "liberal" Christian.

c. Suggest aspects of the story which show its age and its descent from the oral tradition.

2. What connection is made between the Disobedience by Adam and Eve of God's Prohibition, and their awareness of their nakedness?

3. What is added to the story by the Serpent's seduction of Adam by way of Eve? Could he not have seduced Adam directly? Is this story prejudicial to women? Why didn't God create Eve at the same time as Adam? Was she an afterthought?

4. There is no Satan here, only a serpent. Comment on the importance of making a serpent the villain. Would other beasts or reptiles have done as well? Would they have embodied different meanings? Why or why not?

5. There are two trees in the story; what is the significance of the second?

6. Notice that one of Adam's duties included acting as Gardener (verse 15) and as Namer (verse 19 and 20). Why didn't God name His creatures Himself?

7. What is the implication of God's prohibiting the fruit of a tree, and of a tree pleasing to the eye? What kind of fruit was it (it is not an apple)? What other myths are there where eaten or stolen fruits or special trees in special places play important roles? Compare this story to the account in Greek mythology of Pandora's Box.

8. The passage does not furnish much detail about the Lord God. What kind of attributes does the story give him?

9. Evaluate the strength and weakness of Adam and Eve's answers to God's questions. What do the answers show about their position and state of mind?

10. Do you think their punishment is just? Do they deserve what they get? Do they deserve banishment from the Garden in addition to their other punishments? What factors influence your answer to this question?

°*hente:* catch

1. Why in Augustine's view does the temptation proceed by indirect means (via the Serpent and Eve)? What aspects of the story does Augustine add to; what does he choose to emphasize and elaborate upon?

2. Augustine was one of the principal formulators of a symbolic and allegorical mode of interpreting Scripture, one still practiced by all but the most literal of Protestants. To what degree does he seem to be making a literal reading of Genesis; to what degree does he see references in the story to spiritual or psychological attitudes?

3. Section 15 deals directly with a particular doubt which the story raises. What is that doubt? Is it legitimate? Is Augustine's response satisfactory? Why or why not?

1. Does Augustine's explanation of the sexual content of the story have merit? Is he talking about a widely shared or universal attitude toward the body, or does he merely reflect attitudes of the Christian heritage, or of his own heritage?

5. Define Lust. Can it properly be ascribed to Innocent people or is the feeling of such emotion a sign that one is Fallen? Is Shame at nakedness natural or must it be taught? If so, who teaches it to us?

5. Notice Augustine's belief that the Fall proceeds by stages; it is a complex succession of psychological conditions. To what extent is this true? Does it apply to all kinds of disobedience or "sinful" acts, or more to some than others?

5. In *The Canterbury Tales,* how directly does the Parson seem to be following Genesis? What does he add or subtract? What does he emphasize? What aspects of the sermon show its author to be a simple parson rather than a learned cleric of higher rank?

7. How does baptism make a Christian not guilty of original sin? What are the psychological steps by which sin occurs? What does the Parson see as Eve's function in the process of the Fall? Explain temptation, delight, consenting.

7. The fact that temptation is often a function of beauty is mentioned several times ("the fleesh hadde delit in the beautee of the fruyt"). Explain how sins of the eye come about. What aspect of man's nature is the Parson referring to?

. Explain the implications of St. Paul's description of the body as a "prisoun."

. How well does the Parson understand human psychology and attitudes toward temptation and sin?

PART II

The Myth Enters Literature

When Adam delved and Eve span [spun],
Who was then the gentleman?

— *Anonymous, 14th Century*

The Myth Enters Literature

Although *Paradise Lost* is considered a great poem, the weight of its reputation need not intimidate the reader. Although they speak in the Latinate idiom of the 17th century epic poem, Adam, Eve, and Satan are not the stock figures of earlier moral allegory, but substantial dramatic characters, with moral and emotional complexity and conflicting appetites and energies. It is clear that Milton knows a lot about human personality and motivation, about the psychology of the Fall, and about its causes, effects and stages.

Both the dramatic action and conflict and the rich characterization of the protagonists and antagonist, make this account of the Fall the most important and influential model for subsequent variations on this theme. Milton's Satan represents the ambivalence and moral turmoil of the fallen figure: expelled from Heaven for defying God's power (the sin of Pride again), outraged at his loss and impotence, perfectly aware of what he is and therefore of what he has lost, hating the innocence of the primal couple, yet seeing clearly the beauty of their purity. He is thus a moving example of the heroism of intelligent but wrongful rebellion, and of the terror of Evil, of being divided forever from God, and from Innocence, in Hell. Because he knows all this, he becomes, as the fallen one usually does, the most interesting person in the poem—some even say its hero, though that is not Milton's view of the case.

Innocence is less interesting, though not without its own subtlety. Eve knows the meaning of God's prohibition, but has a fatal human weakness—susceptibility to flattery (another form of Pride), and a childish wish to expose herself to danger—"an unsupported flower"—away from Adam's protection. Having fallen, she feels the fear of death, and her jealousy of another Eve whom Adam might find leads her to encourage Adam to sin in turn. Adam falls with more consciousness of what he is doing, choosing to disobey for the sake of his love of Eve. (Feminists may find much to complain of here, for Milton's Paradise is kept in order by the proper and absolute deference of wife to husband.) Their ruin complete, we see them experience predictable consequences: they feel first an ecstatic "high," and fall to "love's disport(ing)," but wake up cold, naked, and guilty; and being unable to sustain or bear their guilt without enmity, they indulge in bitter mutual accusations.

Milton makes a great deal of the proper hierarchy which Divine Providence has ordained, and upon which stability, order, harmony, and moral rectitude and grace depend. The key to that order is proper subordination of weaker to stronger, of angels to God, of men to angels, of women to men. Satan's insurrection violated this order, and he seduces Eve by tempting her to the same violation. His promise that "you shall be as gods" is a suggestion that she rise above her proper place, an offer that only a person weak in Reason, and acting from Pride, would accept.

Thus, while Milton has a modern perception of the psychology of error, of the social dangers of rebellion and the moral dangers of ambition and pride, the poem is firmly traditionalist and conservative. Sin lies in disobedience, and the consequences of sin are fleshly desire and spiritual sterility. Milton's poetry is thus rich enough and his imagination profound enough to offer an interpretation of the Fall myth which goes far beyond its particular literary form or historical setting.

The poem opens with a brief invocation to the Heavenly Muse and a statement, in the manner of the classical epic poem, of what the subject is to be. Milton then begins the narrative with Satan and his lesser followers having just landed from their Fall from Heaven into the Abyss. Satan's first conversation (with Beëlzebub, the angel "next himself in power, and next in crime") asserts his basic position and state of mind: that he is down but not out, that in spite of his defeat and his low situation, his will to oppose God is undiminished (lines 84–124). Beelzebub is not so confident and suggests that perhaps God has allowed Satan's will to remain strong so that he will feel the pangs of his defeat more powerfully (lines 128–155). Satan finally agrees with this view, and concludes that they must figure out a way of continuing the conflict with God by discovering some plan suitable to their anger and rebelliousness.

From PARADISE LOST

John Milton (1608–1674)

From BOOK I

Of Man's first disobedience, and the fruit
Of that forbidden tree whose mortal taste
Brought death into the World, and all our woe,
With loss of Eden, till one greater Man°
Restore us, and regain the blissful seat,   5
Sing, Heavenly Muse, that, on the secret top
Of Oreb, or of Sinai, didst inspire
That shepherd° who first taught the chosen seed
In the beginning how the heavens and earth
Rose out of Chaos: or, if Sion hill   10
Delight thee more, and Siloa's brook that flowed
Fast by the oracle of God, I thence
Invoke thy aid to my adventurous song,

°*one greater Man:* Christo   °*shepherd:* Moses

That with no middle flight intends to soar
Above the Aonian mount, while it pursues   15
Things unattempted yet in prose or rhyme.
And chiefly Thou, O Spirit,° that dost prefer
Before all temples the upright heart and pure,
Instruct me, for Thou know'st; Thou from the first
Wast present, and, with mighty wings outspread,   20
Dove-like sat'st brooding on the vast Abyss,
And mad'st it pregnant: what in me is dark
Illumine, what is low raise and support;
That, to the height of this great argument,
I may assert Eternal Providence,   25
And justify° the ways of God to men.
      Say first—for Heaven hides nothing from thy view,
Nor the deep tract of Hell—say first what cause
Moved our grand Parents, in that happy state,
Favoured of Heaven so highly, to fall off   30
From their Creator, and transgress his will
For one restraint, lords of the World besides.
Who first seduced them to that foul revolt?
      The infernal Serpent; he it was whose guile,
Stirred up with envy and revenge, deceived   35
The mother of mankind, what time° his pride
Had cast him out from Heaven, with all his host
Of rebel Angels, by whose aid, aspiring
To set himself in glory above his peers,
He trusted to have equalled the Most High,   40
If he opposed, and, with ambitious aim
Against the throne and monarchy of God,
Raised impious war in Heaven and battle proud,
With vain attempt. Him the Almighty Power
Hurled headlong flaming from the ethereal sky,   45
With hideous ruin and combustion down
To bottomless perdition, there to dwell
In adamantine chains and penal fire,
Who durst defy the Omnipotent to arms.
      Nine times the space that measures day and night   50
To mortal men, he with his horrid crew
Lay vanquished, rolling in the fiery gulf,
Confounded though immortal. But his doom
Reserved him to more wrath; for now the thought
Both of lost happiness and lasting pain   55

°*Spirit:* the Holy Spirit   °*justify:* show the justice of   °*what time:* after

Torments him: round he throws his baleful° eyes,
That witnessed huge affliction and dismay,
Mixed with obdurate pride and steadfast hate.
At once, as far as Angel's ken, he views
The dismal situation waste and wild.   60
A dungeon horrible, on all sides round,
As one great furnace flamed; yet from those flames
No light, but rather darkness visible
Served only to discover sights of woe,
Regions of sorrow, doleful shades, where peace   65
And rest can never dwell, hope never comes
That comes to all; but torture without end
Still urges, and a fiery deluge, fed
With ever-burning sulphur unconsumed.
Such place Eternal Justice had prepared   70
For those rebellious; here their prison ordained
In utter° darkness, and their portion set,
As far removed from God and light of Heaven
As from the centre° thrice to the utmost pole.
Oh how unlike the place from whence they fell!   75
There the companions of his fall, o'erwhelmed
With floods and whirlwinds of tempestuous fire,
He soon discerns; and, weltering° by his side,
One next himself in power, and next in crime,
Long after known in Palestine, and named   80
Beëlzebub. To whom the Arch-Enemy
And thence in Heaven called Satan, with bold words
Breaking the horrid silence, thus began:
   "If thou beest he—but Oh how fallen! how changed
From him! who in the happy realms of light   85
Clothed with transcendent brightness didst outshine
Myriads though bright—if he whom mutual league,
United thoughts and counsels, equal hope
And hazard in the glorious enterprise,
Joined with me once, now° misery hath joined   90
In equal ruin; into what pit thou seest
From what height fallen: so much the stronger proved
He with his thunder: and till then who knew
The force of those dire arms? Yet not for those,
Nor what the potent Victor in his rage   95
Can else inflict, do I repent, or change,

°*baleful:* threatening evil   °*utter:* outer   °*centre:* earth   °*weltering:*
writhing   °*now:* and now

Though changed in outward lustre, that fixed mind,
And high disdain from sense of injured merit,
That with the Mightiest raised me to contend,
And to the fierce contentions brought along   100
Innumerable force of Spirits armed,
That durst dislike his reign, and, me preferring,
His utmost power with adverse power opposed
In dubious battle on the plains of Heaven,
And shook his throne. What though the field be lost?   105
All is not lost—the unconquerable will,
And study of revenge, immortal hate,
And courage never to submit or yield:
And what is else not to be overcome?
That glory° never shall his wrath or might   110
Extort from me. To bow and sue for grace
With suppliant knee, and deify his power
Who, from the terror of this arm, so late
Doubted° his empire—that were low indeed;
That were an ignominy and shame beneath   115
This downfall; since, by fate, the strength of Gods,
And this empyreal substance, cannot fail;
Since, through experience of this great event,
In arms not worse, in foresight much advanced,
We may with more successful hope resolve   120
To wage by force or guile eternal war,
Irreconcilable to our grand Foe,
Who now triúmphs, and in the excess of joy
Sole reigning holds the tyranny of Heaven."
    So spake the apostate Angel, though in pain,   125
Vaunting aloud, but racked with deep despair;
And him thus answered soon his bold compeer:
    "O Prince, O Chief of many thronèd Powers
That led the embattled Seraphim to war
Under thy conduct, and, in dreadful deeds   130
Fearless, endangered Heaven's perpetual King,
And put to proof his high supremacy,
Whether upheld by strength, or chance, or fate!
Too well I see and rue the dire event
That, with sad overthrow and foul defeat,   135
Hath lost us Heaven, and all this mighty host
In horrible destruction laid thus low,
As far as Gods and Heavenly Essences

°*That glory:*   i.e., submission   °*Doubted:*   was fearful for

Can perish: for the mind and spirit remains
Invincible, and vigour soon returns, 140
Though all our glory extinct,° and happy state
Here swallowed up in endless misery.
But what if He our Conqueror (whom I now
Of force believe almighty, since no less
Than such could have o'erpowered such force as ours) 145
Have left us this our spirit and strength entire,
Strongly to suffer and support our pains,
That we may so suffice° his vengeful ire,
Or do him mightier service as his thralls°
By right of war, whate'er his business be, 150
Here in the heart of Hell to work in fire,
Or do his errands in the gloomy Deep?
What can it then avail though yet we feel
Strength undiminished, or eternal being
To undergo eternal punishment?" 155
    Whereto with speedy words the Arch-Fiend replied:
"Fallen Cherub, to be weak is miserable,
Doing or suffering:° but of this be sure—
To do aught good never will be our task,
But ever to do ill our sole delight, 160
As being the contrary to His high will
Whom we resist. If then his providence
Out of our evil seek to bring forth good,
Our labour must be to pervert that end,
And out of good still to find means of evil; 165
Which ofttimes may succeed so as perhaps
Shall grieve him, if I fail not, and disturb
His inmost counsels from their destined aim.
But see! the angry Victor hath recalled
His ministers of vengeance and pursuit 170
Back to the gates of Heaven: the sulphurous hail,
Shot after us in storm, o'erblown hath laid
The fiery surge that from the precipice
Of Heaven received us falling; and the thunder,
Winged with red lightning and impetuous rage, 175
Perhaps hath spent his shafts, and ceases now
To bellow through the vast and boundless Deep.
Let us not slip° the occasion, whether scorn
Or satiate° fury yield it from our Foe.

°*extinct:* is extinct   °*suffice:* satisfy   °*thralls:* slaves   °*Doing or suffering:*
acting or being acted upon   °*slip:* let slip   °*satiate:* fully satisfied

Seest thou yon dreary plain, forlorn and wild,   180
The seat of desolation, void of light,
Save what the glimmering of these livid flames
Casts pale and dreadful? Thither let us tend
From off the tossing of these fiery waves;
There rest, if any rest can harbour there;   185
And, reassembling our afflicted powers,°
Consult how we may henceforth most offend°
Our enemy, our own loss how repair,
How overcome this dire calamity,
What reinforcement we may gain from hope,   190
If not what resolution from despair."

*   *   *

The fallen angels debate their problem: God's power is too great to afford any hope that their desire for revenge can be fulfilled. Finally, Beelzebub suggests a solution: God's creation, his new World and its new race, Man, may offer less formidable opposition, may lie exposed to assault, and the Earth's "puny inhabitants" may be seduced to the fallen angels' party. The success of such a plan would interrupt God's joy in his victory over Satan, and it would further add to discord by inviting fallen Men to curse "their frail original, and faded bliss." The assemblage of angels acclaim the plan, and Satan takes it upon himself to find out where this new world is, and how it may be attacked.

From BOOK II

. . . Deep on his front engraven
Deliberation sat, and public care;
And princely counsel in his face yet shone,
Majestic, though in ruin. Sage he stood,   305
With Atlantean° shoulders, fit to bear
The weight of mightiest monarchies; his look
Drew audience and attention still as night
Or summer's noontide air, while thus he spake:
    "Thrones and Imperial Powers, Offspring of Heaven,   310
Ethereal Virtues! or these titles now
Must we renounce, and, changing style,° be called
Princes of Hell? for so the popular vote
Inclines—here to continue, and build up here
A growing empire; doubtless! while we dream,   315

°powers: armies   °offend: injure   °Atlantean: like Atlas's   °style: title

And know not that the King of Heaven hath doomed
This place our dungeon—not our safe retreat
Beyond his potent arm, to live exempt
From Heaven's high jurisdiction, in new league
Banded against his throne, but to remain   320
In strictest bondage, though thus far removed,
Under the inevitable curb, reserved
His captive multitude. For He, be sure,
In height or depth, still first and last will reign
Sole king, and of his kingdom lose no part   325
By our revolt, but over Hell extend
His empire, and with iron sceptre rule
Us here, as with his golden those in Heaven.
What sit we then projecting peace and war?
War hath determined us and foiled with loss   330
Irreparable; terms of peace yet none
Voutsafed° or sought; for what peace will be given
To us enslaved, but custody severe,
And stripes,° and arbitrary punishment
Inflicted? and what peace can we return,   335
But, to our power, hostility and hate,
Untamed reluctance, and revenge, though slow,
Yet ever plotting how the Conqueror least
May reap his conquest, and may least rejoice
In doing what we most in suffering feel?   340
Nor will occasion want, nor shall we need
With dangerous expedition to invade
Heaven, whose high walls fear no assault or siege,
Or ambush from the Deep. What if we find
Some easier enterprise? There is a place   345
(If ancient and prophetic fame in Heaven
Err not)—another World, the happy seat
Of some new race, called Man, about this time
To be created like to us, though less
In power and excellence, but favoured more   350
Of Him who rules above; so was His will
Pronounced among the gods, and by an oath
That shook Heaven's whole circumference confirmed.
Thither let us bend all our thoughts, to learn
What creatures there inhabit, of what mould   355
Or substance, how endued, and what their power
And where their weakness: how attempted best,

°*Voutsafed:* vouchsafed   °*stripes:* lashings

By force or subtlety. Though Heaven be shut,
And Heaven's high Arbitrator sit secure
In his own strength, this place may lie exposed,   360
The utmost border of his kingdom, left
To their defence who hold it: here, perhaps,
Some advantageous act may be achieved
By sudden onset—either with Hell-fire
To waste his whole creation, or possess   365
All as our own, and drive, as we are driven,
The puny habitants; or, if not drive,
Seduce them to our party, that their God
May prove their foe, and with repenting hand
Abolish his own works. This would surpass   370
Common revenge, and interrupt His joy
In our confusion, and our joy upraise
In His disturbance; when his darling sons,
Hurled headlong to partake with us, shall curse
Their frail original, and faded bliss—   375
Faded so soon! Advise if this be worth
Attempting, or to sit in darkness here
Hatching vain empires." Thus Beëlzebub
Pleaded his devilish counsel—first devised
By Satan, and in part proposed: for whence,   380
But from the author of all ill, could spring
So deep a malice, to confound the race
Of mankind in one root, and Earth with Hell
To mingle and involve, done all to spite
The great Creator? But their spite still serves   385
His glory to augment. The bold design
Pleased highly those Infernal States, and joy
Sparkled in all their eyes: with full assent
They vote: whereat his speech he thus renews:
"Well have ye judged, well ended long debate,   390
Synod of Gods, and, like to what ye are,
Great things resolved, which from the lowest deep
Will once more lift us up, in spite of fate,
Nearer our ancient seat—perhaps in view
Of those bright confines, whence, with neighboring arms, 395
And opportune excursion, we may chance
Re-enter Heaven; or else in some mild zone
Dwell, not unvisited of Heaven's fair light,
Secure, and at the brightening orient beam
Purge off this gloom: the soft delicious air,   400
To heal the scar of these corrosive fires,

Shall breathe her balm. But, first, whom shall we send
In search of this new World? whom shall we find
Sufficient? who shall tempt with wandering feet
The dark, unbottomed, infinite Abyss, 405
And through the palpable obscure find out
His uncouth° way, or spread his aery flight,
Borne up with indefatigable wings
Over the vast abrupt,° ere he arrive
The happy Isle? What strength, what art, can then 410
Suffice, or what evasion bear him safe
Through the strict senteries° and stations thick
Of Angels watching round? Here he had need
All circumspection: and we now no less
Choice in our suffrage;° for on whom we send 415
The weight of all, and our last hope, relies."
    This said, he sat; and expectation held
His look suspense, awaiting who appeared
To second, or oppose, or undertake
The perilous attempt. But all sat mute, 420
Pondering the danger with deep thoughts; and each
In other's countenance read his own dismay,
Astonished. None among the choice and prime
Of those Heaven-warring champions could be found
So hardy as to proffer or accept, 425
Alone, the dreadful voyage; till at last
Satan, whom now transcendent glory raised
Above his fellows, with monarchal pride
Conscious of highest worth, unmoved thus spake:
    "O Progeny of Heaven! Empyreal Thrones! 430
With reason hath deep silence and demur°
Seized us, though undismayed. Long is the way
And hard, that out of Hell leads up to Light.
Our prison strong, this huge convex° of fire,
Outrageous to devour, immures us round 435
Ninefold; and gates of burning adamant,
Barred over us, prohibit all egress.
These passed, if any pass, the void profound
Of unessential° Night receives him next,
Wide-gaping, and with utter loss of being 440
Threatens him, plunged in that abortive° gulf.

°*uncouth:* unknown °*abrupt:* gap °*senteries:* sentries °*suffrage:* selec-
tion °*demur:* hesitation °*convex:* sphere °*unessential:* having no
essence °*abortive:* dead and deadly

If thence he scape, into whatever world,
Or unknown region, what remains him less
Than unknown dangers, and as hard escape?
But I should ill become this throne, O Peers,   445
And this imperial sovranty, adorned
With splendour, armed with power, if aught proposed
And judged of public moment in the shape
Of difficulty or danger, could deter
Me from attempting. Wherefore do I assume   450
These royalties, and not refuse to reign,
Refusing to accept as great a share
Of hazard as of honour, due alike
To him who reigns, and so much to him due
Of hazard more as he above the rest   455
High honoured sits? Go, therefore, mighty Powers,
Terror of Heaven, though fallen; intend° at home,
While here shall be our home, what best may ease
The present misery, and render Hell
More tolerable; if there be cure or charm   460
To respite, or deceive, or slack the pain
Of this ill mansion: intermit no watch
Against a wakeful foe, while I abroad
Through all the coasts of dark destruction seek
Deliverance for us all. This enterprise   465
None shall partake with me." . . .

This plan does not begin to unfold until Book IV. Satan approaches
Paradise and the Encounter begins.

*   *   *

From BOOK IV

So on he fares, and to the border comes
Of Eden, where delicious Paradise,
Now nearer, crowns with her enclosure green,
As with a rural mound, the champaign head°
Of a steep wilderness, whose hairy sides   135
With thicket overgrown, grotesque and wild,
Access denied; and overhead up-grew
Insuperable height of loftiest shade,
Cedar, and pine, and fir, and branching palm,

°*intend:* consider   °*champaign head:* level top

A sylvan scene, and as the ranks ascend   140
Shade above shade, a woody theatre
Of stateliest view. Yet higher than their tops
The verdurous wall of Paradise up-sprung;
Which to our general sire° gave prospect large
Into his nether empire neighbouring round.   145
And higher than that wall a circling row
Of goodliest trees, loaden with fairest fruit,
Blossoms and fruits at once of golden hue,
Appeared, with gay enamelled colours mixed;
On which the sun more glad impressed his beams   150
Than in fair evening cloud, or humid bow,°
When God hath showered the earth: so lovely seemed
That landskip.° And of pure now purer air
Meets his approach, and to the heart inspires
Vernal delight and joy, able to drive   155
All sadness but despair. . . .

    Now to the ascent of that steep savage hill
Satan had journeyed on, pensive and slow;
But further way found none; so thick entwined,
As one continued brake,° the undergrowth   175
Of shrubs and tangling bushes had perplexed
All path of man or beast that passed that way.
One gate there only was, and that looked east
On the other side: which when the Arch-Felon saw,
Due entrance he disdained, and, in contempt,   180
At one slight bound high overleaped all bound
Of hill or highest wall, and sheer within
Lights on his feet. As when a prowling wolf,
Whom hunger drives to seek new haunt for prey,
Watching where shepherds pen their flocks at eve,   185
In hurdled cotes° amid the field secure,
Leaps o'er the fence with ease into the fold;
Or as a thief, bent to unhoard the cash
Of some rich burgher, whose substantial doors,
Cross-barred and bolted fast, fear no assault,   190
In at the window climbs, or o'er the tiles:
So clomb this first grand Thief into God's fold;
So since into his Church lewd hirelings climb.
Thence up he flew, and on the Tree of Life,

°*general sire:* Adam   °*landskip:* landscape   °*humid bow:* rainbow   °*brake:*
thicket   °*hurdled cotes:* fences made by interweaving branches

The middle tree and highest there that grew,   195
Sat like a cormorant; yet not true life
Thereby regained, but sat devising death
To them who lived; nor on the virtue thought
Of that life-giving plant, but only used
For prospect° what, well used, had been the pledge   200
Of immortality. So little knows
Any, but God alone, to value right
The good before him, but perverts best things
To worst abuse, or to their meanest use.
Beneath him, with new wonder, now he views,   205
To all delight of human sense exposed,
In narrow room Nature's whole wealth; yet more,
A Heaven on Earth: for blissful Paradise
Of God the garden was, by him in the east
Of Eden planted. Eden stretched her line   210
From Auran eastward to the royal towers
Of great Seleucia, built by Grecian kings,
Or where the sons of Eden long before
Dwelt in Telassar. In this pleasant soil
His far more pleasant garden God ordained.   215
Out of the fertile ground he caused to grow
All trees of noblest kind for sight, smell, taste;
And all amid them stood the Tree of Life,
High eminent, blooming ambrosial fruit
Of vegetable gold; and next to life,   220
Our death, the Tree of Knowledge, grew fast by—
Knowledge of good, bought dear by knowing ill.
Southward through Eden went a river large,
Nor changed his course, but through the shaggy hill
Passed underneath ingulfed; for God had thrown   225
That mountain, as his garden-mould, high raised
Upon the rapid current, which, through veins
Of porous earth with kindly thirst up-drawn,
Rose a fresh fountain, and with many a rill
Watered the garden; thence united fell   230
Down the steep glade, and met the nether flood,
Which from his darksome passage now appears,
And now, divided into four main streams,
Runs diverse, wandering many a famous realm
And country whereof here needs no account;   235
But rather to tell how, if Art could tell

°*For prospect:*   for observing

How, from that sapphire fount the crispèd° brooks,
Rolling on orient pearl and sands of gold,
With mazy error° under pendent shades
Ran nectar, visiting each plant, and fed   240
Flowers worthy of Paradise, which not nice Art
In beds and curious knots, but Nature boon°
Poured forth profuse on hill, and dale, and plain,
Both where the morning sun first warmly smote
The open field, and where the unpierced shade   245
Imbrowned the noontide bowers. Thus was this place,
A happy rural seat of various view:
Groves whose rich trees wept odorous gums and balm;
Others whose fruit, burnished with golden rind,
Hung amiable—Hesperian fables true,   250
If true, here only—and of delicious taste.
Betwixt them lawns, or level downs, and flocks
Grazing the tender herb, were interposed,
Or palmy hillock; or the flowery lap
Of some irriguous° valley spread her store,   255
Flowers of all hue, and without thorn the rose.
Another side, umbrageous° grots° and caves
Of cool recess, o'er which the mantling° vine
Lays forth her purple grape, and gently creeps
Luxuriant; meanwhile murmuring waters fall   260
Down the slope hills dispersed, or in a lake,
That to the fringèd bank with myrtle crowned
Her crystal mirror holds, unite their streams.
The birds their quire° apply; airs, vernal airs,
Breathing the smell of field and grove, attune   265
The trembling leaves, while universal Pan,
Knit with the Graces and the Hours in dance,
Led on the eternal Spring. . . .

Enter the Principal Characters:

Two of far nobler shape, erect and tall,
God-like erect, with native honour clad
In naked majesty, seemed lords of all,   290
And worthy seemed; for in their looks divine

°*crispèd:* rippled   °*error:* wandering   °*boon:* plentiful   °*irriguous:*
well-watered   °*umbrageous:* shadow-filled   °*grots:* grottos   °*mantling:*
enveloping   °*quire:* choir

The image of their glorious Maker shone,
Truth, wisdom, sanctitude severe and pure—
Severe, but in true filial freedom placed,
Whence true authority in men: though both   295
Not equal, as their sex not equal seemed;
For contemplation he and valour formed,
For softness she and sweet attractive grace;
He for God only, she for God in him.
His fair large front° and eye sublime° declared   300
Absolute rule; and hyacinthine° locks
Round from his parted forelock manly hung
Clustering, but not beneath his shoulders broad:
She, as a veil down to the slender waist,
Her unadornèd golden tresses wore   305
Dishevelled, but in wanton ringlets waved
As the vine curls her tendrils—which implied
Subjection, but required with gentle sway,
And by her yielded, by him best received,
Yielded with coy submission, modest pride,   310
And sweet, reluctant, amorous delay.
Nor those mysterious parts were then concealed,
Then was not guilty shame: dishonest shame
Of Nature's works, honour dishonourable,
Sin-bred, how have ye troubled all mankind   315
With shows instead, mere shows of seeming pure,
And banished from man's life his happiest life,
Simplicity and spotless innocence!
So passed they naked on, nor shunned the sight
Of God or Angel, for they thought no ill: 320
So hand in hand they passed, the loveliest pair
That ever since in love's embraces met—
Adam the goodliest man of men since born
His sons; the fairest of her daughters Eve.
Under a tuft of shade that on a green   325
Stood whispering soft, by a fresh fountain-side,
They sat them down; and, after no more toil
Of their sweet gardening labour than sufficed
To recommend cool Zephyr, and make ease
More easy, wholesome thirst and appetite   330
More grateful, to their supper-fruits they fell—
Nectarine fruits, which the compliant boughs
Yielded them, sidelong as they sat recline

°*front:* forehead °*sublime:* i.e., looking toward Heaven °*hyacinthine:* dark

On the soft downy bank damasked° with flowers.
The savoury pulp they chew, and in the rind,   335
Still as they thirsted, scoop the brimming stream;
Nor gentle purpose,° nor endearing smiles
Wanted, nor youthful dalliance, as beseems
Fair couple linked in happy nuptial league,
Alone as they. About them frisking played   340
All beasts of the earth, since wild, and of all chase
In wood or wilderness, forest or den.
Sporting the lion ramped,° and in his paw
Dandled the kid; bears, tigers, ounces,° pards,°
Gambolled before them; the unwieldy elephant,   345
To make them mirth, used all his might, and wreathed
His lithe proboscis; close the serpent sly,
Insinuating, wove with Gordian twine
His braided train, and of his fatal guile
Gave proof unheeded. Others on the grass   350
Couched, and, now filled with pasture, gazing sat,
Or bedward ruminating; for the sun,
Declined, was hastening now with prone career
To the Ocean Isles, and in the ascending scale
Of Heaven the stars that usher evening rose: 355
When Satan, still in gaze as first he stood,
Scarce thus at length failed speech recovered sad:
    "O Hell! what do mine eyes with grief behold?
Into our room° of bliss thus high advanced
Creatures of other mould—Earth-born perhaps,   360
Not Spirits, yet to Heavenly Spirits bright
Little inferior—whom my thoughts pursue
With wonder, and could love; so lively shines
In them divine resemblance, and such grace
The hand that formed them on their shape hath poured.   365
Ah! gentle pair, ye little think how nigh
Your change approaches, when all these delights
Will vanish, and deliver ye to woe—
More woe, the more your taste is now of joy:
Happy, but for so happy ill secured   370
Long to continue, and this high seat, your Heaven,
Ill fenced for Heaven to keep out such a foe
As now is entered; yet no purposed foe
To you, whom I could pity thus forlorn,

°*damasked:* decorated   °*purpose:* talk   °*ramped:* pawed the air   °*ounces:*
lynxes   °*pards:* leopards   °*room:* place

Though I unpitied:° League with you I seek,   375
And mutual amity, so strait, so close,
That I with you must dwell, or you with me,
Henceforth. My dwelling haply may not please,
Like this fair Paradise, your sense, yet such
Accept your Maker's work; he gave it me,   380
Which I as freely give. Hell shall unfold,
To entertain you two, her widest gates,
And send forth all her kings; there will be room,
Not like these narrow limits, to receive
Your numerous offspring; if no better place,   385
Thank him who puts me, loath, to this revenge
On you, who wrong me not, for him who wronged.
And, should I at your harmless innocence
Melt, as I do, yet public reason just—
Honour and empire with revenge enlarged   390
By conquering this new World—compels me now
To do what else, though damned, I should abhor."

As Satan watches and listens, Adam speaks of the "one easy prohibition" of their condition, and of the pleasure of "following our delightful
task" of pruning and tending the Garden. Eve speaks of her feeling for
Adam, and how she came to love him: first she saw her own image reflected
in a "liquid plain," but was persuaded by Adam to yield to him even
though he was "less fair, less winning soft, less amiably mild, than that
smooth watery image." But in him she could see:

"How beauty is excelled by manly grace   490
And wisdom, which alone is truly fair."
So spake our general mother, and, with eyes
Of conjugal attraction unreproved,
And meek surrender, half-embracing leaned
On our first father; half her swelling breast   495
Naked met his, under the flowing gold
Of her loose tresses hid. He, in delight
Both of her beauty and submissive charms,
Smiled with superior love, as Jupiter
On Juno smiles when he impregns° the clouds   500
That shed May flowers, and pressed her matron lip
With kisses pure. Aside the Devil turned
For envy: yet with jealous leer malign

°*Though I unpitied:* though I am unpitied (i.e., by God)   °*impregns:* impregnates

Eyed them askance, and to himself thus plained:°
  "Sight hateful, sight tormenting! Thus these two,   505
Imparadised in one another's arms,
The happier Eden, shall enjoy their fill
Of bliss on bliss; while I to Hell am thrust,
Where neither joy nor love, but fierce desire,
Among our other torments not the least,   510
Still unfulfilled, with pain of longing pines!°
Yet let me not forget what I have gained
From their own mouths. All is not theirs, it seems;
One fatal° tree there stands, of Knowledge called,
Forbidden them to taste. Knowledge forbidden?   515
Suspicious, reasonless! Why should their Lord
Envy them that? Can it be sin to know?
Can it be death? And do they only stand
By ignorance? Is that their happy state,
The proof of their obedience and their faith?   520
O fair foundation laid whereon to build
Their ruin! Hence I will excite their minds
With more desire to know, and to reject
Envious commands, invented with design
To keep them low, whom knowledge might exalt   525
Equal with gods. Aspiring to be such,
They taste and die: what likelier can ensue?"

Evening comes to Paradise, and Adam and Eve return to their "blissful bower":

  Thus talking, hand in hand alone they passed
On to their blissful bower. It was a place   690
Chosen by the sovran Planter, when he framed
All things to Man's delightful use. The roof
Of thickest covert was inwoven shade,
Laurel and myrtle, and what higher grew
Of firm and fragrant leaf; on either side   695
Acanthus, and each odorous bushy shrub,
Fenced up the verdant wall; each beauteous flower,
Iris all hues, roses, and jessamine,
Reared high their flourished heads between, and wrought
Mosaic; under foot the violet,   700

°*plained:* complained   °*pines:* (*desire*, line 509) makes me pine   °*fatal:*
death-bringing

Crocus, and hyacinth, with rich inlay
Broidered the ground, more coloured than with stone
Of costliest emblem. Other creature here,
Beast, bird, insect, or worm, durst enter none;
Such was their awe of Man. . . .   705

   Thus at their shady lodge arrived, both stood,   720
Both turned, and under open sky adored
The God that made both Sky, Air, Earth, and Heaven,
Which they beheld, the Moon's resplendent globe,
And starry Pole:° "Thou also mad'st the Night,
Maker Omnipotent; and thou the Day,   725
Which we in our appointed work employed
Have finished happy in our mutual help
And mutual love, the crown of all our bliss
Ordained by thee; and this delicious place,
For us too large, where thy abundance wants°   730
Partakers, and uncropt falls to the ground.
But thou hast promised from us two a race
To fill the earth, who shall with us extol
Thy goodness infinite, both when we wake,
And when we seek, as now, thy gift of sleep."   735
   This said unanimous, and other rites
Observing none, but adoration pure,
Which God likes best, into their inmost bower
Handed they went; and, eased the putting-off
These troublesome disguises which we wear,   740
Straight side by side were laid; nor turned, I ween,
Adam from his fair spouse, nor Eve the rites
Mysterious of connubial love refused:
Whatever hypocrites austerely talk
Of purity, and place, and innocence,   745
Defaming as impure what God declares
Pure, and commands to some, leaves free to all.
Our Maker bids increase; who bids abstain
But our destroyer, foe to God and Man?
Hail, wedded Love, mysterious law, true source   750
Of human offspring, sole propriety°
In Paradise of all things common else!
By thee adulterous lust was driven from men
Among the bestial herds to range; by thee,
Founded in reason, loyal, just, and pure,   755

°*Pole:* sky   °*wants:* lacks   °*propriety:* proprietorship

Relations dear, and all the charities
Of father, son, and brother, first were known.
Far be it that I should write thee sin or blame,
Or think thee unbefitting holiest place,
Perpetual fountain of domestic sweets,   760
Whose bed is undefiled and chaste pronounced,
Present, or past, as saints and patriarchs used.
Here Love his golden shafts employs, here lights
His constant lamp, and waves his purple wings,
Reigns here and revels; not in the bought smile   765
Of harlots—loveless, joyless, unendeared,
Casual fruition; nor in court amours,
Mixed dance, or wanton mask, or midnight ball,
Or serenate, which the starved lover sings
To his proud fair, best quitted with disdain.   770
These, lulled by nightingales, embracing slept,
And on their naked limbs the flowery roof
Showered roses, which the morn repaired. Sleep on,
Blest pair! and, O! yet happiest, if ye seek
No happier state, and know to know no more!   775

*   *   *

In Books V, VI, VII, and VIII, the Angel Raphael comes to Adam
and Eve in Eden. After giving an account of the battle between the two
parties of angels which led to the defeat and casting out of Satan, he
warns Adam of the danger which Satan represents. At the end of Book
VIII Satan is chased out of Paradise by Gabriel, and spends a period of
time circling the earth, hiding from the light. After finding an unwatched
entrance to earth he returns to Hell to continue his plot.

Satan chooses the Serpent, the "subtlest beast of all the field," in
which to hide himself and his "dark suggestions," because "in the wily
snake whatever sleights none would suspicious mark." He realizes that to
enter the body of the Serpent is something of a loss of status, but concludes
that revenge is worth the price:

From BOOK IX

"O foul descent! that I, who erst contended
With Gods to sit the highest, am now constrained
Into a beast, and, mixed with bestial slime,   165
This essence to incarnate and imbrute,
That to the height of deity aspired!

THE MYTH ENTERS LITERATURE   59

But what will not ambition and revenge
Descend to? Who aspires must down as low
As high he soared, obnoxious,° first or last,   170
To basest things. Revenge, at first though sweet,
Bitter ere long back on itself recoils.
Let it; I reck° not, so it light well aimed,
Since higher I fall short,° on him who next
Provokes my envy, this new favourite   175
Of Heaven, this Man of Clay, son of despite,
Whom, us the more to spite, his Maker raised
From dust: spite then with spite is best repaid."
     So saying, through each thicket, dank or dry,
Like a black mist low-creeping, he held on   180
His midnight search, where soonest he might find
The Serpent. Him sleeping soon he found,
In labyrinth of many a round self-rolled,
His head the midst, well stored with subtle wiles:
Not yet in horrid shade or dismal den,   185
Nor nocent° yet, but on the grassy herb,
Fearless, unfeared, he slept. In at his mouth
The Devil entered, and his brutal sense,
In heart or head, possessing soon inspired
With act intelligential; but his sleep   190
Disturbed not, waiting close the approach of morn.

At dawn Adam and Eve awake and go forth to their tending of the
garden. Eve wishes to go alone to show her reliability and, though aware
of the danger, Adam yields to her wishes. She departs with reassurances:

"With thy permission, then, and thus forewarned,
Chiefly by what thy own last reasoning words
Touched only, that our trial, when least sought,   380
May find us both perhaps far less prepared,
The willinger I go, nor much expect
A foe so proud will first the weaker seek;
So bent,° the more shall shame him his repulse."

Eve, however, is overconfident:

O much deceived, much failing, hapless Eve,
Of thy presumed return! event perverse!   405

°*obnoxious:* open, liable   °*reck:* care   °*since . . . short:* since I cannot win
attacking God himself   °*nocent:* harmful   °*So bent:* so intending

Thou never from that hour in Paradise
Found'st either sweet repast or sound repose;
Such ambush, hid among sweet flowers and shades,
Waited, with hellish rancour imminent,
To intercept thy way, or send thee back   410
Despoiled of innocence, of faith, of bliss.
    For now, and since first break of dawn, the Fiend,
Mere° serpent in appearance, forth was come,
And on his quest where likeliest he might find
The only two of mankind, but in them   415
The whole included race, his purposed prey.
In bower and field he sought, where any tuft
Of grove or garden-plot more pleasant lay,
Their tendance° or plantation for delight,
By fountain or by shady rivulet   420
He sought them both, but wished his hap might find
Eve separate; he wished, but not with hope
Of what so seldom chanced, when to his wish,
Beyond his hope, Eve separate he spies,
Veiled in a cloud of fragrance, where she stood,   425
Half-spied, so thick the roses bushing round
About her glowed, oft stooping to support
Each flower of tender stalk, whose head, though gay
Carnation, purple, azure, or specked with gold,
Hung drooping unsustained. Them she upstays   430
Gently with myrtle band, mindless the while
Herself, though fairest unsupported flower,
From her best prop so far, and storm so nigh.
Nearer he drew, and many a walk° traversed
Of stateliest covert,° cedar, pine, or palm;   435
Then voluble° and bold, now hid, now seen
Among thick-woven arborets,° and flowers
Imbordered on each bank, the hand°of Eve: . . .

Much he the place admired, the person more.
As one who, long in populous city pent,   445
Where houses thick and sewers annoy° the air,
Forth issuing on a summer's morn, to breathe
Among the pleasant villages and farms
Adjoined, from each thing met conceives delight—

°*Mere:* pure   °*tendance:* i.e., object of cultivation   °*walk:* path   °*covert:*
cover   °*voluble:* undulating   °*arborets:* shrubs   °*hand:* handiwork
°*annoy:* pollute

The smell of grain, or tedded° grass, or kine,   450
Or dairy, each rural sight, each rural sound—
If chance with nymph-like step fair virgin pass,
What pleasing seemed, for her° now pleases more,
She most, and in her look sums all delight:
Such pleasure took the Serpent to behold   455
This flowery plat,° the sweet recess of Eve
Thus early, thus alone. Her heavenly form
Angelic, but more soft and feminine,
Her graceful innocence, her every air
Of gesture or least action, overawed   460
His malice, and with rapine sweet bereaved
His fierceness of the fierce intent it brought.
That space the Evil One abstracted° stood
From his own evil, and for the time remained
Stupidly good, of enmity disarmed,   465
Of guile, of hate, of envy, of revenge.
But the hot hell that always in him burns,
Though in mid Heaven, soon ended his delight,
And tortures him now more, the more he sees
Of pleasure not for him ordained. Then soon   470
Fierce hate he recollects, and all his thoughts
Of mischief, gratulating,° thus excites:
    "Thoughts, whither have ye led me? with what sweet
Compulsion thus transported to forget
What hither brought us? hate, not love, nor hope   475
Of Paradise for Hell, hope° here to taste
Of pleasure, but all pleasure to destroy,
Save what is in destroying; other joy
To me is lost. Then let me not let pass°
Occasion which now smiles. Behold alone   480
The Woman, opportune to all attempts—
Her husband, for I view far round, not nigh,
Whose higher intellectual more I shun,
And strength, of courage haughty, and of limb
Heroic built, though of terrestrial mould;   485
Foe not informidable, exempt from wound—
I not; so much hath Hell debased, and pain
Enfeebled me, to what I was in Heaven.
She fair, divinely fair, fit love for Gods,
Not terrible, though terror be in love   490

°*tedded:* cut for gathering   °*for her:* on her account   °*plat:* plot   °*abstracted:*
outside of   °*gratulating:* gloating   °*hope:* nor hope   °*pass:* pass up

And beauty, not° approached by stronger hate,
Hate stronger under show of love well feigned—
The way which to her ruin now I tend."
  So spake the Enemy of Mankind, enclosed
In serpent, inmate bad, and toward Eve   495
Addressed his way—not with indented wave,
Prone on the ground, as since, but on his rear,
Circular base of rising folds, that towered
Fold above fold, a surging maze; his head
Crested aloft, and carbuncle his eyes;   500
With burnished neck of verdant gold, erect
Amidst his circling spires, that on the grass
Floated redundant.° . . .

                  . . . With tract° oblique   510
At first, as one who sought access but feared
To interrupt, sidelong he works his way.
As when a ship, by skilful steersman wrought
Nigh river's mouth or foreland, where the wind
Veers oft, as oft so steers, and shifts her sail,   515
So varied he, and of his tortuous train
Curled many a wanton wreath in sight of Eve,
To lure her eye. She, busied, heard the sound
Of rustling leaves, but minded not, as used
To such disport before her through the field   520
From every beast, more duteous at her call
Than at Circean call the herd disguised.
He, bolder now, uncalled before her stood,
But as in gaze admiring. Oft he bowed
His turret° crest and sleek enamelled neck,   525
Fawning, and licked the ground whereon she trod.
His gentle dumb expression turned at length
The eye of Eve to mark his play; he, glad
Of her attention gained, with serpent-tongue
Organic, or impulse of vocal air,   530
His fraudulent temptation thus began:
  "Wonder not, sovran mistress (if perhaps
Thou canst who art sole wonder), much less arm
Thy looks, the heaven of mildness, with disdain,
Displeased that I approach thee thus, and gaze   535
Insatiate, I thus single, nor have feared

°*not:* unless   °*redundant:* in wave-like motion   °*tract:* course   °*turret:*
towering

Thy awful° brow, more awful thus retired.°
Fairest resemblance of thy Maker fair,
Thee all things living gaze on, all things thine
By gift, and thy celestial beauty adore,   540
With ravishment beheld—there best beheld
Where universally admired. But here,
In this enclosure wild, these beasts among,
Beholders rude, and shallow to discern
Half what in thee is fair, one man except,   545
Who sees thee (and what is one?) who shouldst be seen
A Goddess among Gods, adored and served
By Angels numberless, thy daily train?"
    So glozed° the Tempter, and his proem° tuned.
Into the heart of Eve his words made way,   550
Though at the voice much marvelling; at length,
Not unamazed, she thus in answer spake:
    "What may this mean? Language of Man pronounced
By tongue of brute, and human sense expressed!
The first at least of these I thought denied   555
To beasts, whom God on their creation-day
Created mute to all articulate sound;
The latter I demur,° for in their looks
Much reason, and in their actions, oft appears.
Thee, Serpent, subtlest beast of all the field   560
I knew, but not with human voice endued;
Redouble, then, this miracle, and say,
How cam'st thou speakable of° mute, and how
To me so friendly grown above the rest
Of brutal kind that daily are in sight: 565
Say, for such wonder claims attention due."
    To whom the guileful Tempter thus replied:
"Empress of this fair World, resplendent Eve!
Easy to me it is to tell thee all
What thou command'st, and right thou shouldst be obeyed. 570
I was at first as other beasts that graze
The trodden herb, of abject thoughts and low,
As was my food, nor aught but food discerned
Or sex, and apprehended nothing high:
Till on a day, roving the field, I chanced   575
A goodly tree far distant to behold,
Loaden with fruit of fairest colours mixed,

°*awful:* awesome   °*retired:* withdrawn   °*glozed:* flattered   °*proem:* formal
introduction as in an oration   °*demur:* defer decision   °*of:* from being

Ruddy and gold. I nearer drew to gaze;
When from the boughs a savory odour blown,
Grateful to appetite, more pleased my sense   580
Than smell of sweetest fennel, or the teats
Of ewe or goat dropping with milk at even,
Unsucked of lamb or kid, that tend their play.
To satisfy the sharp desire I had
Of tasting those fair apples, I resolved   585
Not to defer; hunger and thirst at once,
Powerful persuaders, quickened at the scent
Of that alluring fruit, urged me so keen.
About the mossy trunk I wound me soon;
For, high from ground, the branches would require   590
Thy utmost reach, or Adam's: round the tree
All other beasts that saw, with like desire
Longing and envying stood, but could not reach.
Amid the tree now got, where plenty hung
Tempting so nigh, to pluck and eat my fill   595
I spared not; for such pleasure till that hour
At feed or fountain never had I found.
Sated at length, ere long I might perceive
Strange alteration in me, to degree
Of Reason in my inward powers, and Speech   600
Wanted not long, though to this shape retained.°
Thenceforth to speculations high or deep
I turned my thoughts, and with capacious mind
Considered all things visible in Heaven,
Or Earth, or Middle, all things fair and good.   605
But all that fair and good in thy divine
Semblance, and in thy beauty's heavenly ray,
United I beheld—no fair to thine
Equivalent or second; which compelled
Me thus, though importune perhaps, to come   610
And gaze, and worship thee of right·declared
Sovran of creatures, universal Dame!"°
     So talked the spirited° sly Snake; and Eve,
Yet more amazed, unwary thus replied:
     "Serpent, thy overpraising leaves in doubt   615
The virtue of that fruit, in thee first proved.
But say, where grows the tree? from hence how far?
For many are the trees of God that grow

°*though . . . retained:* though I remained a serpent in form   °*Dame:* Mistress
spirited: Satan has "inspired" the snake with his spirit.

In Paradise, and various, yet unknown
To us; in such abundance lies our choice   620
As leaves a greater store of fruit untouched,
Still hanging incorruptible,° till men
Grow up to their provision, and more hands
Help to disburden Nature of her bearth."°
   To whom the wily Adder, blithe and glad: 625
"Empress, the way is ready, and not long—
Beyond a row of myrtles, on a flat,
Fast° by a fountain, one small thicket past
Of blowing° myrrh and balm. If thou accept
My conduct,° I can bring thee thither soon."   630
   "Lead, then," said Eve. He, leading, swiftly rolled
In tangles, and made intricate seem straight,
To mischief° swift. Hope elevates, and joy
Brightens his crest, As when a wandering fire,°
Compact° of unctuous° vapour, which the night   635
Condenses, and the cold environs round,
Kindled through agitation to a flame
(Which oft, they say, some evil spirit attends),
Hovering and blazing with delusive light,
Misleads the amazed night-wanderer from his way   640
To bogs and mires, and oft through pond or pool,
There swallowed up and lost, from succour far:
So glistered° the dire Snake, and into fraud°
Led Eve, our credulous mother, to the Tree
Of Prohibition, root of all our woe;   645
Which when she saw, thus to her guide she spake:
   "Serpent, we might have spared our coming hither,
Fruitless to me, though fruit be here in excess,
The credit of whose virtue rest with thee—
Wondrous indeed, if cause of such effects!   650
But of this tree we may not taste nor touch;
God so commanded, and left that command
Sole daughter of his voice: the rest,° we live
Law to ourselves; our Reason is our Law."
   To whom the Tempter guilefully replied: 655
"Indeed! Hath God then said that of the fruit
Of all these garden-trees ye shall not eat,
Yet lords declared of all in Earth or Air?"

°*incorruptible:* undecayed   °*bearth:* what Nature bears ("bear-th")   °*Fast:*
near   °*blowing:* blossoming   °*conduct:* guidance   °*mischief:* evil-doing
°*wandering fire:* will o' the wisp   °*compact:* made up   °*unctuous:* oily
°*glistered:* glittered   °*fraud:* evil acts   °*the rest:* as for the rest

To whom thus Eve, yet sinless: "Of the fruit
Of each tree in the garden we may eat;   660
But of the fruit of this fair tree, amidst
The Garden, God hath said, 'Ye shall not eat
Thereof, nor shall ye touch it, lest ye die.' "
She scarce had said, though brief, when now more bold
The Tempter, but, with show of zeal and love   665
To Man, and indignation at his wrong,
New part puts on, and, as to passion moved,
Fluctuates disturbed, yet comely, and in act
Raised, as of some great matter to begin.
As when of old some orator renowned   670
In Athens or free Rome, where eloquence
Flourished, since mute,° to some great cause addressed,
Stood in himself collected, while each part,
Motion, each act, won audience° ere the tongue
Sometimes in height° began, as no delay   675
Of preface brooking through his zeal of right:
So standing, moving, or to height upgrown,
The Tempter, all impassioned, thus began:
"O sacred, wise, and wisdom-giving Plant,
Mother of science!° now I feel thy power   680
Within me clear, not only to discern
Things in their causes, but to trace the ways
Of highest agents,° deemed however wise.
Queen of this Universe! do not believe
Those rigid threats of death. Ye shall not die.   685
How should ye? By the fruit? it gives you life
To° knowledge. By the Threatener? look on me,
Me who have touched and tasted, yet both live,
And life more perfect have attained than Fate
Meant me, by venturing higher than my lot.   690
Shall that be shut to Man which to the Beast
Is open? or will God incense his ire
For such a petty trespass, and not praise
Rather your dauntless virtue, whom the pain°
Of death denounced,° whatever thing Death be,   695
Deterred not from achieving what might lead
To happier life, knowledge of Good and Evil?
Of good, how just! of evil—if what is evil
Be real, why not known, since easier shunned?

°*since mute:* i.e., no longer practiced   °*audience:* attention   °*height:* high
feeling   °*science:* knowledge   °*highest agents:* e.g., God   °*To:* as well as
°*pain:* penalty   °*denounced:* announced

God therefore cannot hurt ye, and be just;   700
Not just, not God;° not feared then, nor obeyed:
Your fear itself of death removes the fear.
Why then was this forbid! Why but to awe,
Why but to keep ye low and ignorant,
His worshipers? He knows that in the day   705
Ye eat thereof, your eyes that seem so clear,
Yet are but dim, shall perfectly be then
Opened and cleared, and ye shall be as Gods,
Knowing both good and evil, as they know.
That ye should be as Gods, since I as Man,   710
Internal Man, is but proportion meet—
I, of brute, human; ye, of human, Gods.
So ye shall die perhaps, by putting off
Human, to put on Gods—death to be wished,
Though threatened, which no worse than this can bring!   715
And what are Gods, that Man may not become
As they, participating godlike food?
The Gods are first, and that advantage use
On our belief, that all from them proceeds.
I question it; for this fair Earth I see,   720
Warmed by the Sun, producing every kind,
Them nothing; if they° all things, who enclosed
Knowledge of good and evil in this tree,
That whoso eats thereof forthwith attains
Wisdom without their leave? and wherein lies   725
The offence, that Man should thus attain to know?
What can your knowledge hurt him,° or this tree
Impart against his will, if all be his?
Or is it envy? and can envy dwell
In Heavenly breasts? These, these and many more   730
Causes import° your need of this fair fruit.
Goddess humane,° reach then, and freely taste!"
  He ended; and his words, replete with guile,
Into her heart too easy entrance won.
Fixed on the fruit she gazed, which to behold   735
Might tempt alone; and in her ears the sound
Yet rung of his persuasive words, impregned°
With reason, to her seeming,° and with truth.
Meanwhile the hour of noon drew on, and waked

°*Not . . . God:* If not just, then not God   °*if they:* if they produced   °*him:*
God   °*import:* prove   °*humane:* gracious   °*impregned:* impregnated
°*to her seeming:* as she thought

An eager appetite, raised by the smell   740
So savoury of that fruit, which with desire,
Inclinable now grown to touch or taste,
Solicited her longing eye; yet first,
Pausing a while, thus to herself she mused:
  "Great are thy virtues, doubtless, best of fruits,   745
Though kept from Man, and worthy to be admired,
Whose taste, too long forborne, at first assay°
Gave elocution to the mute, and taught
The tongue not made for speech to speak thy praise.
Thy praise he also who forbids thy use   750
Conceals not from us, naming thee the Tree
Of Knowledge, knowledge both of good and evil;
Forbids us then to taste. But his forbidding
Commends thee more, while it infers° the good
By thee communicated, and our want;   755
For good unknown sure is not had, or, had
And yet unknown, is as not had at all.
In plain, then, what forbids he but to know?
Forbids us good, forbids us to be wise!
Such prohibitions bind not. But, if Death   760
Bind us with after-bands, what profits then
Our inward freedom? In the day we eat
Of this fair fruit, our doom is we shall die!
How dies the Serpent? He hath eaten, and lives,
And knows, and speaks, and reasons, and discerns,   765
Irrational till then. For us alone
Was death invented? or to us denied
This intellectual food, for beasts reserved?
For beasts it seems; yet that one beast which first
Hath tasted envies not, but brings with joy   770
The good befallen him, author unsuspect,°
Friendly to Man, far from deceit or guile.
What fear I then? rather, what know to fear
Under this ignorance of good and evil,
Of God or Death, of law or penalty?   775
Here grows the cure of all, this fruit divine,
Fair to the eye, inviting to the taste,
Of virtue° to make wise. What hinders then
To reach, and feed at once both body and mind?"
So saying, her rash hand in evil hour   780
Forth-reaching to the fruit, she plucked, she eat.°

°*assay:* attempt   °*infers:* suggests   °*unsuspect:* reliable   °*virtue:* power
°*eat:* pronounced *et,* ate

Earth felt the wound, and Nature from her seat,
Sighing through all her works, gave signs of woe
That all was lost. Back to the thicket slunk
The guilty Serpent, and well might, for Eve,   785
Intent now only on her taste, naught else
Regarded; such delight till then, as seemed,
In fruit she never tasted, whether true,
Or fancied so through expectation high
Of knowledge; nor was Godhead from her thought.   790
Greedily she ingorged without restraint,
And knew not° eating death. Satiate at length,
And hightened as with wine, jocund and boon,°
Thus to herself she pleasingly began:
　　"O sovran, virtuous, precious of all trees   795
In Paradise! of operation blest
To sapience,° hitherto obscured, infamed,°
And thy fair fruit let hang, as to no end
Created! but henceforth my early care,
Not without song, each morning, and due praise,   800
Shall tend thee, and the fertile burden ease
Of thy full branches, offered free to all;
Till, dieted by thee, I grow mature
In knowledge, as the Gods who all things know;
Though others envy what they cannot give—   805
For, had the gift been theirs, it had not here
Thus grown! Experience, next to thee I owe,
Best guide: not following thee, I had remained
In ignorance; thou open'st Wisdom's way,
And giv'st access, though secret she retire.   810
And I perhaps am secret: Heaven is high—
High, and remote to see from thence distinct
Each thing on Earth; and other care perhaps
May have diverted from continual watch
Our great Forbidder, safe° with all his spies   815
About him. But to Adam in what sort
Shall I appear? Shall I to him make known
As yet my change, and give him to partake
Full happiness with me, or rather not,
But keep the odds of knowledge in my power   820
Without copartner? so to add what wants
In female sex, the more to draw his love,
And render me more equal, and perhaps—

°*knew not:*　knew not she was　　°*boon:*　merry　　°*sapience:*　wisdom　　°*infamed:*
defamed　　　°*safe:*　not dangerous

A thing not undesirable—sometime
Superior; for, inferior, who is free? 825
This may be well; but what if God have seen,
And death ensue? Then I shall be no more;
And Adam, wedded to another Eve,
Shall live with her enjoying, I extinct!
A death to think! Confirmed, then, I resolve 830
Adam shall share with me in bliss or woe.
So dear I love him that with him all deaths
I could endure, without him live no life."

Eve rejoins Adam and tells him what has happened:

Thus Eve with countenance blithe her story told;
But in her cheek distemper flushing glowed.
On the other side, Adam, soon as he heard
The fatal trespass done by Eve, amazed,
Astonied° stood and blank, while horror chill 890
Ran through his veins, and all his joints relaxed.
From his slack hand the garland wreathed for Eve
Down dropt, and all the faded roses shed.
Speechless he stood and pale, till thus at length
First to himself he inward silence broke: 895
"O fairest of Creation, last and best
Of all God's works, creature in whom excelled
Whatever can to sight or thought be formed,
Holy, divine, good, amiable, or sweet!
How art thou lost! how on a sudden lost, 900
Defaced, deflowered, and now to death devote!°
Rather, how hast thou yielded to transgress
The strict forbiddance, how to violate
The sacred fruit forbidden? Some cursèd fraud
Of enemy hath beguiled thee, yet unknown, 905
And me with thee hath ruined; for with thee
Certain my resolution is to die.
How can I live without thee? how forgo
Thy sweet converse, and love so dearly joined,
To live again in these wild woods forlorn? 910
Should God create another Eve, and I
Another rib afford, yet loss of thee
Would never from my heart. No, no! I feel

°*Astonied:* astounded °*devote:* doomed

The link of nature draw me: flesh of flesh,
Bone of my bone thou art, and from thy state   915
Mine never shall be parted, bliss or woe."

Eve persuades Adam to eat the fruit and assures him that death does
not threaten them:

"Were it° I thought death menaced would ensue
This my attempt, I would sustain alone
The worst, and not persuade thee—rather die
Deserted° than oblige° thee with a fact°   980
Pernicious to thy peace, chiefly assured
Remarkably so late of thy so true,
So faithful, love unequaled. But I feel
Far otherwise the event°—not death, but life
Augmented, opened eyes, new hopes, new joys,   985
Taste so divine that what of sweet before
Hath touched my sense, flat seems to this and harsh.
On my experience, Adam, freely taste,
And fear of death deliver to the winds."
　　So saying, she embraced him, and for joy   990
Tenderly wept, much won that he his love
Had so ennobled as of choice to incur
Divine displeasure for her sake, or death.
In recompense (for such compliance bad
Such recompense best merits), from the bough   995
She gave him of that fair enticing fruit
With liberal hand. He scrupled not to eat,
Against his better knowledge, not deceived,
But fondly overcome with female charm.
Earth trembled from her entrails, as again   1000
In pangs, and Nature gave a second groan;
Sky loured, and, muttering thunder, some sad drops
Wept at completing of the mortal Sin
Original; while Adam took no thought,
Eating his fill, nor Eve to iterate   1005
Her former trespass feared, the more to soothe
Him with her loved society; that now,
As with new wine intoxicated both,
They swim in mirth, and fancy that they feel

°*Were it:* if　　°*Deserted:* alone　　°*oblige:* involve　　°*fact:* deed　　°*event:* consequence

Divinity within them breeding wings   1010
Wherewith to scorn the Earth. But that false fruit
Far other operation first displayed,
Carnal desire inflaming. He on Eve
Began to cast lascivious eyes; she him
As wantonly repaid; in lust they burn,   1015
Till Adam thus 'gan Eve to dalliance move:
  "Eve, now I see thou art exact° of taste
And elegant—of sapience no small part;
Since to each meaning savour we apply,
And palate call judicious. I the praise   1020
Yield thee; so well this day thou hast purveyed.
Much pleasure we have lost, while we abstained
From this delightful fruit, nor known till now
True relish, tasting. If such pleasure be
In things to us forbidden, it might be wished   1025
For° this one tree had been forbidden ten.
But come; so well refreshed, now let us play,
As meet° is, after such delicious fare;
For never did thy beauty, since the day
I saw thee first and wedded thee, adorned   1030
With all perfections, so inflame my sense
With ardour to enjoy thee, fairer now
Than ever—bounty of this virtuous tree!"
  So said he, and forbore not glance or toy°
Of amorous intent, well understood   1035
Of Eve, whose eye darted contagious fire.
Her hand he seized, and to a shady bank,
Thick overhead with verdant roof embowered,
He led her, nothing loath; flowers were the couch,
Pansies, and violets, and asphodel,   1040
And hyacinth—Earth's freshest, softest lap.
There they their fill of love and love's disport
Took largely, of their mutual guilt the seal,
The solace of their sin, till dewy sleep
Oppressed them, wearied with their amorous play.   1045
  Soon as the force of that fallacious fruit,
That with exhilarating vapour bland
About their spirits had played, and inmost powers
Made err, was now exhaled, and grosser sleep,
Bred of unkindly° fumes, with conscious dreams   1050

°*exact:* refined   °*For:* instead of   °*meet:* fit   °*toy:* caress   °*unkindly:*
unnatural

Encumbered, now had left them, up they rose
As from unrest, and, each the other viewing,
Soon found their eyes how opened, and their minds
How darkened. Innocence, that as a veil
Had shadowed them from knowing ill, was gone,   1055
Just confidence, and native righteousness,
And honour, from about them, naked left
To guilty Shame: he° covered, but his robe
Uncovered more. So rose the Danite strong,
Herculean Samson, from the harlot-lap   1060
Of Philistean Dalilah, and waked
Shorn of his strength; they destitute and bare
Of all their virtue. Silent, and in face
Confounded, long they sat, as strucken mute;
Till Adam, though not less than Eve abashed,   1065
At length gave utterance to these words constrained:
    "O Eve, in evil hour thou didst give ear
To that false Worm, of whomsoever taught
To counterfeit Man's voice—true in our fall,
False in our promised rising; since our eyes   1070
Opened we find indeed, and find we know
Both good and evil, good lost and evil got:
Bad fruit of knowledge, if this be to know,
Which leaves us naked thus, of honour void,
Of innocence, of faith, of purity,   1075
Our wonted ornaments now soiled and stained,
And in our faces evident the signs
Of foul concupiscence; whence evil store;°
Even shame, the last° of evils; of the first°
Be sure then. How shall I behold the face   1080
Henceforth of God or Angel, erst with joy
And rapture so oft beheld? Those Heavenly Shapes
Will dazzle now this earthly with their blaze
Insufferably bright. Oh, might I here
In solitude live savage, in some glade   1085
Obscured, where highest woods, impenetrable
To star or sunlight, spread their umbrage broad,
And brown° as evening! Cover me, ye pines!
Ye cedars, with innumerable boughs
Hide me, where I may never see them more!   1090
But let us now, as in bad plight, devise

°*he:* shame   °*whence evil store:* whence came abundant evils   °*last:* **worst**
°*first:* lesser   °*brown:* dark

What best may, for the present, serve to hide
The parts of each from other that seem most
To shame obnoxious,° and unseemliest seen—
Some tree, whose broad smooth leaves, together sewed,   1095
And girded on our loins, may cover round
Those middle parts, that° this new comer, Shame,
There sit not, and reproach us as unclean."
So counselled he, and both together went
Into the thickest wood. There soon they chose   1100
The fig-tree°—not that kind for fruit renowned,
But such as, at this day, to Indians known,
In Malabar or Decan° spreads her arms
Branching so broad and long that in the ground
The bended twigs take root, and daughters grow   1105
About the mother tree, a pillared shade
High overarched, and° echoing walks between:
There oft the Indian herdsman, shunning heat,
Shelters in cool, and tends his pasturing herds
At loop-holes cut through thickest shade. Those leaves   1110
They gathered, broad as Amazonian targe,°
And with what skill they had, together sewed,
To gird their waist—vain covering, if to hide
Their guilt and dreaded shame! O how unlike
To that first naked glory! Such of late   1115
Columbus found th' American, so girt
With feathered cincture,° naked else and wild,
Among the trees on isles and woody shores.
Thus fenced, and, as they thought, their shame in part
Covered, but not at rest or east of mind,   1120
They sat them down to weep. Nor only tears
Rained at their eyes, but high winds worse within
Began to rise, high passions—anger, hate,
Mistrust, suspicion, discord—and shook sore
Their inward state of mind, calm region once   1125
And full of peace, now tost and turbulent:
For Understanding ruled not, and the Will
Heard not her lore,° both in subjection now
To sensual Appetite, who, from beneath
Usurping over sovran Reason, claimed   1130
Superior sway. . . .

°*obnoxious:* liable   °*that:* so that   °*fig-tree:* i.e., the banyan tree   °*Malabar*
. . . *Decan:* the whole of India; Malabar, the southwest coast   °*and:* with
°*targe:* shield (the Amazons were the powerful female warriors of Greek mythology)
°*cincture:* girdle   °*lore:* teachings (Understanding's)

Adam concludes that he has admired Eve too much:

> . . . "Thus it shall befall
> Him who, to worth in women overtrusting,
> Lets her will rule: restraint she will not brook;°
> And, left to herself, if evil thence ensue,
> She first his weak indulgence will accuse."
>   Thus they in mutual accusation spent
> The fruitless hours, but neither self-condemning;
> And of their vain contést appeared no end.

1185

QUESTIONS

1. Milton's account gives answers to important questions not dealt with in earlier accounts: the origin of Evil itself, the history of Satan, the events and attitudes which led to Satan's becoming a Serpent. How satisfactory do you find these accounts? What do they add to the meaning of the myth? What makes this history necessary?

2a. The description of the Garden, the Edenic Paradise, in Book IV, contains many effective and important details, and is the primary source of "the Garden Archetype" and hundreds of subsequent references, allusions, and interpretations of this idea in literature. What kinds of animals are in the Garden? How do they get along with each other? What kinds of trees and shrubs grow there?

b. What latitude do the flora and fauna suggest? Is the description botanically realistic, or fantasy? What effect on the philosophic meaning of the poem does the beauty of the Garden have? Could these events have the same meaning if they occurred in a desert or in a rugged mountainous region, both of which have their own beauty? Explain.

3. Classical literature offers a parallel mythic situation, the pastoral place: a rustic countryside, inhabited by innocent shepherds and shepherdesses, piping innocent songs to their sheep, or sometimes to one another. See, for example, the passage from *The Ordeal of Richard Feveral* in Part V. Compare that view of natural innocence with Milton's view of Adam and Eve.

4. What relationship between Man and Nature is suggested by this poem?

5. What are some of the things which make Satan's character interesting, and perhaps heroic? What appeal does he have to the modern reader? Is the modern reader likely to take a different view of his condition than Milton did? Why or why not? What are Satan's special talents and aptitudes? Is rebelliousness a heroic trait?

°*brook:* put up with, endure

. What is Satan's view of his own condition? At what points does he seem most appealing? At what points most repulsive? What aspects of Evil does he portray best? Why does Satan choose the serpent as a disguise?

. What strategy does Satan employ on Eve? What arguments does he make to her? How much of her character does he understand? What special advantages does he have which allow him to persuade her? Is her decision mainly the result of his strength or of her weakness?

. Analyze Satan's arguments (Book IX, 679-732). What validity do they have? What is their weakness? Why is Eve convinced? How does she justify and explain her conversion? Would she have succumbed had Adam been there? Is there any excuse which can be made for her? Is Milton prejudiced against women?

. What persuades Adam to join Eve in sin? What different relationship to Evil is suggested by his Fall that is not present in hers? Do you feel more sympathetic with his fall or hers? What can be said in their defense?

. Although we are accustomed to think about the effects of Evil on Innocence, Milton is aware that Innocence has a special and complex effect of its own on Evil. What is that effect? How does Satan feel when he first sees Adam and Eve? How does he feel when he finds Eve alone?

. How powerful is Innocence against Evil? Can you think of a Confrontation situation where Innocence prevails over Evil, where Evil is "reconverted" back to Innocence? What gives Innocence its particular power?

. What is Milton's view of the place of human sexuality in Paradise? What is the nature of the couple's sexual activity before the Fall—and after? What causes the difference? Do you accept Milton's use of sexuality as an index of one's moral condition? Why or why not? Is Milton's view of this question significantly different from Augustine's? Which do you prefer and why?

. What parts of the poem are most genuine and moving? At what point are you most aware of its historical period?

. In the concluding Books of the poem (X, XI, and XII) Milton tells the subsequent history of the World and suggests some ways in which the Fall has positive and redeeming aspects. Though Adam and Eve are banished by the angel from the Garden, their final redemption by God's grace is implicit in their new condition. What benefits can they gain from their experience? What possibility of Paradise Regained remains? Notice the extensions of this idea in the Redemptive poems given in Part VIII.

PART III

Modern Mythology Begins

Everyone is perfectly willing to learn from unpleasant experience—if only the damage of the first lesson would be repaired.

—*Georg Christoph Lichtenberg*

Modern Mythology Begins

Paradise Lost was published in the middle of the 17th century (1667), a time of changing attitudes toward Nature, and evolving intellectual techniques which have become the basis of modern science. That science which took such long strides forward in the century of Bacon and Newton has become the enemy of literalism in religion and poetry, and has thus caused a change in the ways we understand the Myth of the Fall. By the 18th century, Reason and Nature were seen as allies; skepticism about mysteries made it less and less easy to accept Eden as a literal place and Adam and Eve as actual historical figures. It became easier therefore to treat them and their stories as myth, that is, as figurative representations of some pattern of human experience, some fixed condition of the human psyche. The contents of the old story became metaphors in new systems of thought—devices, symbols, images by which modern mythographers pieced out their own view of the psychological patterns of Innocence and Evil, and the Encounter between them.

Paradise Lost draws its force from the content of Christian belief of its period, but it also looks forward out of that literalism to a more modern pattern. This movement of the myth away from its traditional identification with Christianity is seen clearly in the works of the most original poetic mind of the 18th century, William Blake. Hating the science of Newton, which he saw as contradictory to the genuine spirit of Christian mythology, Blake took upon himself the task of remythologizing the Christian images and figures. He hoped that, as a result, they would retain their emotional power, so that belief in them would prevail in a world becoming more and more analytic, skeptical, and devoted to rationality, and more and more overwhelmed by the "dark Satanic Mills" of industrialism.

Though Blake represents an extreme, and though many later poets used traditional figures in less independent ways, he is the first modern poet—that is, a poet in whose work the contents of traditional myth are always transformed to a greater or lesser degree, by the time in which he lives, by the state of his own mind and feelings, and by the variety and heterogeneity of modern culture. His work typifies modern mythology, which sees the Fall experience as more psychological than religious: the figures and motifs become symbols of stages of individual growth and states of mind, and of the movement of the psyche toward consciousness of itself.

The degree to which Blake redefines traditional elements of the Myth of the Fall is suggested by the two prose passages which follow, the first from *The Marriage of Heaven and Hell,* the second from *A Vision of the Last Judgement.*

From THE MARRIAGE OF HEAVEN AND HELL

William Blake (1757–1827)

THE VOICE OF THE DEVIL

All Bibles or sacred codes have been the causes of the following Errors:

1. That Man has two real existing principles: Viz: a Body & a Soul.
2. That Energy, call'd Evil, is alone from the Body; & that Reason, call'd Good, is alone from the Soul.
3. That God will torment Man in Eternity for following his Energies.

But the following Contraries to these are True:

1. Man has no Body distinct from his Soul; for that Call'd Body is a portion of Soul discern'd by the five Senses, the chief inlets of Soul in this age.
2. Energy is the only life, and is from the Body; and Reason is the bound or outward circumference of Energy.
3. Energy is Eternal Delight.

Those who restrain desire, do so because theirs is weak enough to be restrained; and the restrainer or reason usurps its place & governs the unwilling.
And being restrain'd, it by degrees becomes passive, till it is only the shadow of desire.
The history of this is written in Paradise Lost, & the Governor or Reason is call'd Messiah.
And the original Archangel, or possessor of the command of the heavenly host, is call'd the Devil or Satan, and his children are call'd Sin & Death. . . .

Note: The reason Milton wrote in fetters when he wrote of Angels & God, and at liberty when of Devils & Hell, is because he was a true Poet and of the Devil's party without knowing it.

From A VISION OF THE LAST JUDGEMENT

William Blake

The Combats of Good & Evil is Eating of the Tree of Knowledge. The Combats of Truth & Error is Eating of the Tree of Life; these are not only Universal, but Particular. Each are Personified. There is not an Error but it has a Man for its Agent, that is, it is a Man. There is not a Truth but it has also a Man. Good & Evil are Qualities in Every Man, whether a Good or Evil Man. These are Enemies & destroy one another by every Means in their power, both of deceit & of open Violence. The deist & the Christian are but the Results of these Opposing Natures. Many are deists who would in certain Circumstances have been Christians in outward appearance. Voltaire was one of this number; he was as intolerant as an Inquisitor. Manners make the Man, not Habits. It is the same in Art: by their Works ye shall know them; the Knave who is Converted to Deism & the Knave who is Converted to Christianity is still a Knave but he himself will not know it, tho' Every body else does. Christ comes, as he came at first, to deliver those who were bound under the Knave, not to deliver the Knave. He Comes to deliver Man, the Accused, & not Satan the Accuser. We do not find any where that Satan is Accused of Sin; he is only accused of Unbelief & thereby drawing Man into Sin that he may accuse him. Such is the Last Judgement—a deliverance from Satan's Accusation. Satan thinks that Sin is displeasing to God; he ought to know that Nothing is displeasing to God but Unbelief & Eating of the Tree of Knowledge of Good & Evil.

From THE GATES OF PARADISE

William Blake

EPILOGUE

"To the Accuser who is
The God of This World"

Truly, My Satan, thou art but a Dunce,
And dost not know the Garment from the Man.
Every Harlot was a Virgin once,
Nor can'st thou ever change Kate into Nan.

Tho' thou are Worship'd by the Names Divine   5
Of Jesus & Jehovah, thou art still
The Son of Morn in weary Night's decline,
The lost Traveller's Dream under the Hill.

From POETICAL SKETCHES

William Blake

SONG

Fresh from the dewy hill, the merry year
Smiles on my head, and mounts his flaming car;
Round my young brows the laurel wreathes a shade,
And rising glories beam around my head.

My feet are wing'd, while o'er the dewy lawn   5
I meet my maiden, risen like the morn:
Oh bless those holy feet, like angels' feet;
Oh bless those limbs, beaming with heav'nly light!

Like as an angel glitt'ring in the sky
In times of innocence and holy joy;   10
The joyful shepherd stops his grateful song
To hear the music of an angel's tongue.

So when she speaks, the voice of Heaven I hear:
So when we walk, nothing impure comes near;
Each field seems Eden, and each calm retreat;   15
Each village seems the haunt of holy feet.

But the sweet village, where my black-ey'd maid
Closes her eyes in sleep beneath night's shade,
Whene'er I enter, more than mortal fire
Burns in my soul, and does my song inspire.   20

From SONGS OF INNOCENCE AND EXPERIENCE

William Blake

MOTTO

The Good are attracted by Men's perceptions,
And Think not for themselves;
Till Experience teaches them to catch
And to cage the Fairies & Elves.

And then the Knave begins to snarl   5
And the Hypocrite to howl;
And all his good Friends shew their private ends,
And the Eagle is known from the Owl.

From SONGS OF INNOCENCE

THE ECCHOING GREEN

The Sun does arise,
And make happy the skies;
The merry bells ring
To welcome the Spring;
The skylark and thrush,   5
The birds of the bush,
Sing louder around
To the bells' cheerful sound,
While our sports shall be seen
On the Ecchoing Green.   10

Old John, with white hair,
Does laugh away care,
Sitting under the oak,
Among the old folk.
They laugh at our play,   15
And soon they all say:
"Such, such were the joys
When we all, girls & boys,
In our youth time were seen
On the Ecchoing Green."   20

Till the little ones, weary,
No more can be merry;
The sun does descend,
And our sports have an end.
Round the laps of their mothers   25
Many sisters and brothers,
Like birds in their nest,
Are ready for rest,
And sport no more seen
On the darkening Green.   30

THE SCHOOL BOY

I love to rise in a summer morn
When the birds sing on every tree;
The distant huntsman winds his horn,
And the sky-lark sings with me.
O! what sweet company.   5

But to go to school in a summer morn,
O! it drives all joy away;
Under a cruel eye outworn,
The little ones spend the day
In sighing and dismay.   10

Ah! then at times I drooping sit,
And spend many an anxious hour,
Nor in my book can I take delight,
Nor sit in learning's bower,
Worn thro' with the dreary shower.   15

How can the bird that is born for joy
Sit in a cage and sing?
How can a child, when fears annoy,
But droop his tender wing,
And forget his youthful spring?   20

O! father & mother, if buds are nip'd
And blossoms blown away,
And if the tender plants are strip'd
Of their joy in the springing day,
By sorrow and care's dismay,   25

How shall the summer arise in joy,
Or the summer fruits appear?
Or how shall we gather what griefs destroy,
Or bless the mellowing year,
When the blasts of winter appear?   30

From SONGS OF EXPERIENCE

THE ANGEL

I dreamt a Dream! what can it mean?
And that I was a maiden Queen,
Guarded by an Angel mild:
Witless woe was ne'er beguil'd!

And I wept both night and day,   5
And he wip'd my tears away,
And I wept both day and night
And hid from him my heart's delight.

So he took his wings and fled;
Then the morn blush'd rosy red;   10
I dried my tears, & arm'd my fears
With ten thousand shields and spears.

Soon my Angel came again:
I was arm'd, he came in vain;
For the time of youth was fled,   15
And grey hairs were on my head.

THE GARDEN OF LOVE

I went to the Garden of Love,
And saw what I never had seen:
A Chapel was built in the midst,
Where I used to play on the green.

And the gates of this Chapel were shut,   5
And "Thou shalt not" writ over the door;
So I turn'd to the Garden of Love
That so many sweet flowers bore;

And I saw it was filled with graves,
And tomb-stones where flowers should be;   10
And Priests in black gowns were walking their rounds,
And binding with briars my joys & desires.

A POISON TREE

I was angry with my friend:
I told my wrath, my wrath did end.
I was angry with my foe:
I told it not, my wrath did grow.

And I water'd it in fears,   5
Night and morning with my tears;
And I sunnèd it with smiles
And with soft deceitful wiles.

And it grew both day and night,
Till it bore an apple bright;   10
And my foe beheld it shine,
And he knew that it was mine,

And into my garden stole
When the night had veil'd the pole:
In the morning glad I see   15
My foe outstretch'd beneath the tree.

QUESTIONS

1. Blake calls Satan the Accuser. What does he mean? What view of Sin is
implied in that idea? Compare it with the Genesis story.
2. Blake also says that Satan's Sin was Unbelief, and that the Fall occurred
when man believed his Disbelief. Is this view a reasonable one? What
changes does it cause in our understanding of the Fall story? How does it
change the situation of the Innocent?
3. How does the assertion that "Every Harlot was a Virgin once" relate to
the disdain shown for Satan?
4. What tone does Blake adopt toward Satan?
5. When Blake contrasts Innocence and Experience, what kinds of events or
experiences is he referring to? What have they in common?
6. What kinds of behavior or attitudes does Blake feel deny Innocence?
What kinds of people are least likely to be Innocent?
7. It is easy to sentimentalize the purity and beauty and freshness of childhood. Does Blake do this? Explain.
8. What kinds of situations does Blake believe are detrimental to Love?
9. What circumstances create an earthly Paradise? What makes Eden possible
for every person?

10. Explain the psychological process described in "A Poison Tree." What uses does the poem make of motifs from the Fall myth?

11. These poems refer to children, or to a child's state of mind, as emblematic of the condition of Innocence, a theme taken up in several of the modern works which follow. What makes childhood innocent? What qualities of childhood does Blake emphasize? What do the children in his poems do?

PART IV

The Encounter: Juvenile Division

OK! [whistle] Everybody out of the pool!
Out! Out! Get out! Everybody!

—*Bill Cosby, from "The Apple"*

The Coming of Age: Childhood and Adolescence

Perhaps the commonest treatment of the Myth of the Fall occurs in novels and short stories which deal with some developmental change in a young person's state of mind in which the person passes through stages of learning and disillusionment, to some older and wiser, more fallen but perhaps more mature condition. Short stories by the hundreds have dealt with a single incident causing growth or change of attitude, a moment which usually illustrates the basic psychological forces in the Fall Experience.

Such stories imply a standard set of critical questions which are relatively simple and easy to apply: What Knowledge does the central character have at the end that he lacked at the beginning? What is the person or experience (the Satanic figure) that represents the new Knowledge? How does this person or experience become known to the Innocent? How does the Innocent respond? How does he change after acquiring his Knowledge? What pains or pleasures accompany the change?

Some Very Short Stories

1. Humpty Dumpty sat on a wall,
    Humpty Dumpty had a great fall,
    All the king's horses and all the king's men
    Couldn't put Humpty together again.

2. Jack and Jill went up the hill
    To fetch a pail of water.
    Jack fell down and broke his crown,
    And Jill came tumbling after.

3. Rock-a-bye-baby,
    In a tree top,
    When the wind blows
    The cradle will rock.
    When the bough breaks
    The cradle will fall,
    And down will come baby,
    Cradle and all.

Some Longer Short Stories

The three stories included here are among the best of this particular kind, but almost every writer of fiction has tried his hand at it, and any anthology or collection of short stories will be certain to contain other examples.

Araby is one of the best-known and most admired stories of this type. The object of the narrator's attention and the source of his anguish and pain is not the girl next door, but the only slightly more remote girl across the street. The story tells of his intensity of feeling and of his painful efforts to understand that feeling and understand himself. In terms of the Fall it is important to notice that a natural aspect of time and growth involves the narrator in pains and difficulties which he has not chosen and which he is almost powerless to relieve.

ARABY

James Joyce (1882–1941)

North Richmond Street, being blind,° was a quiet street except at the hour when the Christian Brothers' School set the boys free. An uninhabited house of two storeys stood at the blind end, detached from its neighbours in a square ground. The other houses of the street, conscious of decent lives within them, gazed at one another with brown imperturbable faces.

The former tenant of our house, a priest, had died in the back drawing-room. Air, musty from having been long enclosed, hung in all the rooms, and the waste room behind the kitchen was littered with old useless papers. Among these I found a few paper-covered books, the pages of which were curled and damp: *The Abbot,*° by Walter Scott, *The Devout Communicant* and *The Memoirs of Vidocq.*° I liked the last best because its leaves were yellow. The wild garden behind the house contained a central apple-tree and a few straggling bushes under one of which I found the late tenant's rusty bicycle-pump. He had been a very charitable priest; in his will he had left all his money to institutions and the furniture of his house to his sister.

When the short days of winter came dusk fell before we had well eaten our dinners. When we met in the street the houses had grown som-

---

°*blind:* i.e., a dead end street   °*The Abbot:* a historical novel, full of romance and intrique (1820)   °*The Memoirs of Vidocq:* Vidocq was a famous Chief of Detectives in Paris (1809-1827) .

bre. The space of sky above us was the colour of ever-changing violet and towards it the lamps of the street lifted their feeble lanterns. The cold air stung us and we played till our bodies glowed. Our shouts echoed in the silent street. The career of our play brought us through the dark muddy lanes behind the houses where we ran the gantlet of the rough tribes from the cottages, to the back doors of the dark dripping gardens where odours arose from the ashpits, to the dark odorous stables where a coachman smoothed and combed the horse or shook music from the buckled harness. When we returned to the street light from the kitchen windows had filled the areas. If my uncle was seen turning the corner we hid in the shadow until we had seen him safely housed. Or if Mangan's sister came out on the doorstep to call her brother in to his tea we watched her from our shadow peer up and down the street. We waited to see whether she would remain or go in and, if she remained, we left our shadow and walked up to Mangan's steps resignedly. She was waiting for us, her figure defined by the light from the half-opened door. Her brother always teased her before he obeyed and I stood by the railings looking at her. Her dress swung as she moved her body and the soft rope of her hair tossed from side to side.

Every morning I lay on the floor in the front parlour watching her door. The blind was pulled down to within an inch of the sash so that I could not be seen. When she came out on the doorstep my heart leaped. I ran to the hall, seized my books and followed her. I kept her brown figure always in my eye and, when we came near the point at which our ways diverged, I quickened my pace and passed her. This happened morning after morning. I had never spoken to her, except for a few casual words, and yet her name was like a summons to all my foolish blood.

Her image accompanied me even in places the most hostile to romance. On Saturday evenings when my aunt went marketing I had to go to carry some of the parcels. We walked through the flaring streets, jostled by drunken men and bargaining women, amid the curses of labourers, the shrill litanies of shop-boys who stood on guard by the barrels of pigs' cheeks, the nasal chanting of street-singers, who sang a *come-all-you*° about O'Donovan Rossa,° or a ballad about the troubles in our native land. These noises converged in a single sensation of life for me: I imagined that I bore my chalice safely through a throng of foes. Her name sprang to my lips at moments in strange prayers and praises which I myself did not understand. My eyes were often full of tears (I could not tell why) and at times a flood from my heart seemed to pour itself out into my bosom. I thought little of the future. I did not know whether I would ever speak to her or not or, if I spoke to her, how I could tell her of

---

°*come-all-you:* any popular ballad, so called because many of the first lines began
   this way   °*O'Donovan Rossa:* 19th century Irish rebel

my confused adoration. But my body was like a harp and her words and gestures were like fingers running upon the wires.

One evening I went into the back drawing-room in which the priest had died. It was a dark rainy evening and there was no sound in the house. Through one of the broken panes I heard the rain impinge upon the earth, the fine incessant needles of water playing in the sodden beds. Some distant lamp or lighted window gleamed below me. I was thankful that I could see so little. All my senses seemed to desire to veil themselves and, feeling that I was about to slip from them, I pressed the palms of my hands together until they trembled, murmuring: *O love! O love!* many times.

At last she spoke to me. When she addressed the first words to me I was so confused that I did not know what to answer. She asked me was I going to *Araby*. I forget whether I answered yes or no. It would be a splendid bazaar, she said; she would love to go.

—And why can't you? I asked.

While she spoke she turned a silver bracelet round and round her wrist. She could not go, she said, because there would be a retreat that week in her convent.° Her brother and the two other boys were fighting for their caps and I was alone at the railings. She held one of the spikes, bowing her head towards me. The light from the lamp opposite our door caught the white curve of her neck, lit up her hair that rested there and, falling, lit up the hand upon the railing. It fell over one side of her dress and caught the white border of a petticoat, just visible as she stood at ease.

—It's well for you, she said.

—If I go, I said, I will bring you something.

What innumerable follies laid waste my waking and sleeping thoughts after that evening! I wished to annihilate the tedious intervening days. I chafed against the work of school. At night in my bedroom and by day in the classroom her image came between me and the page I strove to read. The syllables of the word *Araby* were called to me through the silence in which my soul luxuriated and cast an Eastern enchantment over me. I asked for leave to go to the bazaar on Saturday night. My aunt was surprised and hoped it was not some Freemason affair. I answered few questions in class. I watched my master's face pass from amiability to sternness; he hoped I was not beginning to idle. I could not call my wandering thoughts together. I had hardly any patience with the serious work of life which, now that it stood between me and my desire, seemed to me child's play, ugly monotonous child's play.

On Saturday morning I reminded my uncle that I wished to go to the bazaar in the evening. He was fussing at the hallstand, looking for the hat-brush, and answered me curtly:

°*convent:* school run by nuns

—Yes, boy, I know.

As he was in the hall I could not go into the front parlour and lie at the window. I left the house in bad humour and walked slowly towards the school. The air was pitilessly raw and already my heart misgave me.

When I came home to dinner my uncle had not yet been home. Still it was early. I sat staring at the clock for some time and, when its ticking began to irritate me, I left the room. I mounted the staircase and gained the upper part of the house. The high cold empty gloomy rooms liberated me and I went from room to room singing. From the front window I saw my companions playing below in the street. Their cries reached me weakened and indistinct and, leaning my forehead against the cool glass, I looked over at the dark house where she lived. I may have stood there for an hour, seeing nothing but the brown-clad figure cast by my imagination, touched discreetly by the lamplight at the curved neck, at the hand upon the railings and at the border below the dress.

When I came downstairs again I found Mrs. Mercer sitting at the fire. She was an old garrulous woman, a pawnbroker's widow, who collected used stamps for some pious purpose. I had to endure the gossip of the tea-table. The meal was prolonged beyond an hour and still my uncle did not come. Mrs. Mercer stood up to go: she was sorry she couldn't wait any longer, but it was after eight o'clock and she did not like to be out late, as the night air was bad for her. When she had gone I began to walk up and down the room clenching my fists. My aunt said:

—I'm afraid you may put off your bazaar for this night of our Lord.

At nine o'clock I heard my uncle's latchkey in the halldoor. I heard him talking to himself and heard the hallstand rocking when it had received the weight of his overcoat. I could interpret these signs. When he was midway through his dinner I asked him to give me the money to go to the bazaar. He had forgotten.

—The people are in bed and after their first sleep now, he said.

I did not smile. My aunt said to him energetically:

—Can't you give him the money and let him go? You've kept him late enough as it is.

My uncle said he was very sorry he had forgotten. He said he believed in the old saying: *All work and no play makes Jack a dull boy.* He asked me where I was going and, when I had told him a second time he asked me did I know *The Arab's Farewell to his Steed.* When I left the kitchen he was about to recite the opening lines of the piece to my aunt.

I held a florin tightly in my hand as I strode down Buckingham Street towards the station. The sight of the streets thronged with buyers and glaring with gas recalled to me the purpose of my journey. I took my seat in a third-class carriage of a deserted train. After an intolerable delay the train moved out of the station slowly. It crept onward among ruinous houses and over the twinkling river. At Westland Row Station a crowd of people pressed to the carriage doors; but the porters moved them back, saying that it was a special train for the bazaar. I remained alone in the bare carriage. In a few minutes the train drew up beside an improvised wooden platform. I passed out on to the road and saw by the lighted dial of a clock that it was ten minutes to ten. In front of me was a large building which displayed the magical name.

I could not find any sixpenny entrance and, fearing that the bazaar would be closed, I passed in quickly through a turnstile, handing a shilling to a weary-looking man. I found myself in a big hall girdled at half its height by a gallery. Nearly all the stalls were closed and the greater part of the hall was in darkness. I recognized a silence like that which pervades a church after a service. I walked into the centre of the bazaar timidly. A few people were gathered about the stalls which were still open. Before a curtain, over which the words *Café Chantant* were written in coloured lamps, two men were counting money on a salver. I listened to the fall of the coins.

Remembering with difficulty why I had come I went over to one of the stalls and examined porcelain vases and flowered tea-sets. At the door of the stall a young lady was talking and laughing with two young gentlemen. I remarked their English accents and listened vaguely to their conversation.

—O, I never said such a thing!

—O, but you did!

—O, but I didn't!

—Didn't she say that?

—Yes. I heard her.

—O, there's a . . . fib!

Observing me, the young lady came over and asked me did I wish to buy anything. The tone of her voice was not encouraging; she seemed to have spoken to me out of a sense of duty. I looked humbly at the great jars that stood like eastern guards at either side of the dark entrance to the stall and murmured:

—No, thank you.

The young lady changed the position of one of the vases and went back to the two young men. They began to talk of the same subject. Once or twice the young lady glanced at me over her shoulder.

I lingered before her stall, though I knew my stay was useless, to make my interest in her wares seem the more real. Then I turned away slowly and walked down the middle of the bazaar. I allowed the two pennies to fall against the sixpence in my pocket. I heard a voice call from one end of the gallery that the light was out. The upper part of the hall was now completely dark.

Gazing up into the darkness, I saw myself as a creature driven and derided by vanity; and my eyes burned with anguish and anger.

*　　*　　*

There is considerable variety in the ways in which a child encounters the world and its experiences, and considerable variety in the experiences themselves. Most such encounters do not seem large enough or dramatic enough, especially when looked back upon, to offer much matter for fiction. The event may occur quickly and the realization of its meaning may develop along the way, amidst other events and concerns. Most such encounters are not accented by Satanic confrontations or Adamesque heroics. Yet because they occur to all of us—perhaps all the time, but more frequently in childhood—they are the commonplace of short fiction. No modern writer (with the possible exception of J. D. Salinger) has written so well and so movingly as John Updike about the common stuff of small town America—school, family, sports, girls and boys, and the way one grows among these familiarities. *You'll Never Know, Dear, How Much I Love You* is one of the simplest and best of these stories.

YOU'LL NEVER KNOW, DEAR, HOW MUCH I LOVE YOU

John Updike (1932–   )

Carnival! In the vacant lot beyond the old ice plant! Trucks have been unloading all afternoon; the Whirlo-Gig has been unfolded like a giant umbrella, they assembled the baby Ferris wheel with an Erector Set. Twice the trucks got stuck in the mud. Straw has been strewn everywhere. They put up a stage and strung lights. Now, now, gather your pennies; supper is over and an hour of light is left in the long summer day. See, Sammy Hunnenhauser is running; Gloria Gring and her gang have been there all afternoon, they never go home, oh hurry, let me go; how awful it is to have parents that are poor, and slow, and sad!

Fifty cents. The most Ben could beg. A nickel for every year of his life. It feels like plenty. Over the roof of crazy Mrs. Moffert's house, the Ferris wheel tints the air with pink, and the rim of this pink mixes in excitement with the great notched rim of the coin sweating in his hand. This house, then this house, and past the ice plant, and he will be there. Already the rest of the world is there, he is the last, hurrying, hurrying, the balloon is about to take off, the Ferris wheel is lifting; only he will be left behind, on empty darkening streets.

Then there, what to buy? There are not so many people here. Grownups carrying babies mosey glassily on the straw walks. All the booth people,

---

not really gypsies, stare at him, and beckon weakly. It hurts him to ignore the man with the three old softballs, and the old cripple at the merry-go-round, and the fat lady with her plaster Marys, and the skeleton suspended behind a fountain of popcorn. He feels his walking past them as pain. He wishes there were more people here; he feels a fool. All of this machinery assembled to extract from him his pathetic fifty cents. He watches at a distance a thickset man in earnestly rolled-up shirtsleeves twirl a great tinselled wheel with a rubber tongue that patters slower and slower on a circle of nails until it stops between two, and the number there wins. Only a sailor and two boys in yellow silk high-school athletic jackets play. None win. The thick tattooed arm below the rolled-up shirtsleeve carefully sweeps their nickels from a long board divided and numbered as if for hopscotch. The high-school boys, with sideburns and spotty whiskers on their bright pink jaws, put down nickels again leadenly, and this time the man spinning the wheel shouts when it stops, seems more joyful than they, and reaches into his deep apron pocket and pours before them, without counting, a perfect little slipping stack of nickels. Their gums showing as if at a dirty joke, the two boys turn—the shimmer on their backs darts and shifts in cool z's—and walk away, while the man is shouting, "Hey, uh winneh. Hey uh winneh, evvybody wins." His table is bare, and as his mouth continues to form the loud words his eyes lock Ben into a stare of heartbreaking brown blankness that seems to elucidate with paralyzing clarity Ben's state: his dungarees, his fifty cents, his ten years, his position in space, and above the particulars the immense tinted pity, the waste, of being at one little place instead of everywhere, at any time. Then the man looks away, and twirls the wheel for his own amusement.

The fifty-cent piece feels huge to Ben's fingers, a wide oppressive rigidity that must be broken, shattered into twinkling fragments, to merge in the tinsel and splinters of strewn straw. He buys, at the first stand he strikes, a cone of cotton candy, and receives, with the furry pink pasty uncoiling thing, a quarter, a dime, and a nickel: three coins, tripling his wealth.

Now people multiply, crowd in from the houses of the town, that stand beyond the lot on all sides in black forbidding silhouettes like the teeth of a saw. The lights go on; the faces of the houses flee. There is nothing in the lot but light, and at its core, on the stage, three girls wearing white cowboy hats and white spangled skirts and white boots appear, and a man also in white and bearing a white guitar strung with gold. The legs around Ben crush him toward the stage; the smell of mud mingles with the bright sight there. One of the girls coughs into the microphone and twists its neck, so a sharp whine pierces from the loudspeakers and cuts a great crescent through the crowd, leaving silence as harvest. The girls sing, toetapping gingerly: "The other *night,* dear, as I lay *sleep*ing, I dreamt I *held* you in my *arms.*" The spangles on their swishing skirts spring prickles like tears in Ben's eyes. The three voices sob, catch, twang, distend his heart like a rubber band at the highest pitch of their plaint. "—I was mis*taken,* and I *hung* my *head,* a-and *cried."* And then the unbearable rising sugar of the chorus that makes his scalp so tight he fears his head will burst from sweet fullness.

The girls go on to sing other songs, less good, and then they give way to a thin old man in suspenders and huge pants he keeps snapping and looking down and whooping into. He tells horrible jokes that make the nice fat ladies standing around Ben—nice fat factory and dustmop women that made him feel protected—shake with laughter. He fears their quaking, feels threatened from beneath, as if there is a treacherous stratum under this mud and straw. He wanders away, to let the words of "You Are My Sunshine" revolve in his head. "Please don't *take* my *sun*shine *away."* Only the money in his pocket weights him; get rid of it, and he will sail away like a dandelion seed.

He goes to the booth where the wheel is turning, and puts his nickel on the board in a square marked 7, and loses it.

He puts the dime there and it too is taken away.

Squeezed, almost hidden, between the crusty trousered haunches of two adults, he puts down his quarter, as they do, on the inner edge, to be changed. The tattooed man comes along picking up the quarters and pouring, with his wonderfully automatic fingers, the little slipping stacks of five nickels; Ben holds his breath, and to his horror feels his low face catch in the corner of the man's absent-minded eyes. The thick solemn body snags in its smooth progress, and Ben's five nickels are raggedly spaced. Between the second and third there is a gap. A blush cakes Ben's cheeks; his gray-knuckled fingers, as they push out a nickel, are trembling sideways at each other. But the man goes back, and spins the wheel, and Ben loses three nickels one after another. The twittering wheel is a moon-faced god; but Ben feels humanity clouding the space between them, that should be unobstructed. When the tattooed arm—a blue fish, an anchor, the queer word PEACE—comes to sweep in his nickels, he feels the stippled skin breathing thought, and lowers his head against the expected fall of words. Nothing is said, the man moves on, returns to the wheel; but Ben feels puzzled pressure radiating from him, and the pointed eyes of a man in a suit with chalk stripes who has come to stand at the far side of the stand intersect this expanding circle, and Ben, hurrying to pour his money down a narrowing crack, puts down his last two nickels, still on 7.

The rubber tongue leaps into pattering and as the wheel whirls the tattooed man leans backward to hear the one in chalk stripes talk; his tongue patterns silently but a tiny motion of his polished hand, simultaneously with a sideways stab of his eyes, is toward Ben.

The rubber tongue slows, flops, stops at 7—no, 8. He lost, and can leave. The floor of his stomach lifts queerly. "Hey kid." The man with stencilled arms comes over. Ben feels that no matter how fast he would run, those arms would stretch and snare him.

"Huh?"

"How old are you, kid?"

"Ten."

"Whatsamatta with ya, ya daddy rich?"

A titter moves stiffly through the immense adult heads all around. Ben understands the familiar role, that he has undergone a hundred times with teachers and older boys, of being a comic prop. He understands everything, and wants to explain that he knows his eyes are moist and his cheeks red, but that it's because of joy, freedom, not because of losing. But this would be too many words; even the one-word answer "No" sticks to the roof of his mouth and comes loose with a faint tearing noise.

"Here." With his exciting expert touch, the man flicks Ben's two coins back across the painted number. Then he digs into his pocket. He comes up with the usual little stack of five, drops four, but holds the fifth delicately between the tips of two fingers and a thumb, hesitates so that Ben can reread PEACE in blue above his wrist, and then flips the fifth nickel up into his palm and thence down with a plunge into his dirty sagging apron pouch.

"Now move away from the board, kid, move away. Don't come back."

Ben fumbles the coins into his hands and pushes away, his eyes screwed to the sharp edge of painted wood, and shoulders blindly backward through the legs. Yet all the time, in the midst of the heat and water welling up from springs all over his body, he is figuring, and calculates he's been gypped. Forty: he had the quarter and dime and nickel and they gave him back only six nickels: thirty. The injustice, they pretend he's too little to lose and then keep a dime; the waste. The lost dime seems a tiny hole through which everything in existence is draining. As he moves away, his wet knees jarring, trying to hide forever from every sailor and fat woman and high-schooler who witnessed his disgrace, the six nickels make a knobbed weight bumping his thigh through his pocket. The spangles, the splinters of straw and strings of light, the sawtooth peaks of houses showing behind the scattered white heads scented sweetly with mud, are hung like the needles of a Christmas tree with the transparent, tinted globes confusing his eyelashes.

Thus the world, like a bitter coquette, spurns our attempts to give ourselves to her wholly.

*   *   *

Although Seth is only nine years old, he encounters, on this single June day, not one but several chilling Fall experiences. He recognizes not only the isolated portents of flood and storm and night, the tramp from the woods, the dead cow, and the "woman miseries" of Dellie, but also the way they come together in the final question: is the cold weather momentary or permanent, is the summer's beginning illusory? The Farm represents the Garden in the midst of which the Encounter with Time, Death, and Change occurs.

BLACKBERRY WINTER

Robert Penn Warren (1905–   )

It was getting into June and past eight o'clock in the morning, but there was a fire—even if it wasn't a big fire, just a fire of chunks—on the hearth of the big stone fireplace in the living room. I was standing on the hearth, almost into the chimney, hunched over the fire, working my bare toes slowly on the warm stone. I relished the heat which made the skin of my bare legs warp and creep and tingle, even as I called to my mother, who was somewhere back in the dining room or kitchen, and said: "But it's June, I don't have to put them on!"

"You put them on if you are going out," she called.

I tried to assess the degree of authority and conviction in the tone, but at that distance it was hard to decide. I tried to analyze the tone, and then I thought what a fool I had been to start out the back door and let her see that I was barefoot. If I had gone out the front door or the side door she would never have known, not till dinner time anyway, and by then the day would have been half gone and I would have been all over the farm to see what the storm had done and down to the creek to see the flood. But it had never crossed my mind that they would try to stop you from going barefoot in June, no matter if there had been a gully-washer and a cold spell.

Nobody had ever tried to stop me in June as long as I could remember, and when you are nine years old, what you remember seems forever; for you remember everything and everything is important and stands big and full and fills up Time and is so solid that you can walk around and around it like a tree and look at it. You are aware that time passes, that there is a movement in time, but that is not what Time is. Time is not a movement, a flowing, a wind then, but is, rather, a kind of climate in which things are, and when a thing happens it begins to live and keeps on living and stands solid in Time like the tree that you can walk around. And if there is a movement, the movement is not Time itself, any more than a breeze is climate, and all the breeze does is to shake a little the leaves on the tree which is alive and solid. When you are nine, you know that there are things that you don't know, but you know that when you know something you know it. You know how a thing has been and you know that you can go barefoot in June. You do not understand that voice from back in the kitchen which says that you cannot go barefoot outdoors and run to see what has happened and rub your feet over the wet shivery grass and make the perfect mark of your foot in the smooth, creamy, red mud and then muse upon it as though you had suddenly come upon that single mark on the glistening auroral beach of the world. You have never seen a beach, but you have read the book and how the footprint was there.

The voice had said what it had said, and I looked savagely at the black stockings and the strong, scuffed brown shoes which I had brought from my closet as far as the hearth rug. I called once more, "But it's June," and waited.

"It's June," the voice replied from far away, "but it's blackberry winter."

I had lifted my head to reply to that, to make one more test of what was in that tone, when I happened to see the man.

The fireplace in the living room was at the end; for the stone chimney was built, as in so many of the farmhouses in Tennessee at the end of a gable, and there was a window on each side of the chimney. Out of the window on the north side of the fireplace I could see the man. When I saw the man I did not call out what I had intended, but, engrossed by the strangeness of the sight, watched him, still far off, come along the path by the edge of the woods.

What was strange was that there should be a man there at all. That path went along the yard fence, between the fence and the woods which came right down to the yard, and then on back past the chicken runs and on by the woods until it was lost to sight where the woods bulged out and cut off the back field. There the path disappeared into the woods. It led on back, I knew, through the woods and to the swamp, skirted the swamp where the big trees gave way to sycamores and water oaks and willows and tangled cane, and then led on to the river. Nobody ever went back there except people who wanted to gig frogs in the swamp or to fish in the river or to hunt in the woods, and those people, if they didn't have a standing permission from my father, always stopped to ask permission to cross the farm. But the man whom I now saw wasn't, I could tell even at that distance, a sportsman. And what would a sportsman have been doing down there after a storm? Besides, he was coming from the river, and nobody had gone down there that morning. I knew that for a fact, because if anybody had passed, certainly if a stranger had passed, the dogs would have made a racket and would have been out on him. But this man was coming up from the river and had come up through the woods. I suddenly had a vision of him moving up the grassy path in the woods, in the green twilight under the big trees, not making any sound on the path, while now and then, like drops off the eaves, a big drop of water would fall from a leaf or bough and strike a stiff oak leaf lower down with a small, hollow sound like a drop of water hitting tin. That sound, in the silence of the woods, would be very significant.

When you are a boy and stand in the stillness of woods, which can be so still that your heart almost stops beating and makes you want to stand there in the green twilight until you feel your very feet sinking into and clutching the earth like roots and your body breathing slow through its pores like the leaves—when you stand there and wait for the next drop to drop with its small, flat sound to a lower leaf, that sound seems to measure out something, to put an end to something, to begin something, and you cannot wait for it to happen and are afraid it will not happen, and then when it has happened, you are waiting again, almost afraid.

But the man whom I saw coming through the woods in my mind's eye did not pause and wait, growing into the ground and breathing with the enormous, soundless breathing of the leaves. Instead, I saw him moving in the green twilight inside my head as he was moving at that very moment along the path by the edge of the woods, coming toward the house. He was moving steadily, but not fast, with his shoulders hunched a little and his head thrust forward, like a man who has come a long way and has a long way to go. I shut my eyes for a couple of seconds, thinking that when I opened them he would not be there at all. There was no place for him to have come from, and there was no reason for him to come where he was coming, toward our house. But I opened my eyes, and there he was, and he was coming steadily along the side of the woods.

He was not yet even with the back chicken yard.

"Mama," I called.

"You put them on," the voice said.

"There's a man coming," I called, "out back."

She did not reply to that, and I guessed that she had gone to the kitchen window to look. She would be looking at the man and wondering who he was and what he wanted, the way you always do in the country, and if I went back there now she would not notice right off whether or not I was barefoot. So I went back to the kitchen.

She was standing by the window. "I don't recognize him," she said, not looking around at me.

"Where could he be coming from?" I asked.

"I don't know," she said

"What would he be doing down at the river? At night? In the storm?"

She studied the figure out the window, then said, "Oh, I reckon maybe he cut across from the Dunbar place."

That was, I realized, a perfectly rational explanation. He had not been down at the river in the storm, at night. He had come over this morning. You could cut across from the Dunbar place if you didn't mind breaking through a lot of elder and sassafras and blackberry bushes which had about taken over the old cross path, which nobody ever used any more. That satisfied me for a moment, but only for a moment. "Mama," I asked, "what would he be doing over at the Dunbar place last night?"

Then she looked at me, and I knew I had made a mistake, for she was looking at my bare feet. "You haven't got your shoes on," she said.

But I was saved by the dogs. That instant there was a bark which I recognized as Sam, the collie, and then a heavier, churning kind of bark which was Bully, and I saw a streak of white as Bully tore round the corner of the back porch and headed out for the man. Bully was a big, bone-white bull dog, the kind of dog that they used to call a farm bull dog but that you didn't see any more, heavy chested and heavy headed, but with pretty long legs. He could take a fence as light as a hound. He had just cleared the white paling fence toward the woods when my mother ran out to the back porch and began calling, "Here you, Bully! Here you!"

Bully stopped in the path, waiting for the man, but he gave a few more of those deep, gargling, savage barks that reminded you of something down a stone-lined well. The red clay mud, I saw, was splashing up over his white chest and looked exciting, like blood.

The man, however, had not stopped walking even when Bully took the fence and started at him. He had kept right on coming. All he had done was to switch a little paper parcel which he carried from the right hand to the left, and then reach into his pants pocket to get something. Then I saw the glitter and knew that he had a knife in his hand, probably the kind of mean knife just made for devilment and nothing else, with a blade as long as the blade of a frog-sticker, which will snap out ready when you press a button in the handle. That knife must have had a button in the handle, or else how could he have had the blade out glittering so quick and with just one hand?

Pulling his knife against the dogs was a funny thing to do, for Bully was a big, powerful brute and fast, and Sam was all right. If those dogs had meant business, they might have knocked him down and ripped him before he got a stroke in. He ought to have picked up a heavy stick, something to take a swipe at them with and something which they could see and respect when they came at him, but he apparently did not know much about dogs. He just held the knife blade close against the right leg, low down, and kept on moving down the path.

Then my mother had called, and Bully had stopped. So the man let the blade of the knife snap back into the handle, and dropped it into his pocket, and kept on coming. Many women would have been afraid with the strange man who they knew had that knife in his pocket. That is, if they were alone in the house with nobody but a nine-year-old boy. And my mother was alone, for my father had gone off, and Dellie, the cook, was down at her cabin because she wasn't feeling well. But my mother wasn't afraid. She wasn't a big woman, but she was clear and brisk about everything she did and looked everybody and everything right in the eye from her own blue eyes in her tanned face. She had been the first woman in the county to ride a horse astride (that was back when she was a girl and long before I was born), and I have seen her snatch up a pump gun and go out and knock a chicken hawk out of the air like a busted skeet when he came over her chicken yard. She was a steady and self-reliant woman, and when I think of her now after all the years she has been dead, I think of her brown hands, not big but somewhat square for a woman's hands, with square-cut nails. They looked, as a matter of fact, more like a young boy's hands than a grown woman's. But back then it never crossed my mind that she would ever be dead.

She stood on the back porch and watched the man enter the back gate, where the dogs (Bully had leaped back into the yard) were dancing and muttering and giving sidelong glances back to my mother to see if she meant what she had said. The man walked right by the dogs, almost brushing them, and didn't pay them any attention. I could see now that he wore old khaki pants, and a dark wool coat with stripes in it, and a gray felt hat. He had on a gray shirt with blue stripes in it, and no tie. But I could see a tie, blue and reddish, sticking in his side coat-pocket. Everything was wrong about what he wore. He ought to have been wearing blue jeans or overalls, and a straw hat or an old black felt hat, and the coat, granting that he might have been wearing a wool coat and not a jumper, ought not to have had those stripes. Those clothes, despite the fact that they were old enough and dirty enough for any tramp, didn't belong there in our back yard, coming down the path, in Middle Tennessee, miles away from any big town, and even a mile off the pike.

When he got almost to the steps, without having said anything, my mother, very matter-of-factly, said, "Good morning."

"Good morning," he said, and stopped and looked her over. He did not take off his hat, and under the brim you could see the perfectly unmemorable face, which wasn't old and wasn't young, or thick or thin. It was graying and covered with about three days of stubble. The eyes were a kind of nondescript, muddy hazel, or something like that, rather bloodshot. His teeth, when he opened his mouth, showed yellow and uneven. A couple of them had been knocked out. You knew that they had been knocked out, because there was a scar, not very old, there on the lower lip just beneath the gap.

"Are you hunting work?" my mother asked him.

"Yes," he said—not "yes, mam"—and still did not take off his hat.

"I don't know about my husband, for he isn't here," she said, and didn't mind a bit telling the tramp, or whoever he was, with the mean knife in his pocket, that no man was around, "but I can give you a few things to do. The storm has drowned a lot of my chicks. Three coops of them. You can gather them up and bury them. Bury them deep so the dogs won't get at them. In the woods. And fix the coops the wind blew over. And down yonder beyond that pen by the edge of the woods are some drowned poults. They got out and I couldn't get them in. Even after it started to rain hard. Poults haven't got any sense."

"What are them things—poults?" he demanded, and spat on the brick walk. He rubbed his foot over the spot, and I saw that he wore a black, pointed-toe low shoe, all cracked and broken. It was a crazy kind of shoe to be wearing in the country.

"Oh, they're young turkeys," my mother was saying. "And they haven't got any sense. I oughtn't to try to raise them around here with so many chickens, anyway. They don't thrive near chickens, even in separate pens. And I won't give up my chickens." Then she stopped herself and resumed briskly on the note of business. "When you finish that, you can fix my flower beds. A lot of trash and mud and gravel has washed down. Maybe you can save some of my flowers if you are careful."

"Flowers," the man said, in a low, impersonal voice which seemed to have a wealth of meaning, but a meaning which I could not fathom. As I think back on it, it probably was not pure contempt. Rather, it was a kind of impersonal and distant marveling that he should be on the verge of grubbing in a flower bed. He said the word, and then looked off across the yard.

"Yes, flowers," my mother replied with some asperity, as though she would have nothing said or implied against flowers. "And they were very fine this year." Then she stopped and looked at the man. "Are you hungry?" she demanded.

"Yeah," he said.

"I'll fix you something," she said, "before you get started." She turned to me. "Show him where he can wash up," she commanded, and went into the house.

I took the man to the end of the porch where a pump was and where a couple of wash pans sat on a low shelf for people to use before they went into the house. I stood there while he laid down his little parcel wrapped in newspaper and took off his hat and looked around for a nail to hang it on. He poured the water and plunged his hands into it. They were big hands, and strong looking, but they did not have the creases and the earth-color of the hands of men who work outdoors. But they were dirty, with black dirt ground into the skin and under the nails. After he had washed his hands, he poured another basin of water and washed his face. He dried his face, and with the towel still dangling in his grasp, stepped over to the mirror on the house wall. He rubbed one hand over the stubble on his face. Then he carefully inspected his face, turning first one side and then the other, and stepped back and settled his striped coat down on his shoulders. He had the movements of a man who has just dressed up to go to church or a party—the way he settled his coat and smoothed it and scanned himself in the mirror.

Then he caught my glance on him. He glared at me for an instant out of the bloodshot eyes, then demanded in a low, harsh voice, "What you looking at?"

"Nothing," I managed to say, and stepped back a step from him.

He flung the towel down, crumpled, on the shelf, and went toward the kitchen door and entered without knocking.

My mother said something to him which I could not catch. I started to go in again, then thought about my bare feet, and decided to go back of the chicken yard, where the man would have to come to pick up the dead chicks. I hung around behind the chicken house until he came out.

He moved across the chicken yard with a fastidious, not quite finicking motion, looking down at the curdled mud flecked with bits of chicken-droppings. The mud curled up over the soles of his black shoes. I stood back from him some six feet and watched him pick up the first of the drowned chicks. He held it up by one foot and inspected it.

There is nothing deader looking than a drowned chick. The feet curl in that feeble, empty way which back when I was a boy, even if I was a country boy who did not mind hog-killing or frog-gigging, made me feel hollow in the stomach. Instead of looking plump and fluffy, the body is stringy and limp with the fluff plastered to it, and the neck is long and loose like a little string of rag. And the eyes have that bluish membrane over them which makes you think of a very old man who is sick about to die.

The man stood there and inspected the chick. Then he looked all around as though he didn't know what to do with it.

"There's a great big old basket in the shed," I said, and pointed to the shed attached to the chicken house.

He inspected me as though he had just discovered my presence, and moved toward the shed.

"There's a spade there, too," I added.

He got the basket and began to pick up the other chicks, picking each one up slowly by a foot and then flinging it into the basket with a nasty, snapping motion. Now and then he would look at me out of the bloodshot eyes. Every time he seemed on the verge of saying something, but he did not. Perhaps he was building up to say something to me, but I did not wait that long. His way of looking at me made me so uncomfortable that I left the chicken yard.

Besides, I had just remembered that the creek was in flood, over the bridge, and that people were down there watching it. So I cut across the farm toward the creek. When I got to the big tobacco field I saw that it had not suffered much. The land lay right and not many tobacco plants had washed out of the ground. But I knew that a lot of tobacco round the country had been washed right out. My father had said so at breakfast.

My father was down at the bridge. When I came out of the gap in the osage hedge into the road, I saw him sitting on his mare over the heads of the other men who were standing around, admiring the flood. The creek was big here, even in low water; for only a couple of miles away it ran into the river, and when a real flood came, the red water got over the pike where it dipped down to the bridge, which was an iron bridge, and high over the floor and even the side railings of the bridge. Only the upper iron work would show, with the water boiling and frothing red and white around it. That creek rose so fast and so heavy because a few miles back it came down out of the hills, where the gorges filled up with water in no time when a rain came. The creek ran in a deep bed with limestone bluffs along both sides until it got within three quarters of a mile of the bridge, and when it came out from between those bluffs in flood it was boiling and hissing and steaming like water from a fire hose.

Whenever there was a flood, people from half the county would come down to see the sight. After a gully-washer there would not be any work to do anyway. If it didn't ruin your crop, you couldn't plow and you felt like taking a holiday to celebrate. If it did ruin your crop, there wasn't anything to do except to try to take your mind off the mortgage, if you were rich enough to have a mortgage, and if you couldn't afford a mortgage you needed something to take your mind off how hungry you would be by Christmas. So people would come down to the bridge and look at the flood. It made something different from the run of days.

There would not be much talking after the first few minutes of trying to guess how high the water was this time. The men and kids just stood around, or sat their horses or mules, as the case might be, or stood up in the wagon beds. They looked at the strangeness of the flood for an hour or two, and then somebody would say that he had better be getting on home to dinner and would start walking down the gray, puddled limestone pike, or would touch heel to his mount and start off. Everybody always knew what it would be like when he got down to the bridge, but people always came. It was like church or a funeral. They always came, that is, if it was summer and the flood unexpected. Nobody ever came down in winter to see high water.

When I came out of the gap in the bodock hedge, I saw the crowd, perhaps fifteen or twenty men and a lot of kids, and saw my father sitting his mare, Nellie Gray. He was a tall, limber man and carried himself well. I was always proud to see him sit a horse, he was so quiet and straight, and when I stepped through the gap of the hedge that morning, the first thing that happened was, I remember, the warm feeling I always had when I saw him up on a horse, just sitting. I did not go toward him, but skirted the crowd on the far side, to get a look at the creek. For one thing, I was not sure what he would say about the fact that I was barefoot. But the first thing I knew, I heard his voice calling, "Seth!"

I went toward him, moving apologetically past the men, who bent their large, red or thin, sallow faces above me. I knew some of the men, and knew their names, but because those I knew were there in a crowd, mixed with the strange faces, they seemed foreign to me, and not friendly. I did not look up at my father until I was almost within touching distance of his heel. Then I looked up and tried to read his face, to see if he was angry about my being barefoot. Before I could decide anything from that impassive, high-boned face, he had leaned over and reached a hand to me. "Grab on," he commanded.

I grabbed on and gave a little jump, and he said, "Up-see-daisy!" and whisked me, light as a feather, up to the pommel of his McClellan saddle.

"You can see better up here," he said, slid back on the cantle a little to make me more comfortable, and then, looking over my head at the swollen, tumbling water, seemed to forget all about me. But his right hand was laid on my side, just above my thigh, to steady me.

I was sitting there as quiet as I could, feeling the faint stir of my father's chest against my shoulders as it rose and fell with his breath, when I saw the cow. At first, looking up the creek, I thought it was just another big piece of driftwood steaming down the creek in the ruck of water, but all at once a pretty good-size boy who had climbed part way up a telephone pole by the pike so that he could see better yelled out, "Golly-damn, look at that-air cow!"

Everybody looked. It was a cow all right, but it might just as well have been driftwood; for it was dead as a chunk, rolling and roiling down the creek, appearing and disappearing, feet up or head up, it didn't matter which. The cow started up the talk again. Somebody wondered whether it would hit one of the clear places under the top girder of the bridge and get through or whether it would get tangled in the drift and trash that had piled against the upright girders and braces. Somebody remembered how about ten years before so much driftwood had piled up on the bridge that it was knocked off its foundations. Then the cow hit. It hit the edge of the drift against one of the girders, and hung there. For a few seconds it seemed as though it might tear loose, but then we saw that it was really caught. It bobbed and heaved on its side there in a slow, grinding, uneasy fashion. It had a yoke around its neck, the kind made out of a forked limb to keep a jumper behind fence.

"She shore jumped one fence," one of the men said.

And another: "Well, she done jumped her last one, fer a fack."

Then they began to wonder about whose cow it might be. They decided it must belong to Milt Alley. They said that he had a cow that was a jumper, and kept her in a fenced-in piece of ground up the creek. I had never seen Milt Alley, but I knew who he was. He was a squatter and lived up the hills a way, on a shirt-tail patch of set-on-edge land, in a cabin. He was pore white trash. He had lots of children. I had seen the children at school, when they came. They were thin-faced, with straight, sticky-looking, dough-colored hair, and they smelled something like old sour buttermilk, not because they drank so much buttermilk but because that is the sort of smell which children out of those cabins tend to have. The big Alley boy drew dirty pictures and showed them to the little boys at school.

That was Milt Alley's cow. It looked like the kind of cow he would have, a scrawny, old, sway-backed cow, with a yoke around her neck. I wondered if Milt Alley had another cow.

"Poppa," I said, "do you think Milt Alley has got another cow?"

"You say 'Mr. Alley,' " my father said quietly.

"Do you think he has?"

"No telling," my father said.

Then a big gangly boy, about fifteen, who was sitting on a scraggly little old mule with a piece of croker sack thrown across the saw-tooth spine, and who had been staring at the cow, suddenly said to nobody in particular, "Reckin anybody ever et drownt cow?"

He was the kind of boy who might just as well as not have been the son of Milt Alley, with his faded and patched overalls ragged at the bottom of the pants and the mudstiff brogans hanging off his skinny, bare ankles at the level of the mule's belly. He had said what he did, and then looked embarrassed and sullen when all the eyes swung at him. He hadn't meant to say it, I am pretty sure now. He would have been too proud to say it, just as Milt Alley would have been too proud. He had just been thinking out loud, and the words had popped out.

There was an old man standing there on the pike, an old man with a white beard. "Son," he said to the embarrassed and sullen boy on the mule, "you live long enough and you'll find a man will eat anything when the time comes."

"Time gonna come fer some folks this year," another man said.

"Son," the old man said, "in my time I et things a man don't like to think on. I was a sojer and I rode with Gin'l Forrest, and them things we et when the time come, I tell you. I et meat what got up and run when you taken out your knife to cut a slice to put on the fire. You had to knock it down with a carbene butt, it was so active. That-air meat would jump like a bullfrog, it was so full of skippers."

But nobody was listening to the old man. The boy on the mule turned his sullen sharp face from him, dug a heel into the side of the mule and went off up the pike with a motion which made you think that any second you would hear mule bones clashing inside that lank and scrofulous hide.

"Cy Dundee's boy," a man said, and nodded toward the figure going up the pike on the mule.

"Reckin Cy Dundee's young-uns seen times they'd settle fer drownt cow," another man said.

The old man with the beard peered at them both from his weak, slow eyes, first at one and then at the other. "Live long enough," he said, "and a man will settle for what he kin git."

Then there was silence again, with the people looking at the red, foam-flecked water.

My father lifted the bridle rein in his left hand, and the mare turned and walked around the group and was up the pike. We rode on up to our big gate, where my father dismounted to open it and let me myself ride Nellie Gray through. When he got to the lane that led off from the drive about two hundred yards from our house, my father said, "Grab on." I grabbed on, and he let me down to the ground. "I'm going to ride down and look at my corn," he said. "You go on." He took the lane, and I stood there on the drive and watched him ride off. He was wearing cowhide boots and an old hunting coat, and I thought that that made him look very military, like a picture. That and the way he rode.

I did not go to the house. Instead, I went by the vegetable garden and crossed behind the stables, and headed down for Dellie's cabin. I wanted to go down and play with Jebb, who was Dellie's little boy about two years older than I was. Besides, I was cold. I shivered as I walked, and I had gooseflesh. The mud which crawled up between my toes with every step I took was like ice. Dellie would have a fire, but she wouldn't make me put on shoes and stockings.

Dellie's cabin was of logs, with one side, because it was on a slope, set on limestone chunks, with a little porch attached to it, and had a little whitewashed fence around it and a gate with plow points on a wire to clink when somebody came in, and had two big white oaks in the yard and some flowers and a nice privy in the back with some honeysuckle growing over it. Dellie and Old Jebb, who was Jebb's father and who lived with Dellie and had lived with her for twenty-five years even if they never had got married, were careful to keep everything nice around their cabin. They had the name all over the community for being clean and clever Negroes. Dellie and Jebb were what they used to call "white-folks niggers." There was a big difference between their cabin and the other two cabins farther down where the other tenants lived. My father kept the other cabins weatherproof, but he couldn't undertake to go down and pick up after the litter they strewed. They didn't take the trouble to have a vegetable patch like Dellie and Jebb or to make preserves from wild plum, and jelly from crab apple the way Dellie did. They were shiftless, and my father was always threatening to get shed of them. But he never did. When they finally left, they just up and left on their own, for no reason, to go and be shiftless somewhere else. Then some more came. But meanwhile they lived down there, Matt Rawson and his family, and Sid Turner and his, and I played with their children all over the farm when they weren't working. But when I wasn't around they were mean sometimes to Little Jebb. That was because the other tenants down there were jealous of Dellie and Jebb.

I was so cold that I ran the last fifty yards to Dellie's gate. As soon as I had entered the yard, I saw that the storm had been hard on Dellie's flowers. The yard was, as I have said, on a slight slope, and the water running across had gutted the flower beds and washed out all the good black woods-earth which Dellie had brought in. What little grass there was in the yard was plastered sparsely down on the ground, the way the drainage water had left it. It reminded me of the way the fluff was plastered down on the skin of the drowned chicks that the strange man had been picking up, up in my mother's chicken yard.

I took a few steps up the path to the cabin, and then I saw that the drainage water had washed a lot of trash and filth out from under Dellie's house. Up toward the porch, the ground was not clean any more. Old pieces of rag, two or three rusted cans, pieces of rotten rope, some hunks of old dog dung, broken glass, old paper, and all sorts of things like that had washed out from under Dellie's house to foul her clean yard. It looked just as bad as the yards of the other cabins, or worse. It was worse, as a matter of fact, because it was a surprise. I had never thought of all that filth being under Dellie's house. It was not anything against Dellie that the stuff had been under the cabin. Trash will get under any house. But I did not think of that when I saw the foulness which had washed out on the ground which Dellie sometimes used to sweep with a twig broom to make nice and clean.

I picked my way past the filth, being careful not to get my bare feet on it, and mounted to Dellie's door. When I knocked, I heard her voice telling me to come in.

It was dark inside the cabin, after the daylight, but I could make out Dellie piled up in bed under a quilt, and Little Jebb crouched by the hearth, where a low fire simmered. "Howdy," I said to Dellie, "how you feeling?"

Her big eyes, the whites surprising and glaring in the black face, fixed on me as I stood there, but she did not reply. It did not look like Dellie, or act like Dellie, who would grumble and bustle around our kitchen, talking to herself, scolding me or Little Jebb, clanking pans, making all sorts of unnecessary noises and mutterings like an old-fashioned black steam thrasher engine when it has got up an extra head of steam and keeps popping the governor and rumbling and shaking on its wheels. But now Dellie just lay up there on the bed, under the patch-work quilt, and turned the black face, which I scarcely recognized, and the glaring white eyes to me.

"How you feeling?" I repeated.

"I'se sick," the voice said croakingly out of the strange black face which was not attached to Dellie's big, squat body, but stuck out from under a pile of tangled bed-clothes. Then the voice added: "Mighty sick."

"I'm sorry," I managed to say.

The eyes remained fixed on me for a moment, then they left me and the head rolled back on the pillow. "Sorry," the voice said, in a flat way which wasn't question or statement of anything. It was just the empty word put into the air with no meaning or expression, to float off like a feather or a puff of smoke, while the big eyes, with the whites like the peeled white of hard-boiled eggs, stared at the ceiling.

"Dellie," I said after a minute, "there's a tramp up at the house. He's got a knife."

She was not listening. She closed her eyes.

I tiptoed over to the hearth where Jebb was and crouched beside him. We began to talk in low voices. I was asking him to get out his train and play train. Old Jebb had put spool wheels on three cigar boxes and put wire links between the boxes to make a train for Jebb. The box that was the locomotive had the top closed and a length of broom stick for a smoke stack. Jebb didn't want to get the train out, but I told him I would go home if he didn't. So he got out the train, and the colored rocks, and fossils of crinoid stems, and other junk he used for the load, and we began to push it around, talking the way we thought trainmen talked, making a chuck-chucking sound under the breath for the noise of the locomotive and now and then uttering low, cautious toots for the whistle. We got so interested in playing train that the toots got louder. Then, before he thought, Jebb gave a good, loud toot-toot, blowing for a crossing.

"Come here," the voice said from the bed.

Jebb got up slow from his hands and knees, giving me a sudden, naked, inimical look.

"Come here!" the voice said.

Jebb went to the bed. Dellie propped herself weakly up on one arm, muttering, "Come closer."

Jebb stood closer.

"Last thing I do, I'm gonna do it," Dellie said. "Done tole you to be quiet."

Then she slapped him. It was an awful slap, more awful for the kind of weakness which it came from and brought to focus. I had seen her slap Jebb before, but the slapping had always been the kind of easy slap you would expect from a good-natured, grumbling Negro woman like

Dellie. But this was different. It was awful. It was so awful that Jebb didn't make a sound. The tears just popped out and ran down his face, and his breath came sharp, like gasps.

Dellie fell back. "Cain't even be sick," she said to the ceiling. "Git sick and they won't even let you lay. They tromp all over you. Cain't even be sick." Then she closed her eyes.

I went out of the room. I almost ran getting to the door, and I did run across the porch and down the steps and across the yard, not caring whether or not I stepped on the filth which had washed out from under the cabin. I ran almost all the way home. Then I thought about my mother catching me with the bare feet. So I went down to the stables.

I heard a noise in the crib, and opened the door. There was Big Jebb, sitting on an old nail keg, shelling corn into a bushel basket. I went in, pulling the door shut behind me, and crouched on the floor near him. I crouched there for a couple of minutes before either of us spoke, and watched him shelling the corn.

He had very big hands, knotted and graying at the joints, with calloused palms which seemed to be streaked with rust with the rust coming up between the fingers to show from the back. His hands were so strong and tough that he could take a big ear of corn and rip the grains right off the cob with the palm of his hand, all in one motion, like a machine. "Work long as me," he would say, "and the good Lawd'll give you a hand lak cass-ion won't nuthin' hurt." And his hands did look like cast iron, old cast iron streaked with rust.

He was an old man, up in his seventies, thirty years or more older than Dellie, but he was strong as a bull. He was a squat sort of man, heavy in the shoulders, with remarkably long arms, the kind of build they say the river natives have on the Congo from paddling so much in their boats. He had a round bullet-head, set on powerful shoulders. His skin was very black, and the thin hair on his head was now grizzled like tufts of old cotton batting. He had small eyes and a flat nose, not big, and the kindest and wisest old face in the world, the blunt, sad, wise face of an old animal peering tolerantly out on the goings-on of the merely human creatures before him. He was a good man, and I loved him next to my mother and father. I crouched there on the floor of the crib and watched him shell corn with the rusty cast-iron hands, while he looked down at me out of the little eyes set in the blunt face.

"Dellie says she's mighty sick," I said.

"Yeah," he said.

"What's she sick from?"

"Woman-mizry," he said.

"What's woman-mizry?"

"Hit comes on 'em," he said. "Hit just comes on 'em when the time comes."

"What is it?"

"Hit is the change," he said. "Hit is the change of life and time."

"What changes?"

"You too young to know."

"Tell me."

"Time come and you find out everything."

I knew that there was no use in asking him any more. When I asked him things and he said that, I always knew that he would not tell me. So I continued to crouch there and watch him. Now that I had sat there a little while, I was cold again.

"What you shiver fer?" he asked me.

"I'm cold. I'm cold because it's blackberry winter," I said.

"Maybe 'tis and maybe 'tain't," he said.

"My mother says it is."

"Ain't sayen Miss Sallie doan know and ain't sayen she do. But folks doan know everthing."

"Why isn't it blackberry winter?"

"Too late fer blackberry winter. Blackberries done bloomed."

"She said it was."

"Blackberry winter just a leetle cold spell. Hit come and then hit go away, and hit is growed summer of a sudden lak a gunshot. Ain't no tellen hit will go way this time."

"It's June," I said.

"June," he replied with great contempt. "That what folks say. What June mean? Maybe hit is come cold to stay."

"Why?"

"Cause this-here old yearth is tahrd. Hit is tahrd and ain't gonna perduce. Lawd let hit come rain one time forty days and forty nights, 'cause He was tahrd of sinful folks. Maybe this-here old yearth say to the Lawd, Lawd, I done plum tahrd, Lawd, lemme rest. And Lawd say, Yearth, you done your best, you give 'em cawn and you give 'em taters, and all they think on is they gut, and, Yearth, you kin take a rest."

"What will happen?"

"Folks will eat up everthing. The yearth won't perduce no more. Folks cut down all the trees and burn 'em 'cause they cold, and the yearth won't grow no more. I been tellen 'em. I been tellen folks. Sayen, maybe this year, hit is the time. But they doan listen to me, how the yearth is tahrd. Maybe this year they find out."

"Will everything die?"

"Everthing and everbody, hit will be so."

"This year?"

"Ain't no tellen. Maybe this year."

"My mother said it is blackberry winter," I said confidently, and got up.

"Ain't sayen nuthin' agin Miss Sallie," he said.

I went to the door of the crib. I was really cold now. Running, I had got up a sweat and now I was worse.

I hung on the door, looking at Jebb, who was shelling corn again. "There's a tramp came to the house," I said. I had almost forgotten the tramp.

"Yeah."

"He came by the back way. What was he doing down there in the storm?"

"They comes and they goes," he said, "and ain't no tellen."

"He had a mean knife."

"The good ones and the bad ones, they comes and they goes. Storm or sun, light or dark. They is folks and they comes and they goes lak folks."

I hung on the door, shivering.

He studied me a moment, then said, "You git on to the house. You ketch yore death. Then what yore mammy say?"

I hesitated.

"You git," he said.

When I came to the back yard, I saw that my father was standing by the back porch and the tramp was walking toward him. They began talking before I reached them, but I got there just as my father was saying, "I'm sorry, but I haven't got any work. I got all the hands on the place I need now. I won't need any extra until wheat thrashing."

The stranger made no reply, just looked at my father.

My father took out his leather coin purse, and got out a half-dollar. He held it toward the man. "This is for half a day," he said.

The man looked at the coin, and then at my father, making no motion to take the money. But that was the right amount. A dollar a day was what you paid them back in 1910. And the man hadn't even worked half a day.

Then the man reached out and took the coin. He dropped it into the right side pocket of his coat. Then he said, very slowly, and without feeling: "I didn't want to work on your——farm."

He used the word which they would have frailed° me to death for using.

I looked at my father's face and it was streaked white under the sunburn. Then he said, "Get off this place. Get off this place or I won't be responsible."

The man dropped his right hand into his pants pocket. It was the pocket where he kept the knife. I was just about to yell to my father about the knife when the hand came back out with nothing in it. The man gave a kind of twisted grin, showing where the teeth had been knocked out

---

°*frailed:* flailed

above the new scar. I thought that instant how maybe he had tried before to pull a knife on somebody else and had got his teeth knocked out.

So now he just gave that twisted, sickish grin out of the unmemorable, grayish face, and then spat on the brick path. The glob landed just about six inches from the toe of my father's right boot. My father looked down at it, and so did I. I thought that if the glob had hit my father's boot something would have happened. I looked down and saw the bright glob, and on one side of it my father's strong cowhide boots, with the brass eyelets and the leather thongs, heavy boots splashed with good red mud and set solid on the bricks, and on the other side the pointed-toe, broken, black shoes, on which the mud looked so sad and out of place. Then I saw one of the black shoes move a little, just a twitch first, then a real step backward.

The man moved in a quarter circle to the end of the porch, with my father's steady gaze upon him all the while. At the end of the porch, the man reached up to the shelf where the wash pans were to get his little newspaper-wrapped parcel. Then he disappeared around the corner of the house and my father mounted the porch and went into the kitchen without a word.

I followed around the house to see what the man would do. I wasn't afraid of him now, no matter if he did have the knife. When I got around in front, I saw him going out the yard gate and starting up the drive toward the pike. So I ran to catch up with him. He was sixty yards or so up the drive before I caught up.

I did not walk right up even with him at first, but trailed him, the way a kid will, about seven or eight feet behind, now and then running two or three steps in order to hold my place against his longer stride. When I first came up behind him, he turned to give me a look, just a meaningless look, and then fixed his eyes up the drive and kept on walking.

When we had got around the bend in the drive which cut the house from sight, and were going along by the edge of the woods, I decided to come up even with him. I ran a few steps, and was by his side, or almost, but some feet off to the right. I walked along in this position for a while, and he never noticed me. I walked along until we got within sight of the big gate that let on the pike.

Then I said: "Where did you come from?"

He looked at me then with a look which seemed almost surprised that I was there. Then he said, "It ain't none of yore business."

We went on another fifty feet.

Then I said, "Where are you going?"

He stopped, studied me dispassionately for a moment, then suddenly took a step toward me and leaned his face down at me. The lips jerked back, but not in any grin, to show where the teeth were knocked out and to make the scar on the lower lip come white with the tension.

He said: "Stop following me. You don't stop following me and I cut yore throat, you little son-of-a-bitch."

Then he went on to the gate, and up the pike.

That was thirty-five years ago. Since that time my father and mother have died. I was still a boy, but a big boy, when my father got cut on the blade of a mowing machine and died of lockjaw. My mother sold the place and went to town to live with her sister. But she never took hold after my father's death, and she died within three years, right in middle life. My aunt always said, "Sallie just died of a broken heart, she was so devoted." Dellie is dead, too, but she died, I heard, quite a long time after we sold the farm.

As for Little Jebb, he grew up to be a mean and ficey° Negro. He killed another Negro in a fight and got sent to the penitentiary, where he is yet, the last I heard tell. He probably grew up to be mean and ficey from just being picked on so much by the children of the other tenants, who were jealous of Jebb and Dellie for being thrifty and clever and being white-folks' niggers.

Old Jebb lived forever. I saw him ten years ago and he was about a hundred then, and not looking much different. He was living in town then, on relief—that was back in the Depression—when I went to see him. He said to me: "Too strong to die. When I was a young feller just comen on and seen how things wuz, I prayed the Lawd. I said, Oh, Lawd, gimme strength and meke me strong fer to do and to in-dure. The Lawd hearkened to my prayer. He give me strength. I was in-duren proud fer being strong and me much man. The Lawd give me my prayer and my strength. But now He done gone off and fergot me and left me alone with my strength. A man doan know what to pray fer, and him mortal."

Jebb is probably living yet, as far as I know.

That is what has happened since the morning when the tramp leaned his face down at me and showed his teeth and said: "Stop following me. You don't stop following me and I cut yore throat, you little son-of-a-bitch." That was what he said, for me not to follow him. But I did follow him, all the years.

*   *   *

°*ficey:* quarrelsome

Some Verses from the Child's Garden

The peculiar aspect of human consciousness called Memory, which allows us to consider, side by side, recollections from other times and places and present realities is the basis of the following group of poems. Each of them pursues a simple strategy: the knowledge of innocence and youth is juxtaposed in the speaker's mind with the knowledge of age and experience, and the emotional force of the contrast gives the poem its energy and meaning. Whereas the stories by Joyce, Updike, and Warren concentrate on the youth's experience of knowledge, these poems all show very clearly the adult looking back with various emotions to the childish world, with full awareness of the difference between what was and what is.

This stance suggests that we should think about how the Fall is to be lived with, how the Adam figure, expelled by Time, Knowledge, and Process from the Child's Garden, should look back. It is also an essentially historical question: what is the meaning of the past, what is its use to the present, what impact does yesterday have on the way we live and feel today?

FERN HILL

Dylan Thomas (1914–1953)

Now as I was young and easy under the apple boughs
About the lilting house and happy as the grass was green,
   The night above the dingle starry,
     Time let me hail and climb
   Golden in the heydays of his eyes,
And honoured among wagons I was prince of the apple towns
And once below a time I lordly had the trees and leaves
     Trail with daisies and barley
   Down the rivers of the windfall light.

And as I was green and carefree, famous among the barns
About the happy yard and singing as the farm was home,
   In the sun that is young once only,
     Time let me play and be
   Golden in the mercy of his means,
And green and golden I was huntsman and herdsman, the calves

Sang to my horn, the foxes on the hills barked clear and cold,
And the sabbath rang slowly
In the pebbles of the holy streams.

All the sun long it was running, it was lovely, the hay-
Fields high as the house, the tunes from the chimneys, it was air 20
And playing, lovely and watery
And fire green as grass.
And nightly under the simple stars
As I rode to sleep the owls were bearing the farm away,
All the moon long I heard, blessed among stables, the nightjars 25
Flying with the ricks, and the horses
Flashing into the dark.

And then to awake, and the farm, like a wanderer white
With the dew, come back, the cock on his shoulder: it was all
Shining, it was Adam and maiden, 30
The sky gathered again
And the sun grew round that very day.
So it must have been after the birth of the simple light
In the first, spinning place, the spelbound horses walking warm
Out of the whinnying green stable 35
On to the fields of praise.

And honoured among foxes and pheasants by the gay house
Under the new made clouds and happy as the heart was long,
In the sun born over and over,
I ran my heedless ways, 40
My wishes raced through the house high hay
And nothing I cared, at my sky blue trades, that time allows
In all his tuneful turning so few and such morning songs
Before the children green and golden
Follow him out of grace, 45

Nothing I cared, in the lamb white days, that time would take me
Up to the swallow thronged loft by the shadow of my hand,
In the moon that is always rising,
Nor that riding to sleep
I should hear him fly with the high fields 50
And wake to the farm forever fled from the childless land.
Oh as I was young and easy in the mercy of his means,
Time held me green and dying
Though I sang in my chains like the sea.

IN THE OLD DAYS

William Stafford (1914–   )

The wide field that was the rest of the world
came forward at evening, lowered
beyond our window shades; and Mother
spoke from her corner, about the wide field:

How someone whose eyes held another century   5
brought shadows of strange animals
over the mountains, and they were tethered
at night in little groups in the wide field,

And their eyes like wandering sparks
made constellations against the trees;   10
and how, many skies later, my father left
those animals and brought Mother news of the wide field.

Some time, some sunset, our window, she said,
would find itself again with a line of shadows
and the strange call would surround our house   15
and carry us away through the wide field.

Then Mother sang. But we listened, beyond:
we knew that the night she had put into a story was real.

TIME

William Stafford

The years to come (empty boxcars
waiting on a siding while someone forgets
and the tall grass tickles their bellies)
will sometime stay, rusted still;
and a little boy who clambers up,   5
saved by his bare feet, will run
along the top, jump to the last car,
and gaze down at the end into that river
near every town.
                    Once when I was a boy
I took that kind of walk,   10

beyond the last houses, out where the grass
lived, then the tired siding where trains whistled.
The river was choked with old Chevies and Fords.
And that was the day the world ended.

hist, whist

E. E. Cummings (1894–1962)

hist   whist
little ghostthings
tip-toe
twinkle-toe

little twitchy   5
witches and tingling
goblins
hob-a-nob   hob-a-nob

little hoppy happy
toad in tweeds   10
tweeds
little itchy mousies

with scuttling
eyes   rustle and run   and
hidehidehide   15
whisk

whisk   look out for the old woman
with the wart on her nose
what she'll do to yer
nobody knows   20

for she knows the devil   ooch
the devil   ouch
the devil
ach   the great

green   25
dancing
devil
devil

devil
devil   30

    wheeEEE

o by the by

E. E. Cummings

o by the by
has anybody seen
little you-i
who stood on a green
hill and threw   5
his wish at blue

with a swoop and a dart
out flew his wish
(it dived like a fish
but it climbed like a dream)   10
throbbing like a heart
singing like a flame

blue took it my
far beyond far
and high beyond high   15
bluer took it your
but bluest took it our
away beyond where

what a wonderful thing
is the end of a string   20
(murmurs little you-i
as the hill becomes nil)
and will somebody tell
me why people let go

BUBBLES

George Garrett (1929–   )

Not like we used to with pipes
which combined at once the pleasure of
pretending we were smoking with
the chance of a mouthful of soap,

but nowadays with a seagreen liquid,   5
bottled, and a spoon-shaped eyelet
with a handle. You dip it
and in a wave you have

a room that's full of bubbles.
Round and rich, they catch the light   10
in square small patches of color,
and they hover, float and fall

and pop. My children are
pleased and puzzled. It's new
to them. They snatch at globes   15
and find their hands are empty

and the bubble's gone.
Let some stern moralist take on
the task of making sense of this.
I never could explain why balloons   20

burst and playing card towers fall.
I say they're beautiful to see,
however made, by pipe or wand,
and not to have.

Kings might have given ransom   25
to own an air so jeweled and clear,
so nothing filled and handsome.
Children, there are no kings here.

From *Abraham's Knife* by George Garrett. Reprinted by permission of the publisher,
The University of North Carolina Press.

THE ENCOUNTER: JUVENILE DIVISION   *123*

CHILDHOOD IS THE KINGDOM WHERE NOBODY DIES

Edna St. Vincent Millay (1892–1950)

Childhood is not from birth to a certain age and at a certain age
The child is grown, and puts away childish things.
Childhood is the kingdom where nobody dies.

Nobody that matters, that is. Distant relatives of course
Die, whom one never has seen or has seen for an hour,
And they gave one candy in a pink-and-green striped bag, or
a jack-knife,
And went away, and cannot really be said to have lived at all.

And cats die. They lie on the floor and lash their tails,
And their reticent fur is suddenly all in motion
With fleas that one never knew were there,
Polished and brown, knowing all there is to know,
Trekking off into the living world.
You fetch a shoe-box, but it's much too small, because she won't
curl up now:
So you find a bigger box, and bury her in the yard, and weep.

But you do not wake up a month from then, two months,
A year from then, two years, in the middle of the night
And weep, with your knuckles in your mouth, and say Oh, God!
Oh, God!
Childhood is the kingdom where nobody dies that matters,—
mothers and fathers don't die.

And if you have said, "For heaven's sake, must you always be
kissing a person?"
Or, "I do wish to gracious you'd stop tapping on the window
with your thimble!"
Tomorrow, or even the day after tomorrow if you're busy
having fun,
Is plenty of time to say, "I'm sorry, mother."

To be grown up is to sit at the table with people who have died,
who neither listen nor speak;

From *Collected Poems* by Edna St. Vincent Millay. Copyright 1934, 1962, by Edna St. Vincent Millay and Norma Millay Ellis. Published by Harper & Row Publishers, Inc.

Who do not drink their tea, though they always said
Tea was such a comfort.   25

Run down into the cellar and bring up the last jar of rasp-
    berries; they are not tempted.
Flatter them, ask them what was it they said exactly
That time, to the bishop, or to the overseer, or to Mrs. Mason;
They are not taken in.
Shout at them, get red in the face, rise,   30
Drag them up out of their chairs by their stiff shoulders and
    shake them and yell at them;
They are not startled, they are not even embarrassed; they slide
    back into their chairs.

Your tea is cold now.
You drink it standing up,
And leave the house.   35

YOUTH SINGS A SONG OF ROSEBUDS

Countee Cullen (1903–1946)

Since men grow diffident at last,
And care no whit at all
If spring be come, or the fall be past,
Or how the cool rains fall,

I come to no flower but I pluck,   5
I raise no cup but I sip,
For a mouth is the best of sweets to suck;
The oldest wine's on the lip.

If I grow old in a year or two,
And come to the querulous song   10
Of "Alack and aday" and "This was true,
And that, when I was young,"

I must have sweets to remember by,
Some blossom saved from the mire,
Some death-rebellious ember I   15
Can fan into a fire.

From *On These I Stand* by Countee Cullen. Copyright 1927 by Harper & Row, Publishers, Inc.; renewed 1955 by Ida M. Cullen. By permission of the publishers.

DINKY

Theodore Roethke (1908–1963)

O what's the weather in a Beard?
It's windy there, and rather weird,
And when you think the sky has cleared
 —Why, there is Dirty Dinky.

Suppose you walk out in a Storm,   5
With nothing on to keep you warm,
And then step barefoot on a Worm
 —Of course, it's Dirty Dinky.

As I was crossing a hot hot Plain,
I saw a sight that caused me pain,   10
You asked me before, I'll tell you again:
 —It *looked* like Dirty Dinky.

Last night you lay a-sleeping? No!
The room was thirty-five below;
The sheets and blankets turned to snow.   15
 —He'd got in: Dirty Dinky.

You'd better watch the things you do,
You'd better watch the things you do,
You're part of him; he's part of you
 —*You* may be Dirty Dinky.   20

QUESTIONS

a. In *Araby*, what new knowledge does the narrator's experience describe? How aware is the narrator of the process of change in his consciousness at the time the story takes place? How much more aware is he as he looks back? At what points does the reader have a greater awareness of what is happening than the narrator? How does this happen? What phrases suggest this? How are changes in the consciousness of the narrator shown?

b. How aware is the narrator of the sexual aspects of his feelings? What images suggest these? Where is Mangan's sister seen? How many times? What images suggest the narrator's attitude toward her? Why does he fail to buy her a present?

c. How old was the narrator when these events occurred? Why is it significant that a grown man is recalling a boyhood experience that he can look back on as being rather foolish?

d. In Joyce's fiction it is important to relate details of the story to thematic concerns. For example, what is the importance of the setting in North Richmond Street? What significance is there in the descriptions of the house in which the narrator lived, its previous owner, and its backyard?

e. What can the reader tell about the boy's aunt and uncle? What is the importance of his living with them rather than with parents?

f. What is the importance of the bazaar itself? Wouldn't an ordinary store serve the story just as well as a place in which to buy a present?

g. *Dubliners* contains other stories where new levels of awareness and new knowledge are thrust upon people without their seeking it. See particularly *The Sisters, An Encounter, A Painful Case,* and *The Dead.*

a. In *You'll Never Know, Dear, How Much I Love You,* why does Ben feel glad and willing to spend or lose his money? What is important about the attitude he takes toward the carnival?

b. What does the title mean? Why does Updike choose that old song instead of another? Why does it make Ben so happy to hear it?

c. Why would Ben have been happier had the operator of the wheel kept all his money? What would he have felt had he been given back all he had lost?

d. Notice the great number of exactly described details: the names of school children, the roofs of houses, clothing, the feel of the coins clutched in Ben's hand, the booths at the carnival, the booths' keepers, and so forth. What is the effect of these details?

e. How do they support the thematic concerns of the story? We know that Updike admires Joyce. What points of correspondence between this story and *Araby* can you find? What similarities do you find in tone, attitude, style, situation? Are there significant differences? Which story is the more moving, the richer in feeling?

f. Updike has collected a number of stories on the theme of growth in a volume called *Olinger Stories,* which carries the youthful Ben (under other names) forward to middle age. See also the novel, *The Centaur.*

3*a.* In *Blackberry Winter,* what various intimations of a world beyond the Farm and the Summer and Youth does Seth receive?

b. What connects the tramp from the woods, the previous night's storm, the flooded creek, and the visit to Dellie's house? List the effects of the storm which Seth notices.

c. What aspects of his parents' behavior is Seth most aware of? What is the function in the story of their presence and their competence?

d. Explain the title, and the questions about the title which Big Jebb raises.

e. What is the effect of the shift in time and perspective at the end of the story?

f. What is the importance of the discussion of the Milt Alley and Cy Dundee families?

g. What degree of consciousness does Seth have of the meanings of this day's experiences? Where is his own perception shown most clearly? What is his relation to the adult world?

h. Warren's fiction shows a preoccupation with the Fall theme. *All the King's Men* is especially rich in allusions to the Knowledge question. See also the volume of stories edited by Warren and Albert Erskine called *Short Story Masterpieces.* This volume offers a useful collection of stories by a variety of modern writers, many reflecting this motif. See especially J. D. Salinger's *Uncle Wiggily in Connecticut,* Sherwood Anderson's *The Egg,* F. Scott Fitzgerald's *Winter Dreams,* and Henry James's *The Tree of Knowledge.*

4*a.* Describe the attitude taken toward the past by the speaker in each of the poems read in this section. What phrases, images, or words convey that attitude? Which of the attitudes do you find most acceptable, most worthwhile, most satisfactory? Which least? Why?

b. Are any of these poems more complex than others? Do any of them reflect attitudes of greater subtlety or ambiguity than others?

c. What particular aspects of childhood does each poem emphasize? What do they have in common?

d. Define Nostalgia. Is this emotion sentimental? Do any of these poems exaggerate the childhood condition?

e. What aspects of childhood are apparent in the language of these poems?

PART V

The Encounter: Older and then Wiser

The magic of first love is our ignorance that it can ever end.

—*Disraeli*

Heroic Innocence

Each age has its own idea of what innocence is and is not. The 19th century discovered the beauty of childhood and the pathos and pity of the child taken advantage of. Dickens's treatment of David Copperfield innocently encountering the cruel stepfather, Mr. Murdstone, and vicious schoolmasters and thieves is an outstanding example of the triumph of intelligent benevolence over the corruptions offered by life. Dickens's little girls—Little Dorrit, Esther Summerson, and Sissy Jupe, among others— are even more distinguished by the purity with which their spirits resist the cynicisms of society.

George Meredith's novel, *The Ordeal of Richard Feverel,* is a considerable distance from Dickens's in style, attitude, and tone, but its thematic interest is similar. The following passage is a dramatic account of the meeting of two innocents, Richard and Lucy Desborough, in a country garden of rural England. Young love is celebrated with all the appropriate poetic associations and imagery: Romeo and Juliet, Ferdinand and Miranda, the enchanted Paradise in which the Lovers find a new world in each other. Perhaps it is the splendid isolation of this meeting that gives it intensity and vividness; yet there is also an unstated awareness that the beauty and glory of love must touch a more real world at some point. Indeed, as the novel unfolds, Richard and Lucy suffer reality enough. But the reader should notice the mixed tones, the interesting and moving combination of lyric ecstasy and mocking humor, and the way in which detached awareness and a more worldly evaluation of this experience linger on the edges of consciousness while we read.

From THE ORDEAL OF RICHARD FEVEREL

George Meredith (1828–1909)

Chapter XVII: AN ATTRACTION

When Nature has made us ripe for Love it seldom occurs that the Fates are behindhand in furnishing a Temple for the flame.

Above green-flashing plunges of a weir, and shaken by the thunder below, lilies, golden and white, were swaying at anchor among the reeds. Meadow-sweet hung from the banks thick with weed and trailing bramble, and there also hung a daughter of Earth. Her face was shaded by a broad straw-hat with a flexile° brim that left her lips and chin in the sun, and sometimes nodding, sent forth a light of promising eyes. Across her

---

°*flexile:* flexible, pliant

shoulders, and behind flowed large loose curls, brown in shadow, almost golden where the ray touched them. She was simply dressed, befitting decency and the season. On a closer inspection you might see that her lips were stained. This blooming young person was regaling on dewberries. They grew between the bank and the water. Apparently she found the fruit abundant, for her hand was making pretty progress to her mouth. Fastidious youth, which shudders and revolts at woman plumping her exquisite proportions on bread-and-butter, and would (we must suppose) joyfully have her quite scraggy to have her quite poetical, can hardly object to dewberries. Indeed the act of eating them is dainty and induces musing. The dewberry is a sister to the lotos, and an innocent sister. You eat; mouth, eye, and hand are occupied, and the undrugged mind free to roam. And so it was with the damsel who knelt there. The little skylark went up above her, all song, to the smooth southern cloud lying along the blue: from a dewy copse standing dark over her nodding hat, the blackbird fluted, calling to her with thrice mellow note: the kingfisher flashed emerald out of green osiers: a bow-winged heron travelled aloft, searching solitude: a boat slipped towards her, containing a dreamy youth, and still she plucked the fruit, and ate, and mused, as if no fairy prince were invading her territories, and as if she wished not for one, or knew not her wishes. Surrounded by the green shaven meadows, the pastoral summer buzz, the weir-fall's thundering white, amid the breath and beauty of wildflowers, she was a bit of lovely human life in a fair setting: a terrible attraction. The Magnetic Youth leaned round to note his proximity to the weirpiles, and beheld the sweet vision. Stiller and stiller grew Nature, as at the meeting of two electric clouds. Her posture was so graceful that, though he was making straight for the weir, he dared not dip a scull. Just then one most enticing dewberry caught her eye. He was floating by unheeded, and saw that her hand stretched low, and could not gather what it sought. A stroke from his right brought him beside her. The damsel glanced up dismayed, and her whole shape trembled over the brink. Richard sprang from his boat into the water. Pressing a hand beneath her foot, which she had thrust against the crumbling wet sides of the bank to save herself, he enabled her to recover her balance, and gain safe earth, whither, emboldened by the incident, touching her finger's tip, he followed her.

Chapter XVIII: FERDINAND AND MIRANDA°

HE had landed on an Island of the still-vexed Bermoothes. The world lay wrecked behind him: Raynham° hung in mists, remote, a phantom to

---

°*Ferdinand and Miranda:* the innocent lovers of Shakespeare's *The Tempest*
°*Raynham:* the Feverel homestead

the vivid reality of this white hand which had drawn him thither away thousands of leagues in an eye-twinkle. Hark, how Ariel° sung overhead! What splendour in the Heavens! What marvels of beauty about his enchanted head! And, O you Wonder! Fair Flame! by whose light the glories of being are now first seen. . . . Radiant Miranda! Prince Ferdinand is at your feet.

Or is it Adam, his rib taken from his side in sleep, and thus transformed, to make him behold his Paradise, and lose it? . . .

The youth looked on her with as glowing an eye. It was the First Woman to him.

And she—mankind was all Caliban° to her, saving this one princely youth.

So to each other said their changing eyes in the moment they stood together; he pale, and she blushing.

She was indeed sweetly fair, and would have been held fair among rival damsels. On a magic shore, and to a youth educated by a System, strung like an arrow drawn to the head, he, it might be guessed, could fly fast and far with her. The soft rose in her cheeks, the clearness of her eyes, bore witness to the body's virtue; and health, and happy blood was in her bearing. Had she stood before Sir Austin,° among rival damsels, that Scientific Humanist, for the consummation of his System, would have thrown her the handkerchief for his son. The wide summer-hat nodding over her forehead to her brows, seemed to flow with the flowing heavy curls, and those fire-threaded mellow curls, only half-curls, waves of hair, call them, rippling at the ends, went like a sunny red-veined torrent down her back almost to her waist: a glorious vision to the youth, who embraced it as a flower of beauty, and read not a feature. There were curious features of colour in her face for him to have read. Her brows, thick and brownish against a soft skin showing the action of the blood, met in the bend of a bow, extending to the temples long and level: you saw that she was fashioned to peruse the sights of earth, and by the pliability of her brows, that the wonderful creature used her faculty, and was not going to be a statue to the gazer. Under the dark thick brows an arch of lashes shot out, giving a wealth of darkness to the full frank blue eyes, a mystery of meaning—more than brain was ever meant to fathom: richer henceforth than all mortal wisdom to Prince Ferdinand. For when Nature turns artist, and produces contrasts of colour on a fair face, where is the Sage, or what the Oracle, shall match the depth of its lightest look?

Prince Ferdinand was also fair. In his slim boating-attire his figure looked heroic. His hair, rising from the parting to the right of his fore-

---

°*Ariel:* the good spirit of the island Paradise in the play   °*Caliban:* the evil spirit of the island; a deformed, brutal slave   °*Sir Austin (Feverel):* Richard's father, a believer in a System of child raising which Richard and Lucy are about to overthrow

head, in what his admiring Lady Blandish called his plume, fell away slanting silkily to the temples across the nearly imperceptible upward curve of his brows there—felt more than seen, so slight it was—and gave to his profile a bold beauty, to which his bashful breathless air was a flattering charm. An arrow drawn to the head, capable of flying fast and far with her! He leaned a little forward to her, drinking her in with all his eyes, and young Love has a thousand. Then truly the System triumphed, just ere it was to fall; and could Sir Austin have been content to draw the arrow to the head, and let it fly, when it would fly, he might have pointed to his son again, and said to the world, "Match him!" Such keen bliss as the youth had in the sight of her, an innocent youth alone has powers of soul in him to experience.

'O Women!' says THE PILGRIM'S SCRIP,° in one of its solitary outbursts, 'Women, who like, and will have for hero, a rake! how soon are you not to learn that you have taken bankrupts to your bosoms, and that the putrescent gold that attracted you, is the slime of the Lake of Sin.'

If these two were Ferdinand and Miranda, Sir Austin was not Prospero,° and was not present, or their fates might have been different.

So they stood a moment, changing eyes, and then Miranda spoke, and they came down to earth, feeling no less in heaven.

She spoke to thank him for his aid. She used quite common simple words; and used them, no doubt, to express a common simple meaning; but to him she was uttering magic, casting spells, and the effect they had on him was manifested in the incoherence of his replies, which were too foolish to be chronicled.

The couple were again mute. Suddenly Miranda, with an exclamation of anguish, and innumerable lights and shadows playing over her lovely face, clapped her hands, crying aloud, "My book! my book!" and ran to the bank.

Prince Ferdinand was at her side. "What have you lost?" he said.

"My book! my book!" she answered, her long delicious curls swinging across her shoulders to the stream. Then turning to him, divining his rash intention, "Oh, no, no! let me entreat you not to," she said. "I do not so very much mind losing it." And in her eagerness to restrain him, she unconsciously laid her gentle hand upon his arm, and took the force of motion out of him.

"Indeed I do not really care for the silly book," she continued, withdrawing her hand quickly, and reddening. "Pray do not!"

The young gentleman had kicked off his shoes. No sooner was the

---

° *The Pilgrim's Scrip:* Sir Austin's collection of philosophic observations ° *Prospero:* Miranda's magician father

spell of contact broken than he jumped in. The water was still troubled and discoloured by his introductory adventure, and, though he ducked his head with the spirit of a dabchick,° the book was missing. A scrap of paper floating from the bramble just above the water, and looking as if fire had caught its edges and it had flown from one adverse element to the other, was all he could lay hold of, and he returned to land disconsolately, to hear Miranda's murmured mixing of thanks and pretty expostulations.

"Let me try again," he said.

"No, indeed!" she replied, and used the awful threat: "I will run away if you do," which effectually restrained him.

Her eye fell on the fire-stained scrap of paper, and brightened, as she cried, "There—there! you have what I want. It is that. I do not care for the book.—No, please! You are not to look at it. Give it me."

Before her playfully-imperative injunction was fairly spoken, Richard had glanced at the document, and discovered a Griffin between Two Wheatsheaves: his Crest, in silver: and below, O wonderment immense! his own handwriting! remnant of his burnt Offering! a page of the sacrificed Poems! one Blossom preserved from the deadly universal blight.

He handed it to her in silence. She took it, and put it in her bosom.

Who would have said, have thought, that, where all else perished, Odes, fluttering bits of broad-winged Epic, Idyls, Lines, Stanzas, this one Sonnet to the Stars should be miraculously reserved for such a starry fate! passing beatitude!

As they walked silently across the meadow Richard strove to remember the hour, and the mood of mind, in which he had composed the notable production. The stars were invoked, as seeing, and foreseeing, all, to tell him where then his love reclined, and so forth; Hesper° was complacent enough to do so, and described her in a couplet:

> *'Through sunset's amber see me shining fair,*
> *As her blue eyes shine through her golden hair.'*

And surely no words could be more prophetic. Here were two blue eyes, and golden hair; and by some strange chance, that appeared like the working of a divine finger, she had become the possessor of the prophecy, she that was to fulfill it! The youth was too charged with emotion to speak. Doubtless the damsel had less to think of, or had some trifling burden on her conscience, for she seemed to grow° embarrassed. At last she threw up her chin to look at her companion under the nodding brim of her hat (and the action gave her a charmingly freakish air), crying, "But where are you going to? You are wet through. Let me thank you again, and pray leave me, and go home, and change instantly."

°*dabchick:* a small diving bird   °*Hesper:* Hesperus, the evening star, especially Venus

"Wet?" replied the Magnetic muser, with a voice of tender interest, "not more than one foot, I hope? I will leave you while you dry your stocking in the sun."

At this she could not withhold a shy and lovely laugh.

"Not I, but you. You know you saved me, and would try to get that silly book for me, and you are dripping wet. Are you not very uncomfortable?"

In all sincerity he assured her that he was not.

"And you really do not feel that you are wet?"

He really did not: and it was a fact that he spoke truth.

She pursed her sweet dewberry mouth in the most comical way, and her blue eyes lightened laughter out of the half-closed lids.

"I cannot help it," she said, her mouth opening, and sounding harmonious bells of laughter in his ears. "Pardon me, won't you?"

His face took the same soft smiling curves in admiration of her.

"Not to feel that you have been in the water, the very moment after!" she musically interjected, seeing she was excused.

"It's true," he said; and his own gravity then touched him to join a duet with her, which made them no longer feel strangers, and did the work of a month of intimacy. Better than sentiment Laughter opens the breast of Love; opens the whole breast to his full quiver, instead of a corner here and there for a solitary arrow. Hail the occasion Propitious, O ye British young! and laugh, and treat Love as an honest God, and dabble not with the spiritual rouge. These two laughed, and the souls of each cried out to other, 'It is I,' 'It is I.'

They laughed and forgot the cause of their laughter, and the sun dried his light river-clothing, and they strolled towards the blackbird's copse, and stood near a stile, in sight of the foam of the weir, and the many-coloured rings of eddies streaming forth from it.

Richard's boat, meanwhile, had contrived to shoot the weir, and was swinging, bottom upwards, broadside with the current down the rapid backwater.

"Will you let it go?" said the damsel, eyeing it curiously.

"Yes," he replied, and low, as if he spoke in the core of his thought: "What do I care for it now?"

His old life was whirled away with it, dead, drowned. His new life was with her, alive, divine.

She flapped low the brim of her hat. "You must really not come any further," she softly said.

"And will you go, and not tell me who you are?" he asked, growing bold as the fears of losing her came across him: "And will you not tell me before you go," his face burned, "how you came by that—that paper?"

She chose to select the easier question to reply to: "You ought to know me; we have been introduced." Sweet was her winning off-hand affability.

"Then who, in Heaven's name, are you? Tell me! I never could have forgotten you."

"You have, I think," she said demurely.

"Impossible that we could ever have met, and I forget you!"

She looked up to him quickly.

"Do you remember Belthorpe?"

"Belthorpe! Belthorpe!" quoth Richard, as if he had to touch his brain to recollect there was such a place. "Do you mean old Blaize's farm?"

"Then I am old Blaize's niece." She tripped him a soft curtsey.

The Magnetized youth gazed at her. By what magic was it that this divine sweet creature could be allied with that old churl!

"Then what—what is your name?" said his mouth, while his eyes added, "O wonderful creature! How came you to enrich the earth?"

"Have you forgot the Desboroughs of Dorset, too?" she peered at him archly from a side bend of the flapping brim.

"The Desboroughs of Dorset?" a light broke in on him. "And have you grown to this? That little girl I saw there!"

He drew close to her to read the nearest features of the vision. She could no more laugh off the piercing fervour of his eyes. Her volubility fluttered under his deeply wistful look, and now neither voice was high, and they were mutually constrained.

"You see," she murmured, "we are old acquaintances."

Richard, with his eyes still intently fixed on her, returned: "You are very beautiful!"

The words slipped out. Perfect simplicity is unconsciously audacious. Her overpowering beauty struck his heart, and like an instrument that is touched and answers to the touch, he spoke.

Miss Desborough made an effort to trifle with this terrible directness: but his eyes would not be gainsaid, and checked her lips. She turned away from them, her bosom a little rebellious. Praise so passionately spoken, and by one who has been a damsel's first dream, dreamed of nightly many long nights, and clothed in the virgin silver of her thoughts in bud, praise from him is coin the heart cannot reject, if it would. She quickened her steps to the stile.

"I have offended you!" said a mortally wounded voice across her shoulder.

That he should think so were too dreadful.

"Oh, no, no! you would never offend me." She gave him her whole sweet face.

"Then why—why do you leave me?"

"Because," she hesitated, "I must go."

"No. You must not go. Why must you go? Do not go."

"Indeed, I must," she said, pulling at the obnoxious broad brim of her hat; and, interpreting a pause he made for his assent to her sensible resolve, shyly looking at him, she held her hand out, and said, "Good-bye," as if it were a natural thing to say.

The hand was pure white: white and fragrant as the frosted blossom of a May-night. It was the hand whose shadow, cast before, he had last night bent his head reverentially above, and kissed—resigning himself thereupon over to execution for payment of the penalty of such daring: by such bliss well rewarded.

He took the hand, and held it; gazing between her eyes.

"Good-bye," she said again, as frankly as she could, and at the same time slightly compressing her fingers on his in token of adieu. It was a signal for his to close firmly upon hers.

"You will not go?"

"Pray let me," she pleaded, her sweet brows suing in wrinkles.

"You will not go?" Mechanically he drew the white hand nearer his thumping heart.

"I must," she faltered piteously.

"You will not go?"

"Oh yes! yes!"

"Tell me. Do you wish to go?"

The question was subtle. A moment or two she did not answer, and then forswore herself, and said, Yes.

"Do you—do you wish to go?" He looked with quivering eyelids under hers.

A fainter, Yes, responded to his passionate repetition.

"You wish—wish to leave me?" His breath went with the words.

"Indeed I must."

Her hand became a closer prisoner.

All at once an alarming delicious shudder went through her frame. From him to her it coursed, and back from her to him. Forward and back Love's electric messenger rushed from heart to heart, knocking at each, till it surged tumultuously against the bars of its prison, crying out for its mate. They stood trembling in unison, a lovely couple under these fair Heavens of the morning.

When he could get his voice, it was, "Will you go?"

But she had none to reply with, and could only mutely bend upward her gentle wrist.

"Then, farewell," he said, and dropping his lips to the soft fair hand, kissed it, and hung his head, swinging away from her, ready for death.

Strange, that now she was released she should linger by him. Strange, that his audacity, instead of the executioner, brought blushes and timid tenderness to his side, and the sweet words, "You are not angry with me?"

"With you, O Beloved!" cried his soul. "And you forgive me, Fair Charity!"

She repeated her words in deeper sweetness to his bewildered look; and he, inexperienced, possessed by her, almost lifeless with the divine new emotions she had realized in him, could only sigh, and gaze at her wonderingly.

"I think it was rude of me to go without thanking you again," she said, and again proffered her hand.

The sweet Heaven-bird shivered out his song above him. The gracious glory of Heaven fell upon his soul. He touched her hand, not moving his eyes from her, nor speaking, and she with a soft word of farewell, passed across the stile, and up the pathway through the dewy shades of the copse, and out of the arch of the light, away from his eyes.

And away with her went the wild enchantment: he looked on barren air. But it was no more the world of yesterday. The marvellous splendours had sown seeds in him, ready to spring up and bloom at her gaze; and in his bosom now the vivid conjuration of her tones, her face, her shape, makes them leap and illumine him like fitful summer lightnings—ghosts of the vanished Sun.

There was nothing to tell him that he had been making love and declaring it with extraordinary rapidity; nor did he know it. Soft-flushed cheeks! sweet mouth! strange sweet brows! eyes of softest fire! how could his ripe eyes see you, and not plead to keep you? Nay, how could he let you go? And he seriously asks himself that question.

Tomorrow this spot will have a memory—the river, and the meadow, and the white, falling weir: his heart will build a temple here; and the skylark will be its high-priest, and the old blackbird its glossy-gowned chorister, and there will be a sacred repast of dewberries. Today the grass is grass: his heart is chased by phantoms, and finds rest nowhere. Only when the most tender freshness of his flower comes across him, does he taste a moment's calm; and no sooner does it comes than it gives place to keen pangs of fear that she may not be his for ever.

Ere long he learns that her name is Lucy. Ere long he meets Ralph, and discovers that in a day he has distanced him by a sphere. Ere long, he, and Ralph, and the Curate of Lobourne, join in their walks, and raise classical discussions on ladies' hair, fingering a thousand delicious locks, from those of Cleopatra to the Borgia's. "Fair! fair! all of them fair!" sighs the melancholy Curate, "as are those women formed for our perdition! I think we have in this country what will match the Italian, or the Greek." His mind flutters to Mrs. Doria: Richard blushes before the vision of Lucy: and Ralph, whose heroine's hair is a dark luxuriance, dissents, and claims a noble share in the slaughter of men for dark-haired

Wonders. They have no mutual confidences, but they are singularly kind to each other, these three children of instinct.

Chapter XXIII: A DIVERSION PLAYED ON A PENNY-WHISTLE

Away with Systems! Away with a corrupt World! Let us breathe the air of the Enchanted Island!

Golden lie the meadows: golden run the streams: red gold is on the pine-stems. The Sun is coming down to Earth, and walks the fields and the waters.

The Sun is coming down to Earth, and the fields and the waters shout to him golden shouts. He comes, and his heralds run before him, and touch the leaves of oaks, and planes, and beeches, lucid green, and the pine-stems redder gold; leaving brightest foot-prints upon thickly weeded banks, where the foxglove's last upper-bells incline, and brambleshoots wander amid moist rich herbage. The plumes of the woodland are alight; and beyond them, over the open, 'tis a race with the long-thrown shadows; a race across the heaths and up the hills, till, at the farthest bourne of mounted eastern cloud, the heralds of the sun lay rosy fingers, and rest.

Sweet are the shy recesses of the woodland. The ray treads softly there. A film athwart the pathway quivers many-hued against purple shade fragrant with warm pines, deep moss-beds, feathery ferns. The little brown squirrel drops tail, and leaps: the inmost bird is startled to a chance tuneless note. From silence into silence things move.

Peeps of the revelling spendour above, and around, enliven the conscious full heart within. The flaming West, the crimson heights, shower their glories through voluminous leafage. But these are bowers where deep bliss dwells, imperial joy that owes no fealty to yonder glories in which the young lamb gambols, and the spirits of men are glad. Descend, Great Radiance! embrace Creation with beneficent fire, and pass from us! You, and the vice-regal Light that succeeds to you, and all heavenly pageants, are the ministers and the slaves of the throbbing Content within.

For this is the home of the Enchantment. Here, secluded from vexed shores, the Prince and Princess of the Island meet; here like darkling nightingales they sit, and into eyes, and ears, and hands, pour endless ever-fresh treasures of their souls.

Roll on, grinding wheels of the world: cries of ships going down in a calm; groans of a System which will not know its rightful hour of exultation; complain to the Universe. You are not heard here.

He calls her by her name, Lucy: and she, blushing at her great boldness, has called him by his, Richard. Those two names are the key-notes of the wonderful harmonies the Angels sing aloft.

"Lucy! my beloved!"

"O Richard!"

Key-notes of the harmonies Earth even now revolves to, shadowing slowly to its bright-eyed kindred.

Out in the world there, on the skirts of the woodland, a sheep-boy pipes to meditative Eve on a penny-whistle.

Love's musical Instrument is as old, and as poor; it has but two stops; and yet, you see, the Cunning Musician does thus much with it!

Other speech they have little; light foam playing upon waves feeling, and of feeling compact, that bursts only when the sweeping volume is too wild, and is no more than their sigh of tenderness spoken.

Perhaps Love played his tune so well, because their natures had unblunted edges, and were keen for bliss, confiding in it as natural food. To gentlemen and ladies he fine-draws upon the viol, ravishingly; or blows into the mellow bassoon; or rouses the heroic ardours of the trumpet; or, it may be, commands the whole Orchestra for them. And they are pleased. He is still the Cunning Musician. They languish, and taste ecstasy: but it is, however sonorous, an earthly concert. For them the spheres move not to Two Notes. They have lost, or forfeited and never known, the first supersensual spring of the ripe senses into passion; when they carry the soul with them, and have the privileges of spirits to walk disembodied, boundlessly to feel. Or one has it, and the other is a dead body! Ambrosia let them eat, and drink the Nectar: here sit a couple to whom Love's simple Bread and Water is a finer feast.

Pipe, happy sheep-boy, Love! Irradiated Angels, unfold your wings and lift your voices!

They have outflown Philosophy. Their Instinct has shot beyond the ken of Science. Imperiously they know we were made for his Eden: and would you gainsay them who are outside the Gates, and argue from the Fall?

"And this divine Gift was in store for me!"

So runs the internal outcry of each, clasping each: their recurring refrain to the harmonies. How it illumined the years gone by, and suffused the living Future!

"You for me: I for you!"

"We are born for each other!"

They believe that the Angels have been busy about them from their cradles. The celestial hosts have worthily striven to bring them together. And, O Victory! O Wonder! after toil, and pain, and difficulties exceeding, the celestial hosts have succeeded!

"Here we two sit who are written above as one!"

Pipe, happy Love! pipe on to these dear Innocents!

The tide of colour has ebbed from the upper-sky. In the West the sea of sunken fire draws back; and the stars leap forth, and tremble, and retire before the advancing moon, who slips the silver train of cloud from her shoulders, and with her foot upon the pine-tops, surveys Heaven.

"Lucy, did you never dream of meeting me?"

"O Richard! yes; for I remembered you."

"Lucy! and did you pray that we might meet?"

"I did!"

Young as when she looked upon the Lovers in Paradise, the Fair Immortal journeys onward. Fronting her, it is not Night but veiled Day. Full half the sky is flushed. Not Darkness; not Day; the Nuptials of the twain.

"My own! my own for ever! You are pledged to me? Whisper!"

He hears the delicious music.

"And you are mine?"

A soft beam travels to the fern-covert under the pinewood where they sit, and for answer he has her eyes: turned to him an instant, timidly fluttering over the depths of his, and then downcast; for through her eyes her soul is naked to him.

"Lucy! my bride! my life!"

The night-jar spins his dark monotony on the branch of the pine. The soft beam travels round them, and listens to their hearts. Their lips are locked.

Pipe no more, Love, for a time! Pipe as you will you cannot express their first kiss; nothing of its sweetness, and of its sacredness nothing. St. Cecilia° up aloft, before the silver organ-pipes of Paradise, pressing fingers upon all the notes of which Love is but one, from her you may hear it.

So Love is silent. Out in the world there, on the skirts of the woodland, the self-satisfied sheep-boy delivers a last complacent squint down the length of his penny-whistle, and, with a flourish correspondingly wry-faced, he also marches into silence, hailed by supper. The woods are still. There is heard but the night-jar spinning on the pine-branch, circled by moonlight.

*   *   *

°*St. Cecilia:*   patron saint of music

Faithless Women and Other Discouragements

Innocence and youth can, of course, be overrated. One who exaggerates the virtues of innocence and youth, or magnifies the emotions properly attached to them, is guilty of sentimentality, of too much emotion for the cause and occasion. Tennyson's *Locksley Hall* verges on such sentimentality, but it reflects both a melodramatic youthfulness which the Victorians found eminently admirable, and a wide range of disillusionments, bitternesses, and failures of idealism, suffered by the typical young hero of middle-class fiction.

The hero, in a fashion made popular some decades before by Lord Byron, stands apart in splendid isolation, contemplating time, the universe, and his destiny—a destiny which has already included that commonest seed of disillusionment in melodramatic young men, a faithless young woman: "O my cousin, shallow-hearted! O my Amy, mine no more!" Our hero imagines the corruption which Amy's failure of love and idealism has incurred—marriage to a gross husband, narrowness, hypocritical piety. He seems to think, or at least proclaims, that his own future will have a wider scope and be heroic, noble, and fruitful.

LOCKSLEY HALL

Alfred, Lord Tennyson (1809–1892)

Comrades, leave me here a little, while as yet 'tis early morn;
Leave me here, and when you want me, sound upon the bugle horn.

'Tis the place, and all around it, as of old, the curlews call,
Dreary gleams about the moorland flying over Locksley Hall;

Locksley Hall, that in the distance overlooks the sandy tracts,   5
And the hollow ocean-ridges roaring into cataracts.

Many a night from yonder ivied casement, ere I went to rest,
Did I look on great Orion sloping slowly to the west.

Many a night I saw the Pleiads, rising thro' the mellow shade,
Glitter like a swarm of fire-flies tangled in a silver braid.   10

Here about the beach I wander'd, nourishing a youth sublime
With the fairy tales of science, and the long result of time;

When the centuries behind me like a fruitful land reposed;
When I clung to all the present for the promise that it closed;

When I dipt into the future far as human eye could see,
Saw the vision of the world, and all the wonder that would be.—

In the spring a fuller crimson comes upon the robin's breast;
In the spring the wanton lapwing gets himself another crest;

In the spring a livelier iris changes on the burnish'd dove;
In the spring a young man's fancy lightly turns to thoughts of love. 20

Then her cheek was pale and thinner than should be for one so young,
And her eyes on all my motions with a mute observance hung.

And I said, "My cousin Amy, speak, and speak the truth to me,
Trust me, cousin, all the current of my being sets to thee."

On her pallid cheek and forehead came a color and a light, 25
As I have seen the rosy red flushing in the northern night.

And she turn'd—her bosom shaken with a sudden storm of sighs—
All the spirit deeply dawning in the dark of hazel eyes—

Saying, "I have hid my feelings, fearing they should do me wrong";
Saying, "Dost thou love me, cousin?" weeping, "I have loved thee long." 30

Love took up the glass of Time, and turn'd it in his glowing hands;
Every moment, lightly shaken, ran itself in golden sands.

Love took up the harp of Life, and smote on all the chords with might;
Smote the chord of Self, that, trembling, passed in music out of sight.

Many a morning on the moorland did we hear the copses ring, 35
And her whisper throng'd my pulses with the fulness of the spring.

Many an evening by the waters did we watch the stately ships,
And our spirits rush'd together at the touching of the lips.

O my cousin, shallow-hearted! O my Amy, mine no more!
O the dreary, dreary moorland! O the barren, barren shore! 40

Falser than all fancy fathoms, falser than all songs have sung,
Puppet to a father's threat, and servile to a shrewish tongue!°

°Amy has dutifully followed the demands of her parents instead of the truer
promptings of her heart.

Is it well to wish thee happy?—having known me—to decline
On a range of lower feelings and a narrower heart than mine!

Yet it shall be; thou shalt lower to his level day by day,   45
What is fine within thee growing coarse to sympathize with clay.

As the husband is, the wife is; thou art mated with a clown,
And the grossness of his nature will have weight to drag thee down.

He will hold thee, when his passion shall have spent its novel force,
Something better than his dog, a little dearer than his horse.   50

What is this? his eyes are heavy; think not they are glazed with wine.
Go to him, it is thy duty; kiss him, take his hand in thine.

It may be my lord is weary, that his brain is overwrought;
Soothe him with thy finer fancies, touch him with thy lighter thought.

He will answer to the purpose, easy things to understand—   55
Better thou wert dead before me, tho' I slew thee with my hand!

Better thou and I were lying, hidden from the heart's disgrace,
Roll'd in one another's arms, and silent in a last embrace.

Cursed be the social wants that sin against the strength of youth!
Cursed be the social lies that warp us from the living truth!   60

Cursed be the sickly forms that err from honest Nature's rule!
Cursed be the gold that gilds the straiten'd forehead of the fool!

Well—'tis well that I should bluster!—Hadst thou less unworthy proved—
Would to God—for I had loved thee more than ever wife was loved.

Am I mad, that I should cherish that which bears but bitter fruit?   65
I will pluck it from my bosom, tho' my heart be at the root.

Never, tho' my mortal summers to such length of years should come
As the many-winter'd crow that leads the clanging rookery home.

Where is comfort? in division of the records of the mind?
Can I part her from herself, and love her, as I knew her, kind?   70

I remember one that perish'd; sweetly did she speak and move;
Such a one do I remember, whom to look at was to love.

Can I think of her as dead, and love her for the love she bore?
No—she never loved me truly; love is love for evermore.

Comfort? comfort scorn'd of devils! this is truth the poet sings,°   75
That a sorrow's crown of sorrow is remembering happier things.

Drug thy memories, lest thou learn it, lest thy heart be put to proof,
In the dead unhappy night, and when the rain is on the roof.

Like a dog, he hunts in dreams, and thou art staring at the wall,
Where the dying night-lamp flickers, and the shadows rise and fall.   80

Then a hand shall pass before thee, pointing to his drunken sleep,
To thy widow'd marriage-pillows, to the tears that thou wilt weep.

Thou shalt hear the "Never, never," whisper'd by the phantom years,
And a song from out the distance in the ringing of thine ears;

And an eye shall vex thee, looking ancient kindness on thy pain.   85
Turn thee, turn thee on thy pillow; get thee to thy rest again.

Nay, but Nature brings thee solace; for a tender voice will cry.
'Tis a purer life than thine, a lip to drain thy trouble dry.

Baby lips will laugh me down; my latest rival brings thee rest.
Baby fingers, waxen touches, press me from the mother's breast.   90

O' the child too clothes the father with a dearness not his due.
Half is thine and half is his; it will be worthy of the two.

O, I see thee old and formal, fitted to thy petty part,
With a little hoard of maxims preaching down a daughter's heart.

"They were dangerous guides the feelings—she herself was not exempt—   95
Truly, she herself had suffer'd"—Perish in thy self-contempt!

Overlive it—lower yet—be happy! wherefore should I care?
I myself must mix with action, lest I wither by despair.

What is that which I should turn to, lighting upon days like these?
Every door is barr'd with gold, and opens but to golden keys.   100

°Dante in the *Inferno*, V, 121

Every gate is throng'd with suitors, all the markets overflow.
I have but an angry fancy; what is that which I should do?

I had been content to perish, falling on the foeman's ground,
When the ranks are roll'd in vapor, and the winds are laid with sound.

But the jingling of the guinea helps the hurt that Honor feels,   105
And the nations do but murmur, snarling at each other's heels.

Can I but relive in sadness? I will turn that earlier page.
Hide me from my deep emotion, O thou wondrous Mother-Age!

Make me feel the wild pulsation that I felt before the strife,
When I heard my days before me, and the tumult of my life;   110

Yearning for the large excitement that the coming years would yield,
Eager-hearted as a boy when first he leaves his father's field,

And at night along the dusky highway near and nearer drawn,
Sees in heaven the light of London flaring like a dreary dawn;

And his spirit leaps within him to be gone before him then,   115
Underneath the light he looks at, in among the throngs of men;

Men, my brothers, men the workers, ever reaping something new;
That which they have done but earnest of the things that they shall do.

For I dipt into the future, far as human eye could see,
Saw the Vision of the world, and all the wonder that would be;   120

Saw the heavens fill with commerce, argosies of magic sails,°
Pilots of the purple twilight, dropping down with costly bales;

Heard the heavens fill with shouting, and there rain'd a ghastly dew
From the nations' airy navies grappling in the central blue;

Far along the world-wide whisper of the southwind rushing warm,   125
With the standards of the peoples plunging thro' the thunder-storm;

Till the war-drum throbb'd no longer, and the battle-flags were furl'd
In the Parliament of man, the Federation of the world.

°*magic sails:*   balloons

There the common sense of most shall hold a fretful realm in awe,
And the kindly earth shall slumber, lapt in universal law. 130

So I triumph'd ere my passion sweeping thro' me left me dry,
Left me with the palsied heart, and left me with the jaundiced eye;

Eye, to which all order festers, all things here are out of joint.°
Science moves, but slowly, slowly, creeping on from point to point;

Slowly comes a hungry people, as a lion, creeping nigher, 135
Glares at one that nods and winks behind a slowly dying fire.

Yet I doubt not thro' the ages one increasing purpose runs,
And the thoughts of men are widen'd with the process of the suns.°

What is that to him that reaps not harvest of his youthful joys.
Tho' the deep heart of existence beat forever like a boy's? 140

Knowledge comes, but wisdom lingers, and I linger on the shore,
And the individual withers, and the world is more and more.

Knowledge comes, but wisdom lingers, and he bears a laden breast,
Full of sad experience, moving toward the stillness of his rest.

Hark, my merry comrades call me, sounding on the bugle-horn, 145
They to whom my foolish passion were a target for their scorn.

Shall it not be scorn to me to harp on such a moulder'd string?
I am shamed thro' all my nature to have loved so slight a thing.

Weakness to be wroth with weakness! woman's pleasure, woman's pain—
Nature made them blinder motions bounded in a shallower brain. 150

Woman is the lesser man, and all thy passions, match'd with mine,
Are as moonlight unto sunlight, and as water unto wine—

Here at least, where nature sickens, nothing. Ah, for some retreat
Deep in yonder shining Orient, where my life began to beat,

Where in wild Mahratta°-battle fell my father evil-starr'd;— 155
I was left a trampled orphan, and a selfish uncle's ward.

°*out of joint:* see *Hamlet,* I v, 188   °*suns:* years   °*Mahratta:* in India

THE ENCOUNTER: OLDER AND THEN WISER   *147*

Or to burst all links of habit—there to wander far away,
On from island unto island at the gateways of the day.

Larger constellations burning, mellow moons and happy skies,
Breadths of tropic shade and palms in cluster, knots of Paradise.　　160

Never comes the trader, never floats an European flag,
Slides the bird o'er lustrous woodland, swings the trailer° from the crag;

Droops the heavy-blossom'd bower, hangs the heavy-fruited tree—
Summer isles of Eden lying in dark-purple spheres of sea.

There methinks would be enjoyment more than in this march of mind,　165
In the steamship, in the railway, in the thoughts that shake mankind.

There the passions cramp'd no longer shall have scope and breathing space;
I will take some savage woman, she shall rear my dusky race.

Iron jointed, supple-sinew'd, they shall dive, and they shall run,
Catch the wild goat by the hair, and hurl their lances in the sun;　　170

Whistle back the parrot's call, and leap the rainbows of the brooks,
Not with blinded eyesight poring over miserable books—

Fool, again the dream, the fancy! but I *know* my words are wild,
But I count the gray barbarian lower than the Christian child.

I, to herd with narrow foreheads, vacant of our glorious gains,　　175
Like a beast with lower pleasures, like a beast with lower pains!

Mated with a squalid savage—what to me were sun or clime?
I the heir of all the ages, in the foremost files of time—

I that rather held it better men should perish one by one,
Than that earth should stand at gaze like Joshua's moon in Ajalon!°　180

Not in vain the distance beacons. Forward, forward let us range,
Let the great world spin for ever down the ringing grooves of change.

Thro' the shadow of the globe we sweep into the younger day;
Better fifty years of Europe than a cycle of Cathay.°

　　°*trailer:* vine　　°Joshua commanded the moon to stand still in the vale of Ajalon
(Joshua *10*:12-13).　　°*Cathay:* China

Mother-Age,—for mine I knew not,—help me as when life begun; 185
Rift the hills, and roll the waters, flash the lightnings, weigh the sun.

O, I see the crescent promise of my spirit hath not set.
Ancient founts of inspiration well thro' all my fancy yet.

Howsoever these things be, a long farewell to Locksley Hall!
Now for me the woods may wither, now for me the roof-tree fall. 190

Comes a vapor from the margin, blackening over heath and holt,
Cramming all the blast before it, in its breast a thunderbolt.

Let it fall on Locksley Hall, with rain or hail, or fire or snow!
For the mighty wind arises, roaring seaward, and I go.

QUESTIONS

1a. Describe the tone or attitude which Meredith takes toward the encounter in *The Ordeal of Richard Feverel.*
  b. What is the effect of the allusions to Ferdinand and Miranda?
  c. Notice the reference to the importance of laughter as an ingredient of Love. What does Meredith mean in his rejection of "spiritual rouge"?
  d. Does this passage make too much of their meeting? Such intensities are not the modern fashion. Is the passage guilty of sentimentality, making too much of its emotions? If so, where does this feeling appear? If not, what does Meredith do to prevent the moment from falling into bathos?
  e. Describe your attitude toward the elaborate and prolonged attempts of Richard and Lucy to part after their first meeting.
  f. Where does the outside world intrude into this Paradise? Is the encounter touched by alien qualities or awareness or knowledge at all?
  g. What other allusions occur and what is their purpose?
2a. In *Locksley Hall,* what bothers the speaker in the poem, besides the faithlessness and weakness of Amy?
  b. The poem contains a number of shifts of mood and alterations of mind. What points in the poem seem to be turning points, and what are the reasons for these changes?
  c. There are those who say that the speaker in the poem is a shallow, callow youth. Do you think such a description is justified? What aspects of his character suggest such a view?
  d. The hypocrisy of society is a favorite complaint of the speaker in the poem. What particular social forms does he find most distasteful?
  e. The speaker runs through a variety of possible alternatives for his future. What are they? Which seem most convincing?

Peaceable Kingdom, by American "primitivist" Edward Hicks (1780-1849), shows the sense th
some Americans had of the correspondence between the new world and Eden, where the lion a
the lamb could lie down together. In the background, William Penn negotiates peacefully wi
Indians. *(Reprinted by permission, Philadelphia Museum of Art: Bequest of Charles C. Will*
'56-59-1.)

PART VI

Sin in the American Garden

The true Southern watermelon is a boon apart and not to be mentioned with commoner things. It is chief of this world's luxuries, king by the grace of God over all the fruits of the earth. When one has tasted it, he knows what the angels eat. It was not a Southern watermelon that Eve took; we know it because she repented.

—*Mark Twain*

Sin in the American Garden

As has been suggested, the Myth of the Fall is the Myth of America, and themes associated with this Myth are a major part of the works of Hawthorne, Melville, and James. Almost any work of these writers can be usefully treated from this point of view. James's short novels, *The Turn of the Screw* and *Daisy Miller*, both present interesting confrontations between Innocence and Experience, between American simplicity and forthrightness and European subtlety and sophistication. *The Turn of the Screw* plays as much with the innocence of the reader as it does with that of the characters, in order to make the reader himself "feel" the evil in James's words, rather than rely upon the author's "weak specification of it." Excellent shorter works on the same theme are James's stories *The Pupil* and *The Tree of Knowledge*.

Hawthorne is less subtle than James, and his narrative style suggests that he is much more narrowly interested in the emotions and psychology of the human heart, in the ways in which sin, guilt, pride, intellect, fancy, and imagination operate against and with one another. Thus his work represents a kind of moral allegory, a psychodrama in which the emotions are more real than the characters, the spiritual issues more substantial and more powerfully felt than conflict between men. He is therefore difficult to read, and demands of the reader a willingness to accept the reasons for his prejudices and his heavy-handed pursuit of the inner forces of human character.

On the other hand, Hawthorne knew a great deal about the state of mind of a stern, Puritanical, New England people who possessed a land that looked beautiful and Edenic, yet carried the heavy burden of doubt, sin, and the European Calvinist heritage. He also recognized that everywhere the spirit of the time was self-conscious, especially for the artist, requiring him to acknowledge pain and difficulty that the heart could not shrug away.

Of Hawthorne's novels, *The Marble Faun* deals most directly with the effects of a dark, underground Satanic presence on the spirit of the artist, and furnishes a stimulating analysis of the ways in which one's Self and Will make Evil a part of one's own spirit. *The Blithedale Romance* raises similar questions in its account of the ways in which a rural community loses its way. Almost all of Hawthorne's stories carry some reference to this theme—especially *Rappaccini's Daughter, My Kinsman, Major Molineux,* and *The Birthmark*.

We have chosen to include *Egotism: or The Bosom Serpent* because it is less well-known and more obvious, and it makes even fewer gestures than usual toward a conventional story line and action.

From THE MARBLE FAUN

Nathaniel Hawthorne (1804-1864)

CHAPTER XXXVI

A torpor, heretofore unknown to her vivacious though quiet temperament, had possessed itself of the poor girl, like a half-dead serpent knotting its cold, inextricable wreaths about her limbs. It was that peculiar despair, that chill and heavy misery, which only the innocent can experience, although it possesses many of the gloomy characteristics that mark a sense of guilt. It was that heartsickness which, it is to be hoped, we may all of us have been pure enough to feel, once in our lives, but the capacity for which is usually exhausted early, and perhaps with a single agony. It was that dismal certainty of the existence of evil in the world, which, though we may fancy ourselves fully assured of the sad mystery long before, never becomes a portion of our practical belief until it takes substance and reality from the sin of some guide, whom we have deeply trusted and revered, or some friend whom we have dearly loved.

When that knowledge comes, it is as if a cloud had suddenly gathered over the morning light; so dark a cloud that there seems to be no longer any sunshine behind it or above it. The character of our individual beloved one having invested itself with all the attributes of right—that one friend being to us the symbol and representative of whatever is good and true—when he falls, the effect is almost as if the sky fell with him, bringing down in chaotic ruin the columns that upheld our faith. We struggle forth again, no doubt, bruised and bewildered. We stare wildly about us, and discover—or, it may be, we never make the discovery—that it was not actually the sky that has tumbled down, but merely a frail structure of our own rearing, which never rose higher that the housetops, and has fallen because we founded it on nothing. But the crash, and the affright and trouble, are as overwhelming, for the time, as if the catastrophe involved the whole moral world. Remembering these things, let them suggest one generous motive for walking heedfully amid the defilement of earthly ways! Let us reflect that the highest path is pointed out by the pure Ideal of those who look up to us, and who, if we tread less loftily, may never look so high again.

* * *

From EGOTISM:° OR THE BOSOM SERPENT

Nathaniel Hawthorne (1804–1864)

"HERE he comes!" shouted the boys along the street. "Here comes the man with a snake in his bosom!"

This outcry, saluting Herkimer's ears as he was about to enter the iron gate of the Elliston mansion, made him pause. It was not without a shudder that he found himself on the point of meeting his former acquaintance, whom he had known in the glory of youth, and whom now after an interval of five years, he was to find the victim either of a diseased fancy or a horrible physical misfortune.

"A snake in his bosom!" repeated the young sculptor to himself. "It must be he. No second man on earth has such a bosom friend. And now, my poor Rosina, Heaven grant me wisdom to discharge my errand aright! Woman's faith must be strong indeed since thine has not yet failed."

Thus musing, he took his stand at the entrance of the gate and waited until the personage so singularly announced should make his appearance. After an instant or two he beheld the figure of a lean man, of unwholesome look, with glittering eyes and long black hair, who seemed to imitate the motion of a snake; for, instead of walking straight forward with open front, he undulated along the pavement in a curved line. It may be too fanciful to say that something, either in his moral or material aspect, suggested the idea that a miracle had been wrought by transforming a serpent into a man, but so imperfectly that the snaky nature was yet hidden, and scarcely hidden, under the mere outward guise of humanity. Herkimer remarked that his complexion had a greenish tinge over its sickly white, reminding him of a species of marble out of which he had once wrought a head of Envy, with her snaky locks.

The wretched being approached the gate, but, instead of entering, stopped short and fixed the glitter of his eye full upon the compassionate yet steady countenance of the sculptor.

"It gnaws me! It gnaws me!" he exclaimed.

And then there was an audible hiss, but whether it came from the apparent lunatic's own lips, or was the real hiss of a serpent, might admit of a discussion. At all events, it made Herkimer shudder to his heart's core.

"Do you know me, George Herkimer?" asked the snake-possessed.

Herkimer did know him; but it demanded all the intimate and practical acquaintance with the human face, acquired by modelling actual likenesses in clay, to recognize the features of Roderick Elliston in the visage that now met the sculptor's gaze. Yet it was he. It added nothing to the wonder to reflect that the once brilliant young man had undergone this

---

°The physical fact, to which it is here attempted to give a moral signification, has been known to occur in more than one instance. [Hawthorne's note.]

odious and fearful change during the no more than five brief years of Herkimer's abode at Florence. The possibility of such a transformation being granted, it was as easy to conceive it effected in a moment as in an age. Inexpressibly shocked and startled, it was still the keenest pang when Herkimer remembered that the fate of his cousin Rosina, the ideal of gentle womanhood, was indissolubly interwoven with that of a being whom Providence seemed to have unhumanized.

"Elliston! Roderick!" cried he, "I had heard of this; but my conception came far short of the truth. What has befallen you? Why do I find you thus?"

"Oh, 'tis a mere nothing! A snake! A snake! the commonest thing in the world. A snake in the bosom—that's all," answered Roderick Elliston. "But how is your own breast?" continued he, looking the sculptor in the eye with the most acute and penetrating glance that it had ever been his fortune to encounter. "All pure and wholesome? No reptile there? By my faith and conscience, and by the devil within me, here is a wonder! A man without a serpent in his bosom!"

"Be calm, Elliston," whispered George Herkimer, laying his hand upon the shoulder of the snake-possessed. "I have crossed the ocean to meet you. Listen! Let us be private. I bring a message from Rosina—from your wife!"

"It gnaws me! It gnaws me!" muttered Roderick.

With this exclamation, the most frequent in his mouth, the unfortunate man clutched both hands upon his breast as if an intolerable sting or torture impelled him to rend it open and let out the living mischief, even should it be intertwined with his own life. He then freed himself from Herkimer's grasp by a subtle motion, and, gliding through the gate, took refuge in his antiquated family residence. The sculptor did not pursue him. He saw that no available intercourse could be expected at such a moment, and was desirous, before another meeting, to inquire closely into the nature of Roderick's disease and the circumstances that had reduced him to so lamentable a condition. He succeeded in obtaining the necessary information from an eminent medical gentleman.

Shortly after Elliston's separation from his wife—now nearly four years ago—his associates had observed a singular gloom spreading over his daily life, like those chill, gray mists that sometimes steal away the sunshine from a summer's morning. The symptoms caused them endless perplexity. They knew not whether ill health were robbing his spirits of elasticity, or whether a canker of the mind was gradually eating, as such cankers do, from his moral system into the physical frame, which is but the shadow of the former. They looked for the root of this trouble in his shattered schemes of domestic bliss,—wilfully shattered by himself,—but could not be satisfied of its existence there. Some thought that their once brilliant friend was in an incipient stage of insanity, of which his passionate impulses had perhaps been the forerunners; others prognosticated a general blight and gradual decline. From Roderick's own lips they could learn nothing. More than once, it is true, he had been heard to say, clutching his hands convulsively upon his breast,—"It gnaws me! It gnaws me!"—but, by different auditors, a great diversity of explanation was assigned to this ominous expression. What could it be that gnawed the breast of Roderick Elliston? Was it sorrow? Was it merely the tooth of physical disease? Or, in his reckless course, often verging upon profligacy, if not plunging into its depths, had he been guilty of some deed which made his bosom a prey to the deadlier fangs of remorse? There was plausible ground for each of these conjectures; but it must not be concealed that more than one elderly gentleman, the victim of good cheer and slothful habits, magisterially pronounced the secret of the whole matter to be Dyspepsia!°

Meanwhile, Roderick seemed aware how generally he had become the subject of curiosity and conjecture, and, with a morbid repugnance to such notice, or to any notice whatsover, estranged himself from all companionship. Not merely the eye of man was a horror to him; not merely the light of a friend's countenance; but even the blessed sunshine, likewise, which in its universal beneficence typifies the radiance of the Creator's face, expressing his love for all the creatures of his hand. The dusky twilight was now too transparent for Roderick Elliston; the blackest midnight was his chosen hour to steal abroad; and if ever he were seen, it was when the watchman's lantern gleamed upon his figure, gliding along the street, with his hands clutched upon his bosom, still muttering, "It gnaws me! It gnaws me!" What could it be that gnawed him?

After a time, it became known that Elliston was in the habit of resorting to all the noted quacks that infested the city, or whom money would tempt to journey thither from a distance. By one of these persons, in the exultation of a supposed cure, it was proclaimed far and wide, by dint of handbills and little pamphlets on dingy paper, that a distinguished gentleman, Roderick Elliston, Esq., had been relieved of a SNAKE in his stomach! So here was the monstrous secret, ejected from its lurking place into public view, in all its horrible deformity. The mystery was out; but not so the bosom serpent. He, if it were anything but a delusion, still lay coiled in his living den. The empiric's° cure had been a sham, the effect, it was supposed, of some stupefying drug which more nearly caused the death of the patient than of the odious reptile that possessed him. When Roderick Elliston regained entire sensibility, it was to find his misfortune the town talk—the more than nine days' wonder and horror—while, at his bosom, he felt the sickening motion of a thing alive, and the gnawing of that restless fang which seemed to gratify at once a physical appetite and a fiendish spite.

°*Dyspepsia:* indigestion   °*empiric:* quack

He summoned the old black servant, who had been bred up in his father's house, and was a middle-aged man while Roderick lay in his cradle.

"Scipio!" he began; and then paused, with his arms folded over his heart. "What do people say of me, Scipio."

"Sir! my poor master! that you had a serpent in your bosom," answered the servant with hesitation.

"And what else?" asked Roderick, with a ghastly look at the man.

"Nothing else, dear master," replied Scipio, "only that the doctor gave you a powder, and that the snake leaped out upon the floor."

"No, no!" muttered Roderick to himself, as he shook his head, and pressed his hands with a more convulsive force upon his breast, "I feel him still. It gnaws me! It gnaws me!"

From this time the miserable sufferer ceased to shun the world, but rather solicited and forced himself upon the notice of acquaintances and strangers. It was partly the result of desperation on finding that the cavern of his own bosom had not proved deep and dark enough to hide the secret, even while it was so secure a fortress for the loathsome fiend that had crept into it. But still more, this craving for notoriety was a symptom of the intense morbidness which now pervaded his nature. All persons chronically diseased are egotists, whether the disease be of the mind or body; whether it be sin, sorrow, or merely the more tolerable calamity of some endless pain, or mischief among the cords of mortal life. Such individuals are made acutely conscious of a self, by the torture in which it dwells. Self, therefore, grows to be so prominent an object with them that they cannot but present it to the face of every casual passer-by. There is a pleasure—perhaps the greatest of which the sufferer is susceptible—in displaying the wasted or ulcerated limb, or the cancer in the breast; and the fouler the crime, with so much the more difficulty does the perpetrator prevent it from thrusting up its snake-like head to frighten the world; for it is that cancer, or that crime, which constitutes their respective individuality. Roderick Elliston, who, a little while before, had held himself so scornfully above the common lot of men, now paid full allegiance to this humiliating law. The snake in his bosom seemed the symbol of a monstrous egotism to which everything was referred, and which he pampered, night and day, with a continual and exclusive sacrifice of devil worship.

He soon exhibited what most people considered indubitable tokens of insanity. In some of his moods, strange to say, he prided and gloried himself on being marked out from the ordinary experience of mankind, by the possession of a double nature, and a life within a life. He appeared to imagine that the snake was a divinity,—not celestial, it is true, but darkly infernal,—and that he thence derived an eminence and a sanctity, horrid, indeed, yet more desirable than whatever ambition aims at. Thus he drew his misery around him like a regal mantle, and looked down triumphantly upon those whose vitals nourished no deadly monster. Oftener, however, his human nature asserted its empire over him in the shape of a yearning for fellowship. It grew to be his custom to spend the whole day in wandering about the streets, aimlessly, unless it might be called an aim to establish a species of brotherhood between himself and the world. With cankered ingenuity, he sought out his own disease in every breast. Whether insane or not, he showed so keen a perception of frailty, error, and vice, that many persons gave him credit for being possessed not merely with a serpent, but with an actual fiend, who imparted this evil faculty of recognizing whatever was ugliest in man's heart.

For instance, he met an individual, who, for thirty years, had cherished a hatred against his own brother. Roderick, amidst the throng of the street, laid his hand on this man's chest, and looking full into his forbidding face,—

"How is the snake to-day?" he inquired, with a mock expression of sympathy.

"The snake!" exclaimed the brother hater—"what do you mean?"

"The snake! The snake! Does it gnaw you?" persisted Roderick. "Did you take counsel with him this morning when you should have been saying your prayers? Did he sting, when you thought of your brother's health, wealth, and good repute? Did he caper for joy, when you remembered the profligacy of his only son? And whether he stung, or whether he frolicked, did you feel his poison throughout your body and soul, converting everything to sourness and bitterness? That is the way of such serpents. I have learned the whole nature of them from my own!"

"Where is the police?" roared the object of Roderick's persecution, at the same time giving an instinctive clutch to his breast. "Why is this lunatic allowed to go at large?"

"Ha, ha!" chuckled Roderick, releasing his grasp of the man. "His bosom serpent has stung him then!"

Often it pleased the unfortunate young man to vex people with a lighter satire, yet still characterized by somewhat of snake-like virulence. One day he encountered an ambitious statesman, and gravely inquired after the welfare of his boa constrictor; for of that species, Roderick affirmed, this gentleman's serpent must needs be, since its appetite was enormous enough to devour the whole country and constitution. At another time, he stopped a close-fisted fellow, of great wealth, but who skulked about the city in the guise of a scarecrow, with a patched blue surtout,° brown hat, and mouldy boots, scraping pence together, and picking up rusty nails. Pretending to look earnestly at this respectable person's stomach, Roderick assured him that his snake was a copper-head, and had been generated by the immense quantities of that base metal,

---

°*surtout:* overcoat

with which he daily defiled his fingers. Again, he assaulted a man of rubi-
cund visage, and told him that few bosom serpents had more of the devil
in them than those that breed in the vats of a distillery. The next whom
Roderick honored with his attention was a distinguished clergyman, who
happened just then to be engaged in a theological controversy, where
human wrath was more perceptible than divine inspiration.

"You have swallowed a snake in a cup of sacramental wine," quoth he.
"Profane wretch!" exclaimed the divine; but, nevertheless, his hand
stole to his breast.

He met a person of sickly sensibility, who, on some early disap-
pointment, had retired from the world, and thereafter held no intercourse
with his fellow-men, but brooded sullenly or passionately over the irrevocable past. This man's very heart, if Roderick might be believed, had been
changed into a serpent, which would finally torment both him and itself
to death. Observing a married couple, whose domestic troubles were a matter of notoriety, he condoled with both on having mutually taken a house
adder to their bosoms. To an envious author, who depreciated works which
he could never equal, he said that his snake was the slimiest and filthiest
of all the reptile tribe, but was fortunately without a sting. A man of
impure life, and a brazen face, asking Roderick if there were any serpent
in his breast, he told him that there was, and of the same species that
once tortured Don Rodrigo, the Goth.° He took a fair young girl by the
hand, and gazing sadly into her eyes, warned her that she cherished a
serpent of the deadliest kind within her gentle breast; and the world
found the truth of those ominous words, when, a few months afterwards,
the poor girl died of love and shame. Two ladies, rivals in fashionable
life, who tormented one another with a thousand little stings of womanish
spite, were given to understand that each of their hearts was a nest of dim-
inutive snakes, which did quite as much mischief as one great one.

But nothing seemed to please Roderick better than to lay hold of a
person infected with jealousy, which he represented as an enormous green
reptile, with an ice-cold length of body, and the sharpest sting of any snake
save one.

"And what one is that?" asked a by-stander, overhearing him.

It was a dark-browed man who put the question; he had an evasive
eye, which in the course of a dozen years had looked no mortal directly
in the face. There was an ambiguity about this person's character—a stain
upon his reputation—yet none could tell precisely of what nature, although
the city gossips, male and female, whispered the most atrocious sur-
mises. Until a recent period he had followed the sea, and was, in fact, the

---

°*Don Rodrigo, the Goth:* Rodrigo or Roderick was the last of the Visigoth kings
(710–711); he became a legendary Spanish hero. In one legend, he atones for his
sins by suffering an adder's bite; Hawthorne's Roderick is an obvious reference to
the legendary Rodrigo.

very shipmaster whom George Herkimer had encountered, under such singular circumstances, in the Grecian Archipelago.

"What bosom serpent has the sharpest sting?" repeated this man; but he put the question as if by a reluctant necessity, and grew pale while he was uttering it.

"Why need you ask?" replied Roderick, with a look of dark intelligence. "Look into your own breast. Hark! my serpent bestirs himself! He acknowledges the presence of a master fiend!"

And then, as the by-standers afterwards affirmed, a hissing sound was heard, apparently in Roderick Elliston's breast. It was said, too, that an answering hiss came from the vitals of the shipmaster, as if a snake were actually lurking there and had been aroused by the call of its brother reptile. If there were in fact any such sound, it might have been caused by a malicious exercise of ventriloquism on the part of Roderick.

Thus making his own actual serpent—if a serpent there actually was in his bosom—the type of each man's fatal error, or hoarded sin, or unquiet conscience, and striking his sting so unremorsefully into the sorest spot, we may well imagine that Roderick became the pest of the city. Nobody could elude him—none could withstand him. He grappled with the ugliest truth that he could lay his hand on, and compelled his adversary to do the same. Strange spectacle in human life where it is the instinctive effort of one and all to hide those sad realities, and leave them undisturbed beneath a heap of superficial topics which constitute the materials of intercourse between man and man! It was not to be tolerated that Roderick Elliston should break through the tacit compact by which the world has done its best to secure repose without relinquishing evil. The victims of his malicious remarks, it is true, had brothers enough to keep them in countenance; for, by Roderick's theory, every mortal bosom harbored either a brood of small serpents or one overgrown monster that had devoured all the rest. Still the city could not bear this new apostle. It was demanded by nearly all, and particularly by the most respectable inhabitants, that Roderick should no longer be permitted to violate the received rules of decorum by obtruding his own bosom serpent to the public gaze, and dragging those of decent people from their lurking places.

Accordingly, his relatives interfered and placed him in a private asylum for the insane. When the news was noised abroad, it was observed that many persons walked the streets with freer countenances and covered their breasts less carefully with their hands.

His confinement, however, although it contributed not a little to the peace of the town, operated unfavorably upon Roderick himself. In solitude his melancholy grew more black and sullen. He spent whole days —indeed, it was his sole occupation—in communing with the serpent. A conversation was sustained, in which, as it seemed, the hidden monster bore a part, though unintelligibly to the listeners, and inaudible except in a hiss. Singular as it may appear, the sufferer had now contracted a sort of affection for his tormenter, mingled, however, with the intensest loathing and horror. Nor were such discordant emotions incompatible. Each, on the contrary, imparted strength and poignancy to its opposite. Horrible love—horrible antipathy—embracing one another in his bosom, and both concentrating themselves upon a being that had crept into his vitals or been engendered there, and which was nourished with his food, and lived upon his life, and was as intimate with him as his own heart, and yet was the foulest of all created things! But not the less was it the true type of a morbid nature.

Sometimes, in his moments of rage and bitter hatred against the snake and himself, Roderick determined to be the death of him, even at the expense of his own life. Once he attempted it by starvation; but, while the wretched man was on the point of famishing, the monster seemed to feed upon his heart, and to thrive and wax gamesome, as if it were his sweetest and most congenial diet. Then he privily took a dose of active poison, imagining that it would not fail to kill either himself or the devil that possessed him, or both together. Another mistake; for if Roderick had not yet been destroyed by his own poisoned heart nor the snake by gnawing it, they had little to fear from arsenic or corrosive sublimate. Indeed, the venomous pest appeared to operate as an antidote against all other poisons. The physicians tried to suffocate the fiend with tobacco smoke. He breathed it as freely as if it were his native atmosphere. Again, they drugged their patient with opium and drenched him with intoxicating liquors, hoping that the snake might thus be reduced to stupor and perhaps be ejected from the stomach. They succeeded in rendering Roderick insensible; but, placing their hands upon his breast, they were inexpressibly horror stricken to feel the monster wriggling, twining, and darting to and fro within his narrow limits, evidently enlivened by the opium or alcohol, and incited to unusual feats of activity. Thenceforth they gave up all attempts at cure or palliation. The doomed sufferer submitted to his fate, resumed his former loathsome affection for the bosom fiend, and spent whole miserable days before a looking-glass, with his mouth wide open, watching, in hope and horror, to catch a glimpse of the snake's head far down within his throat. It is supposed that he succeeded; for the attendants once heard a frenzied shout, and, rushing into the room, found Roderick lifeless upon the floor.

He was kept but little longer under restraint. After minute investigation, the medical directors of the asylum decided that his mental disease did not amount to insanity, nor would warrant his confinement, especially as its influence upon his spirits was unfavorable, and might produce the evil which it was meant to remedy. His eccentricities were doubtless great; he had habitually violated many of the customs and prejudices of society; but the world was not, without surer ground, entitled to treat him as a madman. On this decision of such competent authority Roderick was released, and had returned to his native city the very day before his encounter with George Herkimer.

As soon as possible after learning these particulars the sculptor, together with a sad and tremulous companion, sought Elliston at his own house. It was a large, somber edifice of wood, with pilasters and a balcony, and was divided from one of the principal streets by a terrace of three elevations, which was ascended by successive flights of stone steps. Some immense old elms almost concealed the front of the mansion. This spacious and once magnificent family residence was built by a grandee of the race early in the past century, at which epoch, land being of small comparative value, the garden and other grounds had formed quite an extensive domain. Although a portion of the ancestral heritage had been alienated, there was still a shadowy enclosure in the rear of the mansion where a student, or a dreamer, or a man of stricken heart might lie all day upon the grass, amid the solitude of murmuring boughs, and forget that a city had grown up around him.

Into this retirement the sculptor and his companion were ushered by Scipio, the old black servant, whose wrinkled visage grew almost sunny with intelligence and joy as he paid his humble greetings to one of the two visitors.

"Remain in the arbor," whispered the sculptor to the figure that leaned upon his arm. "You will know whether, and when, to make your appearance."

"God will teach me," was the reply. "May He support me too!" Roderick was reclining on the margin of a fountain which gushed into the fleckered sunshine with the same clear sparkle and the same voice of airy quietude as when trees of primeval growth flung their shadows across its bosom. How strange is the life of a fountain!—born at every moment, yet of an age coeval with the rocks, and far surpassing the venerable antiquity of a forest.

"You are come! I have expected you," said Elliston, when he became aware of the sculptor's presence.

His manner was very different from that of the preceding day—quiet, courteous, and, as Herkimer thought, watchful both over his guest and himself. This unnatural restraint was almost the only trait that betokened anything amiss. He had just thrown a book upon the grass, where it lay half opened, thus disclosing itself to be a natural history of the serpent tribe, illustrated by life-like plates. Near it lay that bulky volume, the *Ductor Dubitantium* of Jeremy Taylor,° full of cases of conscience, and in which most men, possessed of a conscience, may find something applicable to their purpose.

°*Jeremy Taylor:* English bishop and author (1613–1667) ; the book mentioned was published in 1660.

"You see," observed Elliston, pointing to the book of serpents, while a smile gleamed upon his lips, "I am making an effort to become better acquainted with my bosom friend; but I find nothing satisfactory in this volume. If I mistake not, he will prove to be *sui generis*,° and akin to no other reptile in creation."

"Whence came this strange calamity?" inquired the sculptor.

"My sable friend Scipio has a story," replied Roderick, "of a snake that had lurked in this fountain—pure and innocent as it looks—ever since it was known to the first settlers. This insinuating personage once crept into the vitals of my great grandfather and dwelt there many years, tormenting the old gentleman beyond mortal endurance. In short it is a family peculiarity. But to tell you the truth, I have no faith in this idea of the snake's being an heirloom. He is my own snake, and no man's else."

"But what was his origin?" demanded Herkimer.

Oh, there is poisonous stuff in any man's heart sufficient to generate a brood of serpents," said Elliston with a hollow laugh. "You should have heard my homilies to the good town's-people. Positively, I deem myself fortunate in having bred but a single serpent. You, however, have none in your bosom, and therefore cannot sympathize with the rest of the world. It gnaws me! It gnaws me!"

With this exclamation Roderick lost his self-control and threw himself upon the grass, testifying his agony by intricate writhings, in which Herkimer could not but fancy a resemblance to the motions of a snake. Then, likewise, was heard that frightful hiss, which often ran through the sufferer's speech, and crept between the words and syllables without interrupting their succession.

"This is awful indeed!" exclaimed the sculptor—"an awful infliction, whether it be actual or imaginary. Tell me, Roderick Elliston, is there any remedy for this loathsome evil?"

"Yes, but an impossible one," muttered Roderick, as he lay wallowing with his face in the grass. "Could I for one moment forget myself, the serpent might not abide within me. It is my diseased self-contemplation that has engendered and nourished him."

"Then forget yourself, my husband," said a gentle voice above him; "forget yourself in the idea of another!"

Rosina had emerged from the arbor, and was bending over him with the shadow of his anguish reflected in her countenance, yet so mingled with hope and unselfish love that all anguish seemed but an earthy shadow and a dream. She touched Roderick with her hand. A tremor shivered through his frame. At that moment, if report be trustworthy, the sculptor beheld a waving motion through the grass, and heard a tinkling sound, as if something had plunged into the fountain. Be the truth as it might, it

---

°*sui generis:* unique

is certain that Roderick Elliston sat up like a man renewed, restored to his right mind, and rescued from the fiend which had so miserably overcome him in the battle-field of his own breast.

"Rosina!" cried he, in broken and passionate tones, but with nothing of the wild wail that had haunted his voice so long, "forgive! forgive!"

Her happy tears bedewed his face.

"The punishment has been severe," observed the sculptor. "Even Justice might now forgive; how much more a woman's tenderness! Roderick Elliston, whether the serpent was a physical reptile, or whether the morbidness of your nature suggested that symbol to your fancy, the moral of the story is not the less true and strong. A tremendous Egotism, manifesting itself in your case in the form of jealousy, is as fearful a fiend as ever stole into the human heart. Can a breast, where it has dwelt so long, be purified?"

"Oh yes," said Rosina with a heavenly smile. "The serpent was but a dark fantasy, and what it typified was as shadowy as itself. The past, dismal as it seems, shall fling no gloom upon the future. To give it its due importance we must think of it but as an anecdote in our Eternity."

*　　*　　*

No one ever accused D. H. Lawrence of reticence. In taking on Nathaniel Hawthorne, he sees "that blue-eyed darling" as an illustrative case of the split in consciousness between surface and inner soul, between mind-consciousness and blood-consciousness, between the rationalizing, patronizing weakness of mind and society, and the masculine energies of body and blood. He makes the issue simple, maybe too simple, but he states it with a passion that includes Hawthorne, Mrs. Hawthorne, Hester Prynne, American Puritanical consciousness, and "The American Female" in his denunciation.

The ostensible occasion for this "criticism" is *The Scarlet Letter*, Hawthorne's most respected and widely read novel, and its "heroine," Hester, her illegitimate daughter, Pearl, her sinful and unacknowledged lover, Arthur Dimmesdale, and her former husband, Roger Chillingworth. But one need not know much about Hawthorne to see what Lawrence is getting at.

From STUDIES IN CLASSIC AMERICAN LITERATURE

D. H. Lawrence (1885–1930)

NATHANIEL HAWTHORNE AND "THE SCARLET LETTER"

Nathaniel Hawthorne writes romance.

And what's romance? Usually, a nice little tale where you have every-thing As You Like It, where rain never wets your jacket and gnats never bite your nose and it's always daisy-time. *As You Like It* and *Forest Lovers,* etc. *Morte d'Arthur.*

Hawthorne obviously isn't this kind of romanticist: though nobody has muddy boots in *The Scarlet Letter,* either.

But there is more to it. *The Scarlet Letter* isn't a pleasant, pretty ro-mance. It is a sort of parable, an earthly story with a hellish meaning.

All the time there is this split in the American art and art-con-sciousness. On the top it is as nice as pie, goody-goody and lovey-dovey. Like Hawthorne being such a blue-eyed darling, in life, and Longfellow and the rest such sucking-doves. Hawthorne's wife said she "never saw him in time," which doesn't mean she saw him too late. But always in the "frail effulgence of eternity."

Serpents they were. Look at the inner meaning of their art and see what demons they were.

You must look through the surface of American art, and see the inner diabolism of the symbolic meaning. Otherwise it is all mere childishness.

That blue-eyed darling Nathaniel knew disagreeable things in his inner soul. He was careful to send them out in disguise.

Always the same. The deliberate consciousness of Americans so fair and smooth-spoken, and the underconsciousness so devilish. *Destroy! destroy! destroy!* hums the underconsciousness. *Love and produce! Love and produce!* cackles the upper consciousness. And the world hears only the Love-and-produce cackle. Refuses to hear the hum of destruction underneath. Until such time as it will *have* to hear.

The American has got to destroy. It is his destiny. It is his destiny to destroy the whole corpus of the white psyche, the white consciousness. And he's got to do it secretly. As the growing of a dragon-fly inside a chrysalis or cocoon destroys the larva grub, secretly.

Though many a dragon-fly never gets out of the chrysalis case: dies in-side. As America might.

So the secret chrysalis of *The Scarlet Letter,* diabolically destroying the old psyche inside.

Be good! Be good! warbles Nathaniel. *Be good, and never sin! Be sure your sins will find you out.*

So convincingly that his wife never saw him "as in time."

Then listen to the diabolic undertone of *The Scarlet Letter*.

Man ate of the tree of knowledge, and became ashamed of himself.

Do you imagine Adam had never lived with Eve before that apple episode? Yes he had. As a wild animal with his mate.

It didn't become "sin" till the knowledge-poison entered. That apple of Sodom.

We are divided in ourselves, against ourselves. And that is the meaning of the cross symbol.

In the first place, Adam knew Eve as a wild animal knows its mate, momentaneously, but vitally, in blood-knowledge. Blood-knowledge, not mind-knowledge. Blood-knowledge, that seems utterly to forget, but doesn't. Blood-knowledge, instinct, intuition, all the vast vital flux of knowing that goes on in the dark, antecedent to the mind.

Then came that beastly apple, and the other sort of knowledge started.

Adam began to look at himself. "My hat!" he said. "What's this? My Lord! What the deuce!—And Eve! I wonder about Eve."

Thus starts KNOWING. Which shortly runs to UNDERSTANDING, when the devil gets his own.

When Adam went and took Eve, *after* the apple, he didn't do any more than he had done many a time before, in act. But in consciousness he did something very different. So did Eve. Each of them kept an eye on what they were doing, they watched what was happening to them. They wanted to KNOW. And that was the birth of sin. Not *doing* it, but KNOWING about it. Before the apple, they had shut their eyes and their minds had gone dark. Now, they peeped and pried and imagined. They watched themselves. And they felt uncomfortable after. They felt self-conscious. So they said, "The *act* is sin. Let's hide. We've sinned."

No wonder the Lord kicked them out of the Garden. Dirty hypocrites.

The sin was the self-watching, self-consciousness. The sin, and the doom. Dirty understanding.

Nowadays men do hate the idea of dualism. It's no good, dual we are. The cross. If we accept the symbol, then, virtually, we accept the fact. We are divided against ourselves.

For instance, the blood *hates* being known by the mind. It feels itself destroyed when it is KNOWN. Hence the profound instinct of privacy.

And on the other hand, the mind and the spiritual consciousness of man simply *hates* the dark potency of blood-acts: hates the genuine dark sensual orgasms, which do, for the time being, actually obliterate the mind and the spiritual consciousness, plunge them in a suffocating flood of darkness.

You can't get away from this.

Blood-consciousness overwhelms, obliterates, and annuls mind-consciousness.

Mind-consciousness extinguishes blood-consciousness, and consumes the blood.

We are all of us conscious in both ways. And the two ways are antagonistic in us.

They will always remain so.

That is our cross.

The antagonism is so obvious, and so far-reaching, that it extends to the smallest thing. The cultured, highly-conscious person of to-day *loathes* any form of physical, "menial" work: such as washing dishes or sweeping a floor or chopping wood. This menial work is an insult to the spirit. "When I see men carrying heavy loads, doing brutal work, it always makes me want to cry," said a beautiful, cultured woman to me.

"When you say that, it makes me want to beat you," said I, in reply. "When I see you with your beautiful head pondering heavy thoughts, I just want to hit you. It outrages me."

My father hated books, hated the sight of anyone reading or writing.

My mother hated the thought that any of her sons should be condemned to manual labour. Her sons must have something higher that that.

She won. But she died first.

He laughs longest who laughs last.

There is a basic hostility in all of us between the physical and the mental, the blood and the spirit. The mind is "ashamed" of the blood. And the blood is destroyed by the mind, actually. Hence pale-faces.

At present the mind-consciousness and the so-called spirit triumphs. In America supremely. In America, nobody does anything from the blood. Always from the nerves, if not from the mind. The blood is chemically reduced by the nerves, in American activity.

When an Italian labourer labours, his mind and nerves sleep, his blood acts ponderously.

Americans, when they are *doing* things, never seem really to be doing them. They are "busy about" it. They are always busy "about" something. But truly *immersed* in *doing* something, with the deep blood-consciousness active, that they never are.

They *admire* the blood-conscious spontaneity. And they want to get it in their heads. "Live from the body," they shriek. It is their last mental shriek. *Co-ordinate.*

It is a further attempt still to rationalize the body and blood. "Think about such and such a muscle," they say, "and relax there."

And every time you "conquer" the body with the mind (you can say "heal" it, if you like) you cause a deeper, more dangerous complex or tension somewhere else.

Ghastly Americans, with their blood no longer blood. A yellow spiritual fluid.

The Fall.

There have been lots of Falls.

We *fell* into *knowledge* when Eve bit the apple. Self-conscious knowledge. For the first time the mind put up a fight against the blood. Wanting to UNDERSTAND. That is to intellectualize the blood.

The blood must be *shed,* says Jesus.

Shed on the cross of our own divided psyche.

Shed the blood, and you become mind-conscious. Eat the body and drink the blood, self-cannibalizing, and you become extremely conscious, like Americans and some Hindus. Devour yourself, and God knows what a lot you'll know, what a lot you'll be conscious of.

Mind you don't choke yourself.

For a long time men *believed* that they could be perfected through the mind, through the spirit. They believed, passionately. They had their ecstasy in pure consciousness. They *believed* in purity, chastity, and the wings of the spirit.

America soon plucked the bird of the spirit. America soon killed the *belief* in the spirit. But not the practice. The practice continued with a sarcastic vehemence. America, with a perfect inner contempt for the spirit and the consciousness of man, practises the same spirituality and universal love and KNOWING all the time, incessantly, like a drug habit. And inwardly gives not a fig for it. Only for the *sensation.* The pretty-pretty *sensation* of love, loving all the world. And the nice fluttering aeroplane *sensation* of knowing, knowing, knowing. Then the prettiest of all sensations, the sensation of UNDERSTANDING. Oh, what a lot they understand, the darlings! *So* good at the trick, they are. Just a trick of self-conceit.

The Scarlet Letter gives the show away.

You have your pure-pure young parson Dimmesdale.

You have the beautiful Puritan Hester at his feet.

And the first thing she does is to seduce him.

And the first thing he does is to be seduced.

And the second thing they do is to hug their sin in secret, and gloat over it, and try to understand.

Which is the myth of New England.

Deerslayer° refused to be seduced by Judith Hutter. At least the Sodom apple of sin didn't fetch him. But Dimmesdale was seduced gloatingly. Oh, luscious Sin!

He was such a pure young man.

That he had to make a fool of purity.

°*Deerslayer:* Natty Bumppo, the hero of the novel, *The Deerslayer,* by James Fenimore Cooper (1789–1851)

The American psyche.

Of course, the best part of the game lay in keeping up pure appearances.

The greatest triumph a woman can have, especially an American woman, is the triumph of seducing a man: especially if he is pure. And he gets the greatest thrill of all, in falling.—"Seduce me, Mrs. Hercules."

And the pair of them share the subtlest delight in keeping up pure appearances, when everybody knows all the while. But the power of pure appearances is something to exult in. All America gives in to it. *Look* pure!

To seduce a man. To have everybody know. To keep up appearances of purity. Pure!

This is the great triumph of woman.

A. The Scarlet Letter. Adulteress! The great Alpha. Alpha! Adulteress! The new Adam and Adama! American!

A. Adulteress! Stitched with gold thread, glittering upon the bosom. The proudest insignia.

Put her upon the scaffold and worship her there. Worship her there. The Woman, the Magna Mater. *A.* Adulteress! Abel!

Abel! Abel! Abel! Admirable!

It becomes a farce.

The fiery heart. *A.* Mary of the Bleeding Heart. Mater Adolerata! *A.* Capital *A.* Adulteress. Glittering with gold thread. Abel! Adultery. Admirable!

It is, perhaps, the most colossal satire ever penned. *The Scarlet Letter.* And by a blue-eyed darling of a Nathaniel.

Not Bumppo, however.

The human spirit, fixed in a lie, adhering to a lie, giving itself perpetually the lie.

All begins with *A.*

Adulteress. Alpha. Abel, Adam. *A.* America.

The Scarlet Letter.

"Had there been a Papist among the crowd of Puritans, he might have seen in this beautiful woman, so picturesque in her attire and mien, and with the infant at her bosom, an object to remind him of the image of Divine Maternity, which so many illustrious painters have vied with one another to represent; something which should remind him, indeed, but only by contrast, of that sacred image of sinless Motherhood, whose infant was to redeem the world."

Whose infant was to redeem the world indeed! It will be a startling redemption the world will get from the American infant.

"Here was a taint of deepest sin in the most sacred quality of human life, working such effect that the world was only the darker for this woman's beauty, and more lost for the infant she had borne."

Just listen to the darling. Isn't he a master of apology?

Of symbols, too.

His pious blame is a chuckle of praise all the while.

Oh, Hester, you are a demon. A man *must* be pure, just so that you can seduce him to a fall. Because the greatest thrill in life is to bring down the Sacred Saint with a flop into the mud. Then when you've brought him down, humbly wipe off the mud with your hair, another Magdalen. And then go home and dance a witch's jig of triumph, and stitch yourself a Scarlet Letter with gold thread, as duchesses used to stitch themselves coronets. And then stand meek on the scaffold and fool the world. Who will all be envying you your sin, and beating you because you've stolen an advantage over them.

Hester Prynne is the great nemesis of woman. She is the KNOWING Ligeia° risen diabolic from the grave. Having her own back. UNDERSTANDING.

This time it is Mr. Dimmesdale who dies. She lives on and is Abel.

His spiritual love was a lie. And prostituting the woman to his spiritual love, as popular clergymen do, in his preachings and loftiness, was a tall white lie. Which came flop.

We are so pure in spirit. Hi-tiddly-i-ty!

Till she tickled him in the right place, and he fell.

Flop.

Flop goes spiritual love.

But keep up the game. Keep up appearances. Pure are the pure. To the pure all things, etc.

Look out, Mister, for the Female Devotee. Whatever you do, don't let her start tickling you. She knows your weak spot. Mind your Purity.

When Hester Prynne seduced Arthur Dimmesdale it was the beginning of the end. But from the beginning of the end to the end of the end is a hundred years or two.

Mr. Dimmesdale also wasn't at the end of his resources. Previously, he had lived by governing his body, ruling it, in the interests of his spirit. Now he has a good time all by himself torturing his body, whipping it, piercing it with thorns, macerating himself. It's a form of masturbation. He wants to get a mental grip on his body. And since he can't quite manage it with the mind, witness his fall—he will give it what for, with whips. His will shall *lash* his body. And he enjoys his pains. Wallows in them. To the pure all things are pure.

It is the old self-mutilation process, gone rotten. The mind wanting to get its teeth in the blood and flesh. The ego exulting in the tortures of the mutinous flesh. I, the ego, I *will* triumph over my own flesh. Lash! Lash!

°*Ligeia:* In a story by Edgar Allan Poe, the narrator's first wife, Ligeia, rises "diabolic from the grave."

I am a grand free spirit. *Lash!* I am the master of my soul! *Lash! Lash!* I am the captain of my soul. *Lash!* Hurray! "In the fell clutch of circumstance," etc., etc.

Good-bye Arthur. He depended on women for his Spiritual Devotees, spiritual brides. So, the woman just touched him in his weak spot, his Achilles Heel of the flesh. Look out for the spiritual bride. She's after the weak spot.

It is the battle of wills.

"For the will therein lieth, which dieth not——"

The Scarlet Woman becomes a Sister of Mercy. Didn't she just, in the late war. Oh, Prophet Nathaniel!

Hester urges Dimmesdale to go away with her, to a new country, to a new life. He isn't having any.

He knows there is no new country, no new life on the globe to-day. It is the same old thing, in different degrees, everywhere. *Plus ça change, plus c'est la même chose.*

Hester thinks, with Dimmesdale for her husband, and Pearl for her child, in Australia, maybe, she'd have been perfect.

But she wouldn't. Dimmesdale had already fallen from his integrity as a minister of the Gospel of the Spirit. He had lost his manliness. He didn't see the point of just leaving himself between the hands of a woman and going away to a "new country," to be her thing entirely. She'd only have despised him more, as every woman despises a man who has "fallen" to her; despises him with her tenderest lust.

He stood for nothing any more. So let him stay where he was and dree out his weird.°

She had dished him and his spirituality, so he hated her. As Angel Clare was dished, and hated Tess.° As Jude in the end hated Sue°: or should have done. The women make fools of them, the spiritual men. And when, as men, they've gone flop in their spirituality, they can't pick themselves up whole any more. So they just crawl, and die detesting the female, or the females, who made them fall.

The saintly minister gets a bit of his own back, at the last minute, by making public confession from the very scaffold where she was exposed. Then he dodges into death. But he's had a bit of his own back, on everybody.

" 'Shall we not meet again?' whispered she, bending her face down close to him. 'Shall we not spend our immortal life together? Surely, surely we have ransomed one another with all this woe! Thou lookest far into eternity with those bright dying eyes. Tell me what thou seest!' "

°*dree . . . weird:* endure his fate   °*Angel Clare . . . Tess:* lovers in Thomas Hardy's *Tess of the D'Urbervilles*   °*Jude . . . Sue:* Jude Fawley and Sue Bridehead, the unhappy lovers in Hardy's *Jude the Obscure*

" 'Hush, Hester—hush,' said he, with tremulous solemnity. 'The law we broke!—the sin here so awfully revealed! Let these alone be in thy thoughts. I fear! I fear!' "

So he dies, throwing the "sin" in her teeth, and escaping into death.

The law we broke, indeed. You bet!

Whose law!

But it is truly a law, that man must either stick to the belief he has grounded himself on, and obey the laws of that belief, or he must admit the belief itself to be inadequate, and prepare himself for a new thing.

There was no change in belief, either in Hester or in Dimmesdale or in Hawthorne or in America. The same old treacherous belief, which was really cunning disbelief, in the Spirit, in Purity, in Selfless Love, and in Pure Consciousness. They would go on following this belief, for the sake of the sensationalism of it. But they would make a fool of it all the time. Like Woodrow Wilson, and the rest of modern Believers. The rest of modern Saviours.

If you meet a Saviour, to-day, be sure he is trying to make an innermost fool of you. Especially if the saviour be an UNDERSTANDING WOMAN, offering her love.

Hester lives on, pious as pie, being a public nurse. She becomes at last an acknowledged saint, Abel of the Scarlet Letter.

She would, being a woman. She has had her triumph over the individual man, so she quite loves subscribing to the whole spiritual life of society. She will make herself as false as hell, for society's sake, once she's had her real triumph over Saint Arthur.

Blossoms out into a Sister-of-Mercy Saint.

But it's a long time before she really takes anybody in. People kept on thinking her a witch, which she was.

As a matter of fact, unless a woman is held, by man, safe within the bounds of belief, she becomes inevitably a destructive force. She can't help herself. A woman is almost always vulnerable to pity. She can't bear to see anything *physically* hurt. But let a woman loose from the bounds and restraints of man's fierce belief, in his gods and in himself, and she becames a gentle devil. She becomes subtly diabolic. The colossal evil of the united spirit of Woman. WOMAN, German woman or American woman, or every other sort of woman, in the last war, was something frightening. As every *man* knows.

Woman becomes a helpless, would-be-loving demon. She is helpless. Her very love is a subtle poison.

Unless a man believes in himself and his gods, *genuinely:* unless he fiercely obeys his own Holy Ghost; his woman will destroy him. Woman is the nemesis of doubting man. She can't help it.

And with Hester, after Ligeia, woman becomes a nemesis to man. She bolsters him up from the outside, she destroys him from the inside. And he dies hating her, as Dimmesdale did.

Dimmesdale's spirituality had gone on too long, too far. It had become a false thing. He found his nemesis in woman. And he was done for. Woman is a strange and rather terrible phenomenon, to man. When the subconscious soul of woman recoils from its creative union with man, it becomes a destructive force. It exerts, willy-nilly, an invisible destructive influence. The woman herself may be as nice as milk, to all appearance, like Ligeia. But she is sending out waves of silent destruction of the faltering spirit in men, all the same. She doesn't know it. She can't even help it. But she does it. The devil is in her.

The very women who are most busy saving the bodies of men, and saving the children: these women-doctors, these nurses, these educationalists, these public-spirited women, these female saviours: they are all, from the inside, sending out waves of destructive malevolence which eat out the inner life of a man, like a cancer. It is so, it will be so, till men realize it and react to save themselves.

God won't save us. The women are so devilish godly. Men must save themselves in this strait, and by no sugary means either.

A woman can use her sex in sheer malevolence and poison, while she is *behaving* as meek and good as gold. Dear darling, she is really snow-white in her blamelessness. And all the while she is using her sex as a she-devil, for the endless hurt of her man. She doesn't know it. She will never believe it if you tell her. And if you give her a slap in the face for her fiendishness, she will rush to the first magistrate, in indignation. She is so *absolutely* blameless, the she-devil, the dear, dutiful creature.

Give her the great slap, just the same, just when she is being most angelic. Just when she is bearing her cross most meekly.

Oh, woman out of bounds is a devil. But it is man's fault. Woman never *asked,* in the first place, to be cast out of her bit of an Eden of belief and trust. It is man's business to bear the responsibility of belief. If he becomes a spiritual fornicator and liar, like Ligeia's husband and Arthur Dimmesdale, how *can* a woman believe in him? Belief doesn't go by choice. And if a woman doesn't believe in a *man,* she believes, essentially, in nothing. She becomes, willy-nilly, a devil.

A devil she is, and a devil she will be. And most men will succumb to her devilishness.

Hester Prynne was a devil. Even when she was so meekly going round as a sick-nurse. Poor Hester. Part of her wanted to be saved from her own devilishness. And another part wanted to go on and on in devilishness, for revenge. Revenge! REVENGE! It is this that fills the unconscious spirit of woman to-day. Revenge against man, and against the spirit of man, which has betrayed her into unbelief. Even when she is most sweet and a salvationist, she is her most devilish, is woman. She gives her man the sugar-plum of her own submissive sweetness. And when he's taken this sugar-plum in his mouth, a scorpion comes out of it. After he's taken this Eve to his bosom, oh, so loving, she destroys him inch by inch. Woman and her revenge! She will have it, and go on having it, for decades and decades, unless she's stopped. And to stop her you've got to believe in yourself and your gods, your own Holy Ghost, Sir Man; and then you've got to fight her, and never give in. She's a devil. But in the long run she is conquerable. And just a tiny bit of her wants to be conquered. You've got to fight three-quarters of her, in absolute hell, to get at the final quarter of her that wants a release, at last, from the hell of her own revenge. But it's a long last. And not yet.

"She had in her nature a rich, voluptuous, oriental characteristic—a taste for the gorgeously beautiful." This is Hester. This is American. But she repressed her nature in the above direction. She would not even allow herself the luxury of labouring at fine, delicate stitching. Only she dressed her little sin-child Pearl vividly, and the scarlet letter was gorgeously em-broidered. Her Hecate and Astarte insignia.

"A voluptuous, oriental characteristic——" That lies waiting in Amer-ican women. It is probable that the Mormons are the forerunners of the coming real America. It is probable that men will have more than one wife, in the coming America. That you will have again a half-oriental womanhood, and a polygamy.

The grey nurse, Hester. The Hecate, the hell-cat. The slowly-evolving voluptuous female of the new era, with a whole new submissiveness to the dark, phallic principle.

But it takes time. Generation after generation of nurses and political women and salvationists. And in the end, the dark erection of the images of sex-worship once more, and the newly submissive women. That kind of depth. Deep women in that respect. When we have at last broken this in-sanity of mental-spiritual consciousness. And the women *choose* to experi-ence again the great submission.

"The poor, whom she sought out to be the objects of her bounty, often reviled the hand that was stretched to succour them."

Naturally. The poor hate a salvationist. They smell the devil un-derneath.

"She was patient—a martyr indeed—but she forbore to pray for her enemies, lest, in spite of her forgiving aspirations, the words of the blessing should stubbornly twist themselves into a curse."

So much honesty, at least. No wonder the old witch-lady Mistress Hibbins claimed her for another witch.

"She grew to have a dread of children; for they had imbibed from their parents a vague idea of something horrible in this dreary woman gliding silently through the town, with never any companion but only one child."

"A vague idea!" Can't you see her "gliding silently"? It's not a question of a vague idea imbibed, but a definite feeling directly received.

"But sometimes, once in many days, or perchance in many months, she felt an eye—a human eye—upon the ignominious brand, that seemed to give a momentary relief, as if half her agony were shared. The next instant, back it all rushed again, with a still deeper throb of pain; for in that brief interval she had sinned again. Had Hester sinned alone?"

Of course not. As for sinning again, she would go on all her life silently, changelessly "sinning." She never repented. Not she. Why should she? She had brought down Arthur Dimmesdale, that too-too snow-white bird, and that was her life-work.

As for sinning again when she met two dark eyes in a crowd, why, of course. Somebody who understood as she understood.

I always remember meeting the eyes of a gipsy woman, for one moment, in a crowd, in England. She knew, and I knew. What did we know? I was not able to make out. But we knew.

Probably the same fathomless hate of this spiritual-conscious society in which the outcast woman and I both roamed like meek-looking wolves. Tame wolves waiting to shake off their tameness. Never able to.

And again, that "voluptuous, oriental" characteristic that knows the mystery of the ithyphallic° gods. She would not betray the ithyphallic gods. She would not betray the ithyphallic gods to this white, leprous-white society of "lovers." Neither will I, if I can help it. These leprous-white, seducing, spiritual women, who "understand" so much. One has been too often seduced, and "understood." "I can read him like a book," said my first lover of me. The book is in several volumes, dear. And more and more comes back to me the gulf of dark hate and *other* understanding, in the eyes of the gipsy woman. So different from the hateful white light of understanding which floats like scum on the eyes of white, oh, so white English and American women, with their understanding voices and their deep, sad words, and their profound, *good* spirits. Pfui!

Hester was scared only of one result of her sin: Pearl. Pearl, the scarlet letter incarnate. The little girl. When women bear children, they produce either devils or sons with gods in them. And it is an evolutionary process. The devil in Hester produced a purer devil in Pearl. And the devil in Pearl will produce—she married an Italian Count—a piece of purer devilishness still.

And so from hour to hour we ripe and ripe.

And then from hour to hour we rot and rot.

°*ithyphallic:* literally, "straight phallos."

There was that in the child "which often impelled Hester to ask in bitterness of heart, whether it were for good or ill that the poor little creature had been born at all."

For ill, Hester. But don't worry. Ill is as necessary as good. Malevolence is as necessary as benevolence. If you have brought forth, spawned, a young malevolence, be sure there is a rampant falseness in the world against which this malevolence must be turned. Falseness has to be bitten and bitten, till it is bitten to death. Hence Pearl.

Pearl. Her own mother compares her to the demon of plague, or scarlet fever, in her red dress. But then, plague is necessary to destroy a rotten, false humanity.

Pearl, the devilish girl-child, who can be so tender and loving and *understanding*, and then, when she has understood, will give you a hit across the mouth, and turn on you with a grin of sheer diabolic jeering.

Serves you right, you shouldn't be *understood*. That is your vice. You shouldn't want to be loved, and then you'd not get hit across the mouth. Pearl will love you: marvelously. And she'll hit you across the mouth: oh, so neatly. And serves you right.

Pearl is perhaps the most modern child in all literature.

Old-fashioned Nathaniel, with his little-boy charm, he'll tell you what's what. But he'll cover it with smarm.

Hester simply *hates* her child, from one part of herself. And from another, she cherishes her child as her one precious treasure. For Pearl is the continuing of her female revenge on life. But female revenge hits both ways. Hits back at its own mother. The female revenge in Pearl hits back at Hester, the mother, and Hester is simply livid with fury and "sadness," which is rather amusing.

"The child could not be made amenable to rules. In giving her existence a great law had been broken; and the result was a being whose elements were perhaps beautiful and brilliant, but all in disorder, or with an order peculiar to themselves, amidst which the point of variety and arrangement was difficult or impossible to discover."

Of course, the order is peculiar to themselves. But the point of variety is this: "Draw out the loving, sweet soul, draw it out with marvelous understanding; and then spit in its eye."

Hester, of course, didn't at all like it when her sweet child drew out her motherly soul, with yearning and deep understanding: and then spit in the motherly eye, with a grin. But it was a process the mother had started.

Pearl had a peculiar look in her eyes: "a look so intelligent, yet so inexplicable, so perverse, sometimes so malicious, but generally accompanied by a wild flow of spirits, that Hester could not help questioning at such moments whether Pearl was a human child."

A little demon! But her mother, and the saintly Dimmesdale, had borne her. And Pearl, by the very openness of her perversity, was more straightforward than her parents. She flatly refuses any Heavenly Father, seeing the earthly one such a fraud. And she has the pietistic Dimmesdale on toast, spits right in his eye: in both his eyes.

Poor, brave, tormented little soul, always in a state of recoil, she'll be a devil to men when she grows up. But the men deserve it. If they'll let themselves be "drawn," by her loving understanding, they deserve that she shall slap them across the mouth the moment they *are* drawn. The chickens! Drawn and trussed.

Poor little phenomenon of a modern child, she'll grow up into the devil of a modern woman. The nemesis of weak-kneed modern men, craving to be love-drawn.

The third person in the diabolic trinity, or triangle, of the Scarlet Letter, is Hester's first husband, Roger Chillingworth. He is an old Elizabethan physician, with a grey beard and a long-furred coat and a twisted shoulder. Another healer. But something of an alchemist, a magician. He is a magician on the verge of modern science, like Francis Bacon.

Roger Chillingworth is of the old order of intellect, in direct line from the mediæval Roger Bacon alchemists. He has an old, intellectual belief in the dark sciences, the Hermetic philosophies. He is no Christian, no selfless aspirer. He is not an aspirer. He is the old authoritarian in man. The old male authority. But without passional belief. Only intellectual belief in himself and his male authority.

Shakespeare's whole tragic wail is because of the downfall of the true male authority, the ithyphallic authority and masterhood. It fell with Elizabeth. It was trodden underfoot with Victoria.

But Chillingworth keeps on the *intellectual* tradition. He hates the spiritual aspirers, like Dimmesdale, with a black, crippled hate. He is the old male authority, in intellectual tradition.

You can't keep a wife by force of an intellectual tradition. So Hester took to seducing Dimmesdale.

Yet her only marriage, and her last oath, is with the old Roger. He and she are accomplices in pulling down the spiritual saint.

"Why dost thou smile so at me—" she says to her old, vengeful husband. "Art thou not like the Black Man that haunts the forest around us? Hast thou not enticed me into a bond which will prove the ruin of my soul?"

"Not thy soul!" he answered with another smile. "No, not thy soul"

It is the soul of the pure preacher, that false thing, which they are after. And the crippled physician—this other healer—blackly vengeful in his old, distorted male authority, and the "loving" woman, they bring down the saint between them.

A black and complementary hatred, akin to love, is what Chillingworth feels for the young, saintly parson. And Dimmesdale responds, in a hideous kind of love. Slowly the saint's life is poisoned. But the black old physician smiles, and tries to keep him alive. Dimmesdale goes in for self-torture, self-lashing, lashing his own white, thin, spiritual saviour's body. The dark old Chillingworth listens outside the door and laughs, and prepares another medicine, so that game can go on longer. And the saint's very soul goes rotten. Which is the supreme triumph. Yet he keeps up appearances still.

The black, vengeful soul of the crippled, masterful male, still dark in his authority: and the white ghastliness of the fallen saint! The two halves of manhood mutually destroying one another.

Dimmesdale has a "coup" in the very end. He gives the whole show away by confessing publicly on the scaffold, and dodging into death, leaving Hester dished, and Roger as it were, doubly cuckolded. It is a neat revenge.

Down comes the curtain, as in Ligeia's poem.

But the child Pearl will be on in the next act, with her Italian Count and a new brood of vipers. And Hester greyly Abelling, in the shadows, after her rebelling.

It is a marvellous allegory. It is to me one of the greatest allegories in all literature, *The Scarlet Letter*. Its marvellous under-meaning! And its perfect duplicity.

The absolute duplicity of that blue-eyed *Wunderkind* of a Nathaniel. The American wonder-child, with his magical allegorical insight.

But even wonder-children have to grow up in a generation or two. And even SIN becomes stale.

QUESTIONS

1. Is Lawrence's tone proper to the spirit of his subject, or too extreme?
2. What matters exercise Lawrence's most extreme passions? What makes him most furious? What is he in favor of?
3. Though he makes a very large and general attack on a national habit, is there any way to verify or reject his view on the basis of hard evidence? What other books validate or refute his charges?
4. Lawrence's view of the proper relationship between man and woman is very much out of fashion today. What is his view of that relationship and why does he think it so important? Why has it become so unpopular?
5. Literary criticism which is so heavily ideological is also out of fashion (if it was ever in). Do you think Lawrence is a fair critic of Hawthorne? Is his attitude toward the writer a legitimate one? What does Lawrence seem to think literature is?

PART VII

Psychoanalysis and the Fall

Late resounds what early sounds.

—Goethe

Psychoanalysis and the Fall

Psychoanalysis has revealed still another way in which the Myth of the Fall is true. Not only has it been able to validate the psychological force of myth in general, but it has had particular success in showing the important relationships between the child's experiences and the adult's attitudes. Specifically, the ways in which the child learns to live without the blissful, instinctual satisfactions of the mother's womb and breast, the ways in which that transition to independence, self-sufficiency, and membership in the community of man are accomplished, are the essential determiners of whether an adult will be happy, stable, and loving, or hostile and sick. What Blake knew in his bones we have now documented and confirmed. What poets sing, scientists come after to verify. It is a nice reversal: Science, having taken away the original force of religious belief in the Fall, now returns it to us.

In the passages and poems that follow we see that the Myth of the Fall is the crucial experience in human development—the way we do or do not learn to live and love determines whether as adults we can accept the present or whether we refuse it by looking back in anger. We see that unless we attach ourselves in love to other fallen human beings, we cannot redeem the necessary loss of the all-sufficient Mother in the Garden.

From MARGINALIA

W. H. Auden (1907–)

Few can remember
clearly when innocence came
to a sudden end,
the moment at which we ask
for the first time: *Am I loved?*

*   *   *

Erik Erikson is a follower of Sigmund Freud, whose work has emphasized the stages of growth and development which a child and adolescent encounter. The passage here is from *Childhood and Society.*°

From CHILDHOOD AND SOCIETY

Erik H. Erikson (1902–   )

As the child's radius of awareness, co-ordination, and responsiveness expands, he meets the educative patterns of his culture, and thus learns the basic modalities° of human existence, each in personally and culturally significant ways. These basic modalities are admirably expressed in "basic" English, which is so precise when it comes to the definition of interpersonal patterns. To our great relief, therefore, we can at this point take recourse to some of the simplest English words instead of inventing new Latin combinations.

To get (when it does not mean "to fetch") means to receive and to accept what is given. This is the first social modality learned in life; and it sounds simpler than it is. For the groping and unstable newborn organism learns this modality only as it learns to regulate its organ systems in accordance with the way in which the maternal environment integrates its methods of child care.

It is clear, then, that the optimum total situation implied in the baby's readiness to get which is given is his mutual regulation with a mother who will permit him to develop and co-ordinate his means of getting as she develops and co-ordinates her means of giving. There is a high premium of libidinal pleasure on this co-ordination—a libidinal pleasure which one feels is only insufficiently formulated by the term "oral." The mouth and the nipple seem to be mere centers of a general aura of warmth and mutuality which are enjoyed and responded to with relaxation not only by these focal organs, but by both total organisms. The mutuality of relaxation thus developed is of prime importance for the first experience of friendly otherness. One may say (somewhat mystically, to be sure) that in thus *getting what is given,* and in learning to *get somebody to do* for him what he wishes to have done, the baby also develops the necessary ego groundwork to *get to be* a giver. Where this fails, the situation falls apart into a variety of attempts at controlling by

---

°For an interesting psychoanalytic view of the Myth of the Fall, see: John Wren-Lewis's "Love's Coming of Age" in *Psychoanalysis Observed,* edited by Charles Rycroft, Penguin, 1968.   °*modalities:* methods and means

duress or fantasy rather than by reciprocity. The baby will try to get by random activity what he cannot get by central suction; he will exhaust himself or he will find his thumb and damn the world. The mother too may try to force matters by urging the nipple into the baby's mouth, by nervously changing hours and formulas, or being unable to relax the initially painful procedure of suckling.

There are, of course, methods of alleviating such a situation, of maintaining reciprocity by giving to the baby what he can get through good artifical nipples and of making up for what is missed orally through the satiation of other than oral receptors: his pleasure in being held, warmed, smiled at, talked to, rocked, etc. We cannot afford to relax our remedial inventiveness. However, it seems (here as elsewhere) that if we expend a fraction of our curative energy on thoughtful prevention, we may abet the cure and make it simpler.

Now to the second stage, during which the ability to make a more active and directed approach, and the pleasure derived from it, grow and ripen. The teeth develop, and with them the pleasure in biting *on* hard things, in biting *through* things, and in biting pieces *off* things. With a little configurational play we can see that the biting mode serves to subsume a variety of other activities (as did the first incorporative mode). The eyes, first part of a relatively passive system of accepting impressions as they come along, have now learned to focus, to isolate, to "grasp" objects from the vaguer background, and to follow them. The organs of hearing have similarly learned to discern significant sounds, to localize them, and to guide an appropriate change in position (lifting and turning the head, lifting and turning the upper body). The arms have learned to reach out and the hands to grasp more purposefully.

With all of this a number of interpersonal patterns are established which center in the social modality of *taking* and *holding on to* things —things which are more or less freely offered and given, and things which have more or less of a tendency to slip away. As the baby learns to change positions, to roll over, and very gradually to sit up, he must perfect the mechanisms of grasping, investigating, and appropriating all that is within his reach. . . .

At this stage, however, not even the kindest environment can save the baby from a traumatic change—one of the severest because the baby is so young and the difficulties encountered are so diffuse. I refer to the general development of impulses and mechanisms of active prehension,° the eruption of the teeth and the proximity of this process to that of weaning and to the increasing separation from the mother, who may go back to work, or be pregnant again, or both.

°*prehension:* taking hold

For it is here that "good" and "evil" enter the baby's world, unless his basic trust in himself and others has already been shaken in the first stage by unduly provoked or prolonged paroxysms of rage and exhaustion. It is, of course, impossible to know what the infant feels, as his teeth "bore from within"—in the very oral cavity which until then was the main seat of pleasure, and a seat mainly of pleasure; and what kind of masochistic dilemma results from the fact that the tension and pain caused by the teeth, these inner saboteurs, can be alleviated only by biting harder. This, in turn, adds a social dilemma to a physical one. For where breast feeding lasts into the biting stage (and, all in all, this has been the rule on earth) it is now necessary to learn how to continue sucking without biting, so that the mother may not withdraw the nipple in pain or anger. Our clinical work indicates that this point in the individual's early history can be the origin of an evil dividedness, where anger against the gnawing teeth, and anger against the withdrawing mother, and anger with one's impotent anger all lead to a forceful experience of sadistic and masochistic confusion leaving the general impression that once upon a time one destroyed one's unity with a maternal matrix. This earliest catastrophe in the individual's relation to himself and to the world is probably the ontogenetic° contribution to the Biblical saga of paradise, where the first people on earth forfeited forever the right to pluck without effort what had been put at their disposal; they bit into the forbidden apple, and made God angry. We must understand that the profundity as well as the universality of this subject makes it seem the more important that the early unity should be a deep and satisfactory one and that a baby should be exposed to the unavoidable "evil" in human nature gently and reassuringly, and without avoidable aggravation.

In regard to the first oral state, we spoke of a mutual regulation of the baby's pattern of accepting things and the mother's (the culture's) way of giving them. There are stages, however, which are marked by such unavoidable development of rage and anger that mutual regulation by complementary behavior cannot be the pattern for meeting them. The rages of teething, the tantrums of muscular and anal impotence, the failures of falling, etc.—all are situations in which the intensity of the impulse leads to its own defeat. Parents and cultures use and exploit just these infantile encounters with inner gremlins for the reinforcement of their outer demands. But parents and cultures must also meet these stages by seeing to it that as little as possible of the original mutuality is lost in the process of moving from phase to phase. Weaning, therefore, should not mean sudden loss of the breast and loss of the mother's reassuring presence too, unless, of course, the cultural situation is a

---

°*ontogenetic:* pertaining to the life cycle of a single organism

homogeneous one and other women can be depended on to sound and feel pretty much like the mother. A drastic loss of accustomed mother love without proper substitution at this time can lead (under otherwise aggravating conditions) to acute infantile depression or to a mild but chronic state of mourning which may give a depressive undertone to the whole remainder of life. But even under the most favorable circumstances, this stage leaves a residue of a primary sense of evil and doom and of a universal nostalgia for a lost paradise.

The oral stages, then, form in the infant the springs of the *basic sense of trust* and the *basic sense of mistrust* which remain the autogenic° source of both primal hope and of doom throughout life.

*   *   *

How Children Fail is an important and influential work which shows how often and how unwittingly schools and teachers encourage the wrong kinds of growth, failing to create positive and useful attitudes toward new experience—i.e., toward the inevitable processes of life.

From HOW CHILDREN FAIL

John Holt (1926–   )

December 3, 1958

The other day I decided to talk to the other section about what happens when you don't understand what is going on. We had been chatting about something or other, and everyone seemed in a relaxed frame of mind, so I said, "You know, there's something I'm curious about, and I wonder if you'd tell me." They said, "What?" I said, "What do you think, what goes through your mind, when the teacher asks you a question and you don't know the answer?"

It was a bombshell. Instantly a paralyzed silence fell on the room. Everyone stared at me with what I have learned to recognize as a tense expression. For a long time there wasn't a sound. Finally Ben, who is bolder than most, broke the tension, and also answered my question, by saying in a loud voice, "Gulp!"

°*autogenic:* self-produced

He spoke for everyone. They all began to clamor, and all said the same thing, that when the teacher asked them a question and they didn't know the answer they were scared half to death. I was flabbergasted—to find this in a school which people think of as progressive; which does its best not to put pressure on little children; which does not give marks in the lower grades; which tries to keep children from feeling that they're in some kind of race.

I asked them why they felt gulpish. They said they were afraid of failing, afraid of being kept back, afraid of being called stupid, afraid of feeling themselves stupid. Stupid. Why is it such a deadly insult to these children, almost the worst thing they can think of to call each other? Where do they learn this?

Even in the kindest and gentlest of schools, children are afraid, many of them a great deal of the time, some of them almost all the time. This is a hard fact of life to deal with. What can we do about it?

*   *   *

Selma Fraiberg is Professor of Child Psychoanalysis at the University of Michigan Medical School. She has published numerous articles and essays on child development.

THE ORIGINS OF HUMAN BONDS
Selma Fraiberg (1918–   )

I

Konrad Lorenz has called it "the bond"°—the enduring ties that unite members of a species in couples, in groups, and in complex social organizations. This personal bond is not the exclusive prerogative of man or of mammals. Stable and permanent partnerships for the propagation of young can also be found among some species of fish—and these partnerships endure beyond the period of spawning and the raising of young. Among greylag geese there are elderly couples which have raised their broods and remain demonstrative to each other and solicitous of each other's welfare in an exclusive and cozy domesticity that has outlived the biological purpose of union. Lorenz has described genuine grief reactions among widowed geese. Similar accounts exist of the fidelity of jackdaw couples, even after prolonged separation.

° In *On Aggression*, Harcourt, Brace & World, 1967.

Yet, within the same species that produce permanent bonds among members, *fighting* among members is a common occurrence, regulated by formal rules of conduct and ritual forms of triumph and appeasement. It seems that the "problem" of aggression, which we like to believe was invented by the moral intelligence of man, is no less a "problem" to every species that possesses the bond. Conflicts between the claims of love and the claims of aggression did not originate with our own intelligent species. The devotion and fidelity of the greylag goose, for instance, is maintained through elaborate rituals designed to divert aggression from the partner. Even the device of the scapegoat appears in a simplified form among some species of fish and is ubiquitous among all species that exhibit bond behavior. To put it simply, aggression in these species is channeled away from the partner in order to preserve the bond.

The parallels between these phenomena and the data of human development and human behavior are striking. In the course of development, the child modifies his aggressive urges through love of his human partners. If a child, for one or another reason, becomes deprived of human partners or of the conditions for attachment, the result may be a lack of inhibitions of aggressive impulses or of the capacity to regulate aggression. In the psychoanalytic view, conflicts between love and hate are central in the human personality. The need to preserve love from the destructive forces of aggression has produced in man great love, great works, and the highest moral attainments. The modification of aggression in the service of love has produced an infinite variety of redirected action and mental mechanisms which serve to discharge the drive tendencies through substitute goals. And while the same conflicts between love and hate can also produce neurotic symptoms in the human personality, it is well to remember that there is a vast range in which man can find successful solutions to these conflicts without resorting to disease.

This essay is not intended as a review of Lorenz's book. Rather, I shall attempt to take up some problems in human psychology that Lorenz has illuminated from the biological side. Naturally, at a time when the most intelligent of animals seems bent on the extermination of his own species, a study of the natural history of aggression and its relationship to the love bonds should prove instructive. This is not to say that the solutions that have evolved among sea animals and birds or even the higher mammals are applicable to human society. When Lorenz urges us to regard the lessons from biology with modesty, he is not suggesting, of course, that we employ the rituals of waterfowl to regulate our daily aggressions or our foreign policy. He is telling us that there is an evolutionary tendency at work which has produced increasingly complex and effective means of regulating aggression, that the tendency is at work within human society in ways that we cannot easily recognize without following the biological narrative, and that there are as many portents for human solutions to the ancient problems of aggression as there are, at this point in our history, portents of disaster.

II

At the center of Lorenz's book is a paradox. (1) Intraspecific aggression—fighting between members of the same species—is a characteristic of some species, but not of others. (2) The bond appears *only* in those species which also manifest intraspecific aggression. (3) There are species that have intraspecific aggression and no bond, but conversely there are no species that have the bond and do not also have intraspecific aggression. (4) Within those species which have evolved enduring attachments among members, there are biological mechanisms for inhibiting aggression under certain conditions and there are ritual forms of courtship and greeting ceremonials among members in which the characteristic motor patterns of aggression have undergone a transformation in the service of love.

It appears, then, that there are phylogenetic° links between aggression and love. The coexistence of intraspecific aggression and the bond in certain species should inform us of the biological purpose and earliest interdependence of two instinctual drives which have evolved as polar and antagonistic. This is the territory that Lorenz explores.

Among the human psychologies, psychoanalysis maintains its original position with regard to the instinctual drives. In 1920, when the earlier libido theory was modified by Freud, aggression was given full status as an instinctual drive; a two-drive theory (sexual and aggressive) has remained central to psychoanalytic theory since that time. While recent advances in psychoanalytic theory have been in the area of ego psychology, psychoanalytic ego psychology has, on the whole, remained firmly rooted in biological foundations. Thus, it is the ego's role as a regulator of drives, the ego as the agency of adaptation, the ego as the mediator between drives and the demands of conscience, that define ego for psychoanalysis.

Now, it matters a great deal whether we include drives in our theory or not. If we believe that an aggressive drive is part of the biological inheritance of man, we add another dimension of meaning to conflict. It means that we grant motivational force to aggression as an instinctual drive that can, at times, be independent of objective circumstances. We thus have the means to explain what the behaviorists cannot well explain, the ubiquitous conflicts of love and hate, the admixture of aggression in the most sublime love, the "store" of aggression in human personality which can be triggered by a militant slogan or a boxing match or the buzzing of a mosquito. In this view the instinctual drive is given; it cannot be abolished—although it *can* be brought into the service of human

---

°*phylogenetic:* pertaining to the evolutionary history of a particular species

aspirations by inhibiting those tendencies of the drive that can lead to destructive purpose.

We can learn, then, from the study of biology that the biological "purpose" of aggression is not murder. The killing of a member of one's own species is rarely encountered outside of human society. When it occurs among animals in the wild state, it is accidental. When it occurs in a zoo or an animal laboratory it can be demonstrated that some component in the instinctual organization was deprived of a vital nutriment for functioning or of the stimulus for release, and that the intricate network which transmits signals within the instinct groups broke down. In one example given by Lorenz, hens that were surgically deafened for experimental purposes killed their newly hatched chicks by furious pecking. The hen, who does not "know" her young, normally responds to the call notes of the newly hatched chicks, which elicit appropriate maternal behavior. The deafened hens, unable to receive the signals of their young, reacted to the stimulus of the "strange object" and unleashed the aggression—heightened in this period by the necessities of brood defense—against the brood itself.

Lorenz defines aggression as "the fighting instinct in beast and man which is directed *against* members of the same species." Intraspecific aggression usually occurs in the service of survival. By warding off competitors within the species, aggression maintains living space and an equitable access to the food supply. Aggression is essential for defense of the brood; in any given species the primary tender of the brood, whether male or female, is endowed with the highest amount of aggressivity. With some rare exceptions, intraspecific fighting is limited to subduing the opponent or causing him to take flight. Lorenz describes ritual expressions of appeasement and submission in the loser of the fight as well as ritual forms of triumph (the "triumph ceremony") in the winner. Lorenz and other ethologists° have collected thousands of examples from various species and have analyzed the components of each action in order to determine the specific patterns and variations. Each species, it appears, has its own forms of appeasement and triumph, and the ritual performance becomes a common language in which each gesture, each subtle nuance, has a sign function that is "understood" by every other member of the species. Among wolves and dogs, for example, the submissive gesture is the offering of the vulnerable, arched side of the neck to the aggressor. This is by no means an analogue to a "death wish" in the animal; it is the signal, "I give up," and it derives its function as a signal from the opposite behavior in fighting in which the animal protects the vulnerable region by averting his head. The triumph ritual among dogs is the lateral shaking of the head, the "shaking-to-death"

°*ethologists:* students of comparative cultural or group behavior

gesture with mouth closed. At the end of this ceremony, the loser retreats and the victor marches off.

This ritualization of innate aggressive patterns is one of the most important links between instinct and the social forms that derive from instinct. The motor patterns for aggression are innate; when another instinctual need is manifested simultaneously, or external circumstances alter the aim of the drive, the innate motor pattern is still produced, but with some slight variation that endows it with another function and another meaning that is "understood" in the common language of the species.

What prevents a fight to the death within a given species? By what means can an animal check the intensity of his aggression before it destroys a member of his own species? There are inhibitions in animals, Lorenz tells us, that are themselves instinctual in their nature. There are inhibitions against killing an animal of one's own species or eating the flesh of a dead animal of the species. Nearly all species have inhibitions against attacking females or the young of the species. The inhibitions are so reliable that Lorenz regards a dog who attacks a female as aberrant and warns the reader against trusting such an animal with children. As we follow Lorenz we see that certain values which for humans are "moral imperatives" have antecedents in the instinctual inhibitions of animals.

Now if we grant that a certain quantity of energy is expended in an aggressive act, an inhibition of aggressive action can leave a quantity of undischarged energy in an animal that does not have a repertoire of behaviors or mental mechanisms for blocking discharge. In this dilemma the most common solution among animals is "redirection," to use the ethological term. That is, the animal switches his goal and discharges aggression on a substitute object. In one of many examples given by Lorenz, a female fish wearing the glorious colors of her "nuptial dress" entices a male. In the cichlid, the colors worn by the female are also the very colors that elicit aggression in the species. The excited male plows toward the female, clearly intent on ramming her. Within a few inches of the female he brakes, swerves, and directs his attack to a hapless bystander, a male member of the species. The foe vanquished, the victorious fish presents himself to his bride in a triumph ceremony, which serves as a prologue to the sexual act.

In this example, the inhibition is provided by the claims of another instinct, the sexual drive, and discharge of aggression is redirected toward another member of the species—an "indifferent object," as we would see it. This is a very simple example of conflict between two drives in a species less complex than our own. The claims of each drive must be satisfied, but the aggressive drive cannot satisfy itself upon the sexual object without obstructing the aim of the sexual drive. Redirection of the aggressive drive toward substitute goals provides the solution.

We can of course immediately recognize the behavior of "redirection" as a component of human behavior: in its simplest form it is analogous to "taking it out on" another person or an indifferent object, "displacing" the anger. Among humans the behavior of "redirection" has evolved into complex mental mechanisms in which drives are directed to substitute aims, as in sublimation, in defense mechanisms, and also at times in symptoms. In striking analogy with the drive conflicts of the unintelligent animals, it is the necessity among humans to divert aggression away from the object of love that creates one of the strong motives for the displacement, inhibition, and even repression of aggressive impulses. This means, of course, that the mental mechanisms available to humans not only permit redirection of the drives toward objectives that are far removed from "motor discharge of aggression," but that the drive energy is available in part for investing the substitute act with meaning far removed from "the fighting instinct." Where aggressive and sexual impulses enter into a work of art, for example, the original impulses undergo a qualitative change and the product in the work itself becomes a metaphor, a symbolic representation of the biological aims.

I do not wish to strain the analogies between "redirection" in animals and in humans. When complex mental acts intervene between a drive and its expression, as in human behavior, we are clearly dealing with another order of phenomenon. It is, for example, the human capacity for symbolic thought that makes it possible for the ego to block discharge of a drive or, more marvelous still, to exclude from consciousness (as in repression) the idea associated with the impulse. In non-human species, where there are no ideas and, properly speaking, no state that corresponds to "consciousness" in humans, there are no equivalents for repression.

Yet, we will find it arresting to see, in Lorenz's animal data, simple forms of symbolic action, a preliminary sketch for a design that becomes marvelously extended and elaborated in human thought. This is the process called "ritualization" in animals which we have already touched on in connection with the ceremonies of appeasement and triumph in animals. Lorenz presents us with an impressive body of data to show how courtship ceremonies among many species have evolved through the ritualization of aggression.

Any one of the processes that lead to redirection may become ritualized in the course of evolution. In the cichlid we saw earlier how aggression against the female is diverted and discharged against another member of the species in the courtship pattern. Among cranes there is a kind of tribal greeting and appeasement ceremony in which "redirected aggression" is simply pantomimed. The bird performs a *fake* attack on any substitute object, preferably a nearby crane who is not a friend, or even on a harmless goose, or on a piece of wood or stone which he seizes with his beak and throws three of four times into the air. In other words, the ritual redirection of aggression has evolved into a symbolic action.

Among greylag geese and other species, the redirected fighting and its climax are ritually observed in courtship, but they have also been generalized into a greeting ceremonial within the species as a whole. Greylag geese, male or female, greet each other ritually by performing the triumph ceremony. It is the binding ceremony of the group, and the performance of this rite with another member of the group renews and cements the bond, like the handshake or password of a secret society or a tribal ceremonial.

And here we reach the central part of Lorenz's thesis, the evolution of the personal bond. We recall that Lorenz and other ethologists have demonstrated that personal ties among members of a species—"the bond"—appear only among species in which aggression against members of the same species also occurs. Using the greylag goose as model, Lorenz shows how redirected forms of aggression become ritualized, then follow an evolutionary course to become the binding force among members of the group. Thus, among the greylag goose, a species with strong intraspecific aggression, stable and enduring friendships and lifelong fidelity exist between mates. These are bonds which are relatively independent of survival needs or procreation. Unlike partnerships found in some other species, these bonds are not seasonal or circumstantially determined. The mate, the friend, among greylags is individually recognized, and valued; he cannot be exchanged with any other partner. Loss of the friend or mate produces genuine mourning in the bereaved partner. And the ceremonial that binds these birds in pairs and in groups, the ritual greeting, the ritual wooing, the bond of love, is the triumph ceremony which originated in fighting and through redirection and ritualization evolved into a love ceremonial which has the effect of binding partners and groups. Aggression is made over in the service of love.

In the model of the greylag goose, Lorenz traces the pattern of the triumph ceremony in fine detail. The phylogenetic origins of the pattern are probably similar to those described in the cichlid: that is, a conflict between the subject's sexual aims and aggressive aims toward the same object finds a solution in the redirection of aggression toward another, "indifferent" object. The pattern evolved as a condition for mating and, through ritualization, became part of the courtship ceremonial. In the further evolution of the ritual fight, the triumph ceremony acquired a sign function for the affirmation of love; within the species it became a binding ritual. The ceremony, as Lorenz points out, has become independent of sexual drives and has become a bond which embraces the whole family and whole groups of individuals, in any season.

Lorenz adduces a large number of examples to show the evolution of greeting rituals from the motor patterns of aggression. Among certain birds, the "friendly" confrontation and exchange of signals is barely distinguishable from the threatening stance and gestures of the same species (thus, for example, the expressive movement which accompanies cackling among geese). But close observation and motivational analysis show a detail, such as a half-turn of the head or body, which alters the "meaning" of the motor pattern so that the sign value of the pattern is taken as friendly. The human smile, Lorenz suggests, probably originated in the same way: the baring of the teeth in the primal threatening gesture has been made over into the friendly smile, the uniquely human tribal greeting. No other animal has evolved the act of smiling from the threatening gesture of tooth baring.

Moreover, these greeting patterns, which are found among all species which have personal bonds, are not dependent upon learning. Given certain eliciting stimuli the baby animal produces the greeting sign as part of his innate inventory of behaviors. If one bends over a newly hatched gosling, says Lorenz, and speaks to it "in an approximate goosy voice," the newborn baby goose utters the greeting sound of its species! Similarly, given certain "eliciting stimuli" the human baby in the first weeks of life produces our tribal greeting sign, the smile.

All of this means that in the process of redirection and the ritualization of aggression in the service of love, a new pattern emerges which acquires full status as an instinct and a high degree of autonomy from the aggressive and sexual instincts from which it derived. Not only are the patterns of love part of an autonomous instinct group, but they have a motive force equal to or greater than that of aggression under a wide range of conditions, and are capable of opposing and checking and redirecting aggression when the aims of aggression conflict with those of love.

While we can speak, then, of innate tendencies that produce characteristic forms of attachment in a particular species, it is very important to stress that these patterns of attachment will not emerge if certain eliciting stimuli are not provided by the environment. In the case of the newborn gosling, the cry of greeting is elicited by the call notes of the species, usually provided by the mother. Lorenz, by producing these sounds experimentally, elicited the greeting sounds from the newborn gosling and actually produced in hand-reared geese a permanent attachment to himself; he became the "mother." In experiments which Lorenz describes in *On Aggression* and elsewhere he was able to produce nearly all of the characteristics of early attachment behavior in young geese by providing the necessary signals during the critical phase of attachment.

In other experiments in which baby geese were reared in isolation from their species and otherwise deprived of the conditions for attachment, an aberrant bird was produced, a solitary creature that seemed unaware of its surroundings, unresponsive to stimuli—a creature, in fact, which avoided stimuli as if they were painful. It is worth mentioning in this context that Harry Harlow in certain experiments with monkeys accidentally produced an aberrant group of animals with some of the same characteristics of stimulus avoidance. In his now famous experiments in which baby monkeys were reared with dummy mothers (a cloth "mother," a wire "mother") the animals became attached to the dummy mothers in a striking parody of the species' attachment behavior, but the animals also produced a group of pathological symptoms that were never seen among mother-reared monkeys. They were strangely self-absorbed, made no social contact with other members of the species, would sit in their cages and stare fixedly into space, circle their cages in a repetitive, stereotyped manner, and clasp their heads in their hands or arms and rock for long periods. Some of them chewed and tore at their own flesh until it bled. When these animals reached sexual maturity they were unable to copulate. In the rare circumstance under which a female could be impregnated by a normal male from another colony, the female ignored her young after birth or tried to kill them.

To those of us who are working in the area of human infancy and early development, these studies of attachment behavior in animals and the correlate studies of animals deprived of attachment have had a sobering effect. For there are some striking parallels between them and our own studies of normal development and of certain aberrant patterns in early childhood which I will describe later as "the diseases of non-attachment." In all these studies of animal behavior and human infancy, we feel as if we are about to solve an ancient riddle posed by the polar drives of love and aggression.

III

In the earliest years of psychoanalysis, Freud discovered that conflicts between the claims of love and the claims of aggression were central to all personality development. As early as 1905 he demonstrated through the study of a five-year-old boy, "Little Hans," how the animal phobias of early childhood represent a displacement of aggressive and libidinous impulses from the love objects, the parents, to a symbol of dangerous impulses, the animal. The phobia served the function of keeping the dangerous impulses in a state of repression and of preserving the tender feelings toward the parents in a state of relative harmony. This is not to say, of course, that conflicts between drives must lead to neurotic solutions. There are other solutions available in childhood, among them the redirection of hostile impulses in play and in the imagination. But in all these instances of normal development and even in the case of childhood neuroses, the motive for redirection of hostile impulses is love. *It is because the loved person is valued above all other things that the child gradually modifies his aggressive impulses and finds alternative modes of expression that are sanctioned by love.*

In all this we can see an extraordinary correspondence between the regulation of human drives and the phylogenetic origins of the love bond as constructed from the data of comparative ethology. Perhaps it might even strike us as a banal statement that human aggression should be modified by love. We are accustomed to take human bonds as a biological datum in human infancy. There would be no point in writing this essay if it were not for another story that is emerging from the study of a large body of data in psychoanalysis, psychiatry, and psychology on the diseases of non-attachment.

The group of disorders that I am here calling "the diseases of non-attachment" are, strictly speaking, diseases of the ego, structural weaknesses or malformations which occur during the formative period of ego development, the first eighteen months of life. These disorders are not classified as neuroses. A neurosis, properly speaking, can only exist where there is ego organization, where there is an agency that is capable of self-observation, self-criticism, and the regulation of internal needs and of the conditions for their expression. In a neurosis there may be disorders in love relationships, but there is no primary incapacity of human attachments. Similarly, we need to discriminate between the diseases of non-attachment and psychoses. In a psychosis there may be a breakdown or rupture of human bonds and disorders of thinking which are related to the loss of boundaries between "self" and "not self"—all of which may testify to structural weakness in ego organization—but this breakdown does not imply a primary incapacity of human attachments.

The distinguishing characteristic of the diseases of non-attachment is the incapacity of the person to form human bonds. In personal encounter with such an individual there is an almost perceptible feeling of intervening space, of remoteness, of "no connection." The life histories of people with such a disease reveal no single significant human relationship. The narrative of their lives reads like a vagrant journey with chance encounters and transient partnerships. Since no partner is valued, any one partner can be exchanged for any other; in the absence of love, there is no pain in loss. Indeed, the other striking characteristic of such people is their impoverished emotional range. There is no joy, no grief, no guilt, and no remorse. In the absence of human ties, a conscience cannot be formed; even the qualities of self-observation and self-criticism fail to develop. Many of these people strike us as singularly humorless, which may appear to be a trifling addition to this long catalogue of human deficits, but I think it is significant. For smiling and laughter, as Lorenz tells us, are among the tribal signs that unite the members of the human fraternity, and somewhere in the lonely past of these hollow men and women, the sign was not passed on.

Some of these men and women are to be found in institutions for the mentally ill, a good many of them are part of the floating populations of prisons. A very large number of them have settled inconspicuously in the disordered landscape of a slum, or a carnie show, or underworld enterprises where the absence of human connections can afford vocation and specialization. For the women among them, prostitution affords professional scope for the condition of emotional deadness. Many of them marry and produce children, or produce children and do not marry. And because tenderness or even obligatory parental postures were never a part of their experience, they are indifferent to their young, or sometimes "inhumanly cruel," as we say, except that cruelty to the young appears to be a rare occurrence outside of the human race.

A good many of these hollow men remain anonymous in our society. But there are conditions under which they rise from anonymity and confront us with dead, unsmiling faces. The disease of emotional poverty creates its own appetite for powerful sensation. The deadness within becomes the source of an intolerable tension—quite simply, I think, the ultimate terror of not-being, the dissolution of self. The deadness within demands at times powerful psychic jolts in order to affirm existence. Some get their jolts from drugs. Others are driven to perform brutal acts. We can learn from Jean Genet of the sense of exalted existential awareness that climaxes such acts. Victims of such acts of brutality are chosen indiscriminately and anonymously. There is no motive, as such, because the man who has no human connections does not have specific objects for his hatred. When caught for his crimes, he often brings new horror to the case in his confession. There is no remorse, often no self-defense. The dead voice recounts the crime in precise detail. There was no grievance against the victim: ". . . he was a very nice gentleman. . . . I thought so right up to the minute I slit his throat," said one of the killers in Truman Capote's *In Cold Blood*.

Among those who are driven to brutal acts we can sometimes see how aggression and sexuality are fused in a terrible consummatory experience. It is as if the drives themselves are all that can be summoned from the void, and the violent discharge of these drives becomes an affirmation of being, like a scream from the tomb. Yet it would be a mistake to think that such criminals are endowed with stronger sexual urges than others. For the sober clinical truth is that these are men without potency and women without sexual desire, under any of the conditions that normally favor sexual response. These men and women who have never experienced human bonds have a diffuse and impoverished sexuality. When it takes the form of a violent sexual act it is not the sexual component that gives terrible urgency to the act, but the force of aggression; the two drives are fused in the act. When we consider the ways in which, in early childhood, the love bond normally serves the redirection of aggression from the love object, we obtain a clue: the absence of human bonds can promote a morbid alliance between sexual and aggressive drives and a mode of discharge in which a destructive form of aggression becomes the condition under which the sexual drive becomes manifest.

From these descriptions we can see that the diseases of non-attachment give rise to a broad range of disordered personalities. But if I have emphasized the potential for crime and violence in this group, I do not wish to distort the picture. A large number of these men and women distinguish themselves in no other way than in that they exhibit an attitude of indifference to life and an absence of human connections.

The hollow man can inform us considerably about the problem we are pursuing, the relations between the formation of human love bonds and the regulation of the aggressive drive. In those instances where we have been able to obtain histories of such patients, it appears that there were never any significant human ties, as far back as memory or earlier records could inform us. Often the early childhood histories told a dreary story of lost and broken connections. A child would be farmed out to relatives, or foster parents, or institutions: the blurred outlines of one family faded into those of another, as the child, already anonymous, shifted beds and families in monotonous succession. The change of address would be factually noted in an agency record. Or it might be a child who had been reared in his own family, a family of "no connections," unwanted, neglected, and sometimes brutally treated. In either case, by the time these children entered school, the teachers, attendance officers, or school social workers would be reporting for the record such problems as "impulsive, uncontrolled behavior," "easily frustrated," "can't get close to him," "doesn't seem to care about anything." Today we see many of these children in Head Start programs. These are the three- and four-year olds who seem unaware of other people or things, silent, unsmiling, poor ghosts of children who wander through a brightly painted nursery as if it were a cemetery. Count it a victory if, after six months of work with such a child, you can get him to smile in greeting or learn your name.

Once extensive study was begun on the problems of unattached children, some of the missing links in etiology° appeared. We now know that if we fail in our work with these children, if we cannot bring them into a human relationship, their future is predictable. They become, of course, the permanently unattached men and women of the next generation. But beyond this we have made an extraordinary and sobering discovery. An unattached child, even at the age of three or four, cannot easily attach himself even when he is provided with the most favorable conditions for the formation of a human bond. The most expert clinical workers and foster parents can testify that to win such a child, to make him care, to

---

°*etiology:* assigning causes or origins

become important to him, to be needed by him, and finally to be loved by him, is the work of months and years. Yet all of this, including the achievement of a binding love for a partner, normally takes place, without psychiatric consultation, in ordinary homes and with ordinary babies, during the first year of life.

This brings us to another part of the story, and to further links with the biological studies of Lorenz. Research into the problems of attachment and non-attachment has begun to move further and further back into early childhood, and finally to the period of infancy. Here too it is pathology that has led the way and informed us more fully of the normal course of attachment behavior in children.

IV

Since World War II, a very large number of studies have appeared which deal with the absence or rupture of human ties in infancy. There is strong evidence to indicate that either of these two conditions can produce certain disturbances in the later functioning of the child and can impair to varying degrees the capacity of the child to bind himself to human partners later in childhood. A number of these studies were carried out in infant institutions. Others followed children who had spent their infancy and early years in a succession of foster homes. In each of the studies that I shall refer to here, the constitutional adequacy of the baby at birth was established by objective tests. When control groups were employed, as they were in some of the studies, there was careful matching of the original family background. These investigations have been conducted by some of the most distinguished men and women working in child psychoanalysis, child psychiatry, and pediatrics—among them Anna Freud, Dorothy Burlingham, René Spitz, John Bowlby, William Goldfarb, Sally Provence, and Rose Lipton.

The institutional studies have enabled us to follow the development of babies who were reared without any possibility of establishing a human partnership. Typically, even in the best institutions, a baby is cared for by a corps of nurses and aides, and three such corps, working in shifts, have responsibility for large groups of babies in a ward.° The foster-home studies, on the other hand, together with studies of "separation effects," have enabled us to investigate a group of babies and young children who had known mothering and human partnerships at one or another period

---

°We should carefully distinguish this kind of group care from that provided babies and young children in a *kibbutz*. The *kibbutz* baby has a mother and is usually breastfed by her. Studies show that the *kibbutz* baby is attached to his mother and that the mother remains central in his early development. The group care of the *kibbutz* does not deprive the baby of mothering, whereas such deprivation is the crucial point of the studies I cite in this essay. [Author's note.]

of early development and who suffered loss of the mother and often repeated separations from a succession of substitute mothers. In one set of studies, then, the groups of babies had in common the experience of no human partnerships; in the other, the babies had suffered ruptures of human ties in early development.

Within these two large groups the data from all studies confirm each other in these essential facts: children who have been deprived of mothering, and who have formed no personal human bonds during the first two years of life, show permanent impairment of the capacity to make human attachments in later childhood, even when substitute families are provided for them. The degree of impairment is roughly equivalent to the degree of deprivation. Thus, if one constructs a rating scale, with the institutions studied by Spitz at the lowest end of the scale and the institution studied by Provence and Lipton at the other end of the scale, measurable differences may be discerned between the two groups of babies in their respective capacity to respond to human stimulation. But even in the "better" institution of the Provence and Lipton study, there is gross retardation in all areas of development when compared with a control group, and permanent effects in the kind and quality of human attachments demonstrated by these children in foster homes in later childhood. In the Spitz studies, the degree of deprivation in a hygienic and totally impersonal environment was so extreme that the babies deteriorated to the mental level of imbeciles at the end of the second year and showed no response to the appearance of a human figure. The motion picture made of these mute, solemn children, lying stuporous in their cribs, is one of the little-known horror films of our time.

As the number of studies has increased in recent years and come to encompass more diverse populations and age groups, we have become able to see the "variables" at work here. (A "variable"—a monstrous term to use when one is speaking of human babies—signifies in this case the degree and kind of deprivation.) They can be tested in the following way. As we group the findings on all the follow-up studies it becomes clear that the *age* at which the child suffered deprivation of human ties is closely correlated to certain effects in later personality and the capacity to sustain human ties. For example, in some of the studies, children had suffered maternal deprivation or rupture of human connections at various stages in early childhood. As we sort out the data we see a convergence of signs showing that the period of greatest vulnerability with respect to later development is in the period under two years of life. When, for any reason, a child has spent the whole or a large part of his infancy in an environment that could not provide him with human partners or the conditions for sustained human attachments, the later development of this child demonstrates measurable effects in three areas: (1) Children thus deprived show varying degrees of impairment in the capacity to attach themselves to substitute parents or, in fact, to any persons. They seem to form their relationships on the basis of need and satisfaction of need (a characteristic of the infant's earliest relationship to the nurturing person). One "need-satisfying person" can substitute for another, quite independently of his personal qualities. (2) There is impairment of intellectual function during the first eighteen months of life which remains consistent in follow-up testing of these children. Specifically, it is conceptual thinking that remains depressed even when favorable environments are provided for such children in the second and third years of life. Language itself, which was grossly retarded in all the infant studies of these children, improves to some extent under more favorable environmental conditions but remains nevertheless an area of retardation. (3) Disorders of impulse control, particularly in the area of aggression, are reported in all follow-up studies of these children.

The significance of these findings goes far beyond the special case of infants reared in institutions or in a succession of foster homes. The institutional studies tell us how a baby develops in an environment that cannot provide a mother, or, in fact, any human partners. But there are many thousands of babies reared in pathological homes, who have, in effect, no mother and no significant human attachments during the first two years of life. A mother who is severely depressed, or a psychotic, or an addict, is also, for all practical purposes, a mother who is absent from her baby. A baby who is stored like a package with neighbors and relatives while his mother works may come to know as many indifferent caretakers as a baby in the lowest grade of institution and, at the age of one or two years, can resemble in all significant ways the emotionally deprived babies of such an institution.

V

The information available to us from all of these studies indicates that the period of human infancy is the critical period for the establishment of human bonds. From the evidence, it appears that a child who fails to make the vital human connections in infancy will have varying degrees of difficulty in making them in later childhood. In all of this there is an extraordinary correspondence with the findings of ethologists regarding the critical period for attachment in animals.

If I now proceed to construct some parallels, I should also make some cautious discriminations between attachment behavior in human infancy and that in animals. The phenomenon of "imprinting," for example, which Lorenz describes, has no true equivalent in human infancy. When Lorenz hand-rears a gosling he elicits an attachment from the baby goose by producing the call notes of the mother goose. In effect he produces the code signal that releases an instinctual response. The unlocking of the instinctual code guarantees that the instinct will attach itself to *this* object, the producer of the signal. The registration of certain key characteristics of the object gives its own guarantees that this object and no other can elicit the specific instinctual response. From this point on, the baby gosling accepts Dr. Lorenz as its "mother"; the attachment of the baby animal to Lorenz is selective and permanent. The conditions favoring release of instinctual behavior are governed by a kind of biological timetable. In the case of attachment behavior, there is a critical period in the infancy of the animal that favors imprinting. Following this period the instinct wanes and the possibility of forming a new and permanent attachment ends.

It is not difficult to find analogies to this process in the attachment behavior of the human infant, but the process of forming human bonds is infinitely more complex. The development of attachment behavior in human infancy follows a biological pattern, but we have no true equivalents for "imprinting" because the function of memory in the first eighteen months of a human baby's life is far removed from the simple registrations of stimuli that take place in the baby animal. Yet even the marvelous and uniquely human achievements of cognitive development are dependent upon adequacy in instinctual gratification, for we can demonstrate through a large body of research that where need satisfaction is not adequate there will be impairment in memory and consequently in all the complex functions of human intelligence.

Similarly, there is no single moment in time in which the human infant—unlike the lower animals—makes his attachment to his mother. There is no single act or signal which elicits the permanent bond between infant and mother. Instead, we have an extended period in infancy for the development of attachment behavior and a sequential development that leads to the establishment of human bonds. By the time a baby is eight or nine months old he demonstrates his attachment by producing all of the characteristics that we identify as human love. He shows preference for his mother and wants repeated demonstrations of her love; he can only be comforted by his mother, he initiates games of affection with her, and he shows anxiety, distress, and even grief if a prolonged separation from her takes place.

I do not wish to give the impression that this process is so complex or hazardous that only extraordinary parents can produce a baby with strong human bonds. It is achieved regularly by ordinary parents with ordinary babies without benefit of psychiatric consultation. It requires no outstanding measures beyond satisfaction of a baby's biological needs in the early period of infancy through feeding, comfort in distress, and the provision of nutriments for sensory and motor experience—all of which are simply "givens" in a normal home. But above all it requires that there be human partners who become for the baby the embodiment of need satisfaction, comfort, and well-being. All of this, too, is normally given in ordinary families, without any reflection on the part of the parents that they are engaged in initiating a baby into the human fraternity.

Finally, where the attachment of a baby animal to its mother is guaranteed by interlocking messages and responses on an instinctual basis, we have no such instinctual code to guarantee the attachment of a human infant to his mother. This means, of course, that there are an infinite number of normal variations in patterns of mothering and great diversity in the mode of communication between baby and mother. Any of a vast number of variations in the pattern can be accommodated in the human baby's development and still ensure that a human bond will be achieved. The minimum guarantee for the evolution of the human bond is prolonged intimacy with a nurturing person, a condition that was once biologically insured through breast feeding. In the case of the bottle-fed baby, the insurance must be provided by the mother herself, who "builds in" the conditions for intimacy and continuity of the mothering experience. As bottle feeding has become common among all social groups in our society, continuity of the nurturing experience becomes more and more dependent upon the personality of the mother and environmental conditions that favor, or fail to favor, intimacy between the baby and his mother.

The bond which is ensured in a moment of time between a baby animal and its mother is, in the case of the human baby, the product of a complex sequential development, a process that evolves during the first eighteen months of life. The instinctual patterns are elicited through the human environment, but they do not take the form of instinctual release phenomena in terms of a code and its unlocking. What we see in the evolution of the human bond is a *language* between partners, a "dialogue," as Spitz puts it, in which messages from the infant are interpreted by his mother and messages from the mother are taken as signals by the baby. This early dialogue of "need" and "an answer to need" becomes a highly differentiated signal system in the early months of life; it is, properly speaking, the matrix of human language and of the human bond itself.

The dialogue begins with the cry that brings a human partner. Long before the human baby experiences the connection between his cry and the appearance of a human face, and long before he can use the cry as a signal, he must have had the experience in which the cry is "answered." Need and the expressive vocalization of need set up the dialogue between the baby and his human partners. Normally, too, there is a range of expressive signs in a baby's behavior which his mother interprets through her intimacy with him—the empty mouthing: "He's hungry"; fretful sounds: "He's cranky, he's ready for his nap"; a complaining sound: "He wants company"; arms extended: "He wants to be picked up." Sometimes the mother's interpretation may not be the correct one, but she has acted upon the baby's signal in some way, and this is the crucial point. The baby learns that his signals bring mother and bring need satisfaction in a specific or general way.

The institutional baby has no partner who is tuned in to his signals. As Provence and Lipton demonstrate in their institutional study, since there is no one to read the baby's signs there is finally no motive for producing signals. The expressive vocalizations drop out or appear undifferentiated in these babies. And long after they have been moved to homes with foster families, speech development remains impoverished.

The animal baby makes a selective response to his mother in the early hours of life, and distinguishes his mother from other members of the species. The human baby discovers the uniqueness of his mother in a succession of stages throughout the first year. How do we know this? Among other ways, through the study of the smiling response of the human infant. Our tribal greeting sign, the smile, undergoes a marvelous course of differentiation in the first year. Since the smile connotes "recognition," among other things, we may study differential smiling as one of the signs in the evolution of attachment behavior. In this way Peter Wolff of Harvard has found that the human baby in the third and fourth weeks of life will smile selectively in response to his mother's voice. Wolff can demonstrate experimentally that no other voice and no other sounds in the same frequency range will elicit the baby's smile. Wolff's finding should end the controversy over the "gas smile," and mothers who always disagreed with pediatricians on this score are thus vindicated in their wisdom.

At about eight weeks of age, the baby smiles in response to the human face. As René Spitz has demonstrated, the smile is elicited by the configuration of the upper half of the human face. A mask, representing eyes and forehead, will also elicit the baby's smile at this age. The baby of this age does not yet make a *visual* discrimination among his mother's face, other familiar faces, and strange faces. But between the age of six weeks and eight months the smile of the baby grows more and more selective, and at about eight months of age the baby demonstrates through his smile a clear discrimination of the mother's face from the faces of other familiar persons or the face of a stranger. Presented with a strange face at eight months, the baby will typically become solemn, quizzical, or unfriendly, and may even set up a howl. This means that a form of recognition memory for familiar faces has emerged in the infant. But in order that recognition memory appear, there must be thousands of repetitions in the presentation of certain faces, to produce the indelible tracing of *this* face with *these* characteristics, which can be later discriminated from all other faces with the general characteristic of the human face. This does not mean that a mother or other family members need to be constantly in the baby's perceptual field; it does not mean that, if someone else occasionally takes over the care of the baby, his memory capacity will be impaired.

But it does mean that there must be one or more persons who remain central and stable in the early experience of the baby so that the conditions for early memory function be present. And it means, too, that such a central person must be associated with pleasure and need gratification because memory itself must be energized through the emotional import of experience. By the time a baby is eight months old, the mother is discriminated from all other persons, and the baby shows his need for her and his attachment to her by distress when she leaves him and by grief reactions when absence is prolonged beyond his tolerance. At this stage, when the mother has become the indispensable human partner, we can speak of love, and under all normal circumstances this love becomes a permanent bond, one that will embrace not only the mother but other human partners and, in a certain sense, the whole human fraternity.

The baby who is deprived of human partners can also be measured by his smile, or by the absence of a smile. If the human deprivation is extreme, no smile appears at any stage of infancy. In the institution studied by Provence and Lipton the babies smiled at the appearance of a human face, and while the smile was rarely joyful or rapturous, it was a smile. But whereas at a certain age babies normally discriminate among human faces by producing a *selective* smile, the institutional babies smiled indifferently at all comers. There was nothing in the last months of the first year or even in the second year to indicate that these babies discriminated among the various faces that presented themselves, nothing to indicate that one person was valued above other persons. There was no reaction to the disappearance or loss of any one person in this environment. In short, there was no attachment to any one person. And in this study, as in others, it was seen that even when families were found for these children in the second or third year of life there was a marked incapacity to bind themselves to any one person.

These were the same babies who showed a consistent type of mental retardation in follow-up studies. In the areas of abstract thinking and generalization these children and, in fact, institutional babies in all studies, demonstrated marked impairment in later childhood. In ways that we still do not entirely understand, this disability in thinking is related to impoverishment in the structures that underlie memory in the first year of life. The diffusion and lack of focus in the early sense-experience of these infants, and the absence of significant human figures which normally register as the first mental traces, produce an unstable substratum for later and more complex mental acts.

The third generalization to be drawn from all these studies has to do with "impulse control," and specifically the control of aggression. From all reports, including those on the model institution directed and studied by Anna Freud and Dorothy Burlingham and the "good" institution investigated by Provence and Lipton, it emerges that such children show marked impulsivity, intolerance of frustration, and rages and tantrums far beyond the age in childhood where one would normally expect such behavior. Over twenty years ago Anna Freud drew the lesson from her institutional study that the problems of aggression in these children were due to the absence of intimate and stable love ties. Under the most favorable circumstances, the group care provided by the institution usually cannot produce durable love bonds in an infant. Everything we have learned since this sobering study by Anna Freud has confirmed her findings twice over.

And this brings us back full circle to Lorenz's study of aggression and the bond. The progressive modification of the aggressive drive takes place under the aegis of the love drives. Where there are no human bonds there is no motive for redirection, for the regulation and control of aggressive urges. The parallel with animal studies is exact.

VI

If we read our evidence correctly, the formation of the love bond takes place during human infancy. The later capacity of the ego to regulate the aggressive drive is very largely dependent upon the quality and the durability of these bonds. The absence of human bonds in infancy or the rupture of human bonds in early life can have permanent effects upon the later capacity for human attachments and for the regulation of aggression.

It would be a mistake, of course, to blame all human ills on failure in early nurture. There are other conditions in the course of human development which can affect the capacity to love and the regulation of drives. Yet, the implications of maternal deprivation studies are far-reaching and, if properly interpreted, carry their own prescription for the prevention of the diseases of non-attachment. As I see it, the full significance of the research on the diseases of non-attachment may be this: We have isolated a territory in which the diseases of non-attachment originate. These bondless men, women, and children constitute one of the largest aberrant populations in the world today, contributing far beyond their numbers to social disease and disorder. These are the people who are unable to fulfill the most ordinary human obligations in work, in friendship, in marriage, and in child-rearing. The condition of non-attachment leaves a void in the personality where conscience should be. Where there are no human attachments there can be no conscience. As a consequence, the hollow men and women contribute very largely to the criminal population. It is this group, too, that produces a particular kind of criminal, whose crimes, whether they be petty or atrocious, are always characterized by indifference. The potential for violence and destructive acts is far greater among these bondless men and women; the absence of human bonds leaves a free "unbound" aggression to pursue its erratic course.

The cure for such diseases is not simple. All of us in clinical work can testify to that. But to a very large extent, the diseases of non-attachment can be eradicated at the source, by ensuring stable human partnerships for every baby. If we take the evidence seriously we must look upon a baby deprived of human partners as a baby in deadly peril. This is a baby who is being robbed of his humanity.

QUESTIONS

. Evaluate Erikson's argument which brings the forbidden fruit back into the process of child raising. What are the strengths and weaknesses of using mythology in this way? How convincing do you find Erikson's account?

. What is the purpose of Selma Fraiberg's discussion of animal behavior? What has it to do with human behavior? Evaluate the uses of such analogies.

. Explain what "intraspecific aggression" is. Where does it occur and where does it not occur?

. What are some of the ways in which aggressive behavior is modified or redirected in animals and in humans? When is aggression functional (useful)? What are the commonest examples of functional and non-functional aggression?

. What is "ritualization?" Suggest some examples of the process in human behavior.

. What is the primary motive in a child for a redirection of aggressive energies?

. What are "the diseases of non-attachment"? How useful or accurate do you think the term "disease" is in this context? Discuss.

. What connections is there between the behavior patterns of greylag geese and the Myth of the Fall?

. What are the terms or components of the "dialogue" between mother and baby?

. Do the arguments made by Erickson and Fraiberg suggest that the Fall can be sufficiently understood in scientific terms to allow its effects to be calculated and predicted, and its time(s) and places(s) to be chosen by parents and teachers? What are the advantages and liabilities of this idea? What kinds of childhood events does a person remember most clearly?

PART VIII

Fall Poems

Experience is not what happens to a man. It is what a man does with what happens to him.

—*Aldous Huxley*

Elements of the Fall

The poems in the following section all demonstrate the continuing utility to poets of the mythology of the Fall. The poems refer to the elements of the myth with varying degrees of explicitness, some referring directly to the characters in the story or to its setting, others alluding more generally to the traditional imagery. Similarly, the poems take differing but analogous views of the particular kind of Fall that they describe: death, self-consciousness, mutability, or the transiency of the human condition.

When all is said and done, however, one finds more than ample evidence that as cultural history, evolution, and perhaps progress continue, we may be more and more able to reach, through the support of psychoanalysis and the special insights of poets, a stronger sense of redemption and a clear understanding that the condition of man is to *know*.

The Fall Again: Bitter

The first poems take the pessimistic and bitter view, suggesting that the Fall is more or less what the Old Testament said it was, a harsh and inescapable imprinting of Original Sin upon the soul of Man, a condition of human life for which Man must show daily penitence and respect. To keep his self-sufficiency under these conditions, Man must either bitterly lament the cost, or tragically affirm the knowledge.

THE BEGINNING

Wallace Stevens (1879–1955)

So summer comes in the end to these few stains
And the rust and rot of the door through which she went.

The house is empty. But here is where she sat
To comb her dewy hair, a touchless light,

Perplexed by its darker iridescences.   5
This was the glass in which she used to look

At the moment's being, without history,
The self of summer perfectly perceived,

And feel its country gayety and smile
And be surprised and tremble, hand and lip.   10

This is the chair from which she gathered up
Her dress, the carefulest, commodious weave

Inwoven by a weaver to twelve bells° . . .
The dress is lying, cast-off, on the floor.

Now, the first tutoyers° of tragedy   15
Speak softly, to begin with, in the eaves.

°*twelve bells:* perhaps a reference to noon, the beginning of the day's decline
°*tutoyers:* In French, the verb "tutoyer" refers grammatically to use of the second person (you) familiar form, rather than the formal form; here the meaning is "familiar," "personal."

WHY SHOULD NOT OLD MEN BE MAD?

William Butler Yeats (1865-1939)

Why should not old men be mad?
Some have known a likely lad
That had a sound fly-fisher's wrist
Turn to a drunken journalist;
A girl that knew all Dante once   5
Live to bear children to a dunce;
A Helen of social welfare dream,
Climb on a wagonette to scream.
Some think it a matter of course that chance
Should starve good men and bad advance,   10
That if their neighbours figured plain,
As though upon a lighted screen,
No single story would they find
Of an unbroken happy mind,
A finish worthy of the start.   15
Young men know nothing of this sort,
Observant old men know it well;
And when they know what old books tell,
And that no better can be had,
Know why an old man should be mad.   20

ADAM'S CURSE

William Butler Yeats

WE sat together at one summer's end,
That beautiful mild woman, your close friend,
And you and I, and talked of poetry.
I said: 'A line will take us hours maybe;
Yet if it does not seem a moment's thought,   5
Our stitching and unstitching has been naught.

Better go down upon your marrow-bones
And scrub a kitchen pavement, or break stones
Like an old pauper, in all kinds of weather;
For to articulate sweet sounds together   10

Is to work harder than all these, and yet
Be thought an idler by the noisy set
Of bankers, schoolmasters, and clergymen
The martyrs call the world.'

                    And thereupon
That beautiful mild woman for whose sake   15
There's many a one shall find out all heartache
On finding that her voice is sweet and low
Replied: 'To be born woman is to know—
Although they do not talk of it at school—
That we must labour to be beautiful.'   20

I said: 'It's certain there is no fine thing
Since Adam's fall but needs much labouring.
There have been lovers who thought love should be
So much compounded of high courtesy
That they would sigh and quote with learned looks   25
Precedents out of beautiful old books;
Yet now it seems an idle trade enough.'

We sat grown quiet at the name of love;
We saw the last embers of daylight die,
And in the trembling blue-green of the sky   30
A moon, worn as if it had been a shell
Washed by time's waters as they rose and fell
About the stars and broke in days and years.

I had a thought for no one's but your ears:
That you were beautiful, and that I strove   35
To love you in the old high way of love;
That it had all seemed happy, and yet we'd grown
As weary-hearted as that hollow moon.

APRIL MORTALITY

Léonie Adams (1899–   )

Rebellion shook an ancient dust,
    And bones bleached dry of rottenness
Said: Heart, be bitter still, nor trust
    The earth, the sky, in their bright dress.

Heart, heart, dost thou not break to know   5
    This anguish thou wilt bear alone?

We sang of it an age ago,
  And traced it dimly upon stone.

With all the drifting race of men
  Thou also art begot to mourn
That she is crucified again,
  The lonely Beauty yet unborn.

And if thou dreamest to have won
  Some touch of her in permanence,
'Tis the old cheating of the sun,
  The intricate lovely play of sense.

Be bitter still, remember how
  Four petals, when a little breath
Of wind made stir the pear-tree bough,
  Blew delicately down to death.

ORIGINAL SIN

Robinson Jeffers (1887–1962)

The man-brained and man-handed ground-ape, physically
The most repulsive of all hot-blooded animals
Up to that time of the world: they had dug a pitfall
And caught a mammoth, but how could their sticks and stones
Reach the life in that hide? They danced around the pit
  shrieking
With ape excitement, flinging sharp flints in vain, and the
  stench of their bodies
Stained the white air of dawn; but presently one of them
Remembered the yellow dancer, wood-eating fire
That guards the cave-mouth: he ran and fetched him, and
  others
Gathered sticks at the wood's edge; they made a blaze
And pushed it into the pit, and they fed it high, around the
  mired sides
Of their huge prey. They watched the long hairy trunk
Waver over the stifle-trumpeting pain,
And they were happy.

Meanwhile the intense color and nobility of sunrise,
Rose and gold and amber, flowed up the sky. Wet rocks were 15
shining, a little wind
Stirred the leaves of the forest and the marsh flag-flowers; the
soft valley between the low hills
Became as beautiful as the sky; while in its midst, hour after
hour, the happy hunters
Roasted their living meat slowly to death.
                                    These are the people.
This is the human dawn. As for me, I would rather
Be a worm in a wild apple than a son of man.   20
But we are what we are, and we might remember
Not to hate any person, for all are vicious;
And not to be astonished at any evil, all are deserved;
And not fear death; it is the only way to be cleansed.

SPRING AND FALL
TO A YOUNG CHILD

Gerard Manley Hopkins (1844–1889)

Márgarét,° are you grieving
Over Goldengrove unleaving°?
Leáves, líke the things of man, you
With your fresh thoughts care for, can you?
Áh! Ás the heart grows older   5
It will come to such sights colder
By and by, nor spare a sigh
Though worlds of wanwood° leafmeal° lie;
And yet you wíll weep and know why.
Now no matter, child, the name: 10
Sórrow's spríngs áre the same.
Nor mouth had, no nor mind, expressèd
What heart heard of, ghost guessed:
It ís the blight man was born for,
It is Margaret you mourn for.   15

°*Márgarét:* The stress marks are Hopkins's; some syllables that do not normally get
stress are purposely given stress.
°*unleaving:* losing its leaves   °*wanwood:* fallen, dead leaves   °*leafmeal:* like
"piecemeal," leaf by leaf gradually

AS NEAR TO EDEN

Robert Francis (1901–   )

Hearing the cry I looked to see a bird
Among the boughs that overhung the stream.
No bird was there. The cry was not a bird's.
Then I looked down and saw the snake and saw
The frog. Half of the frog was free to cry.   5
The other half the snake had in its jaws.
The snake was silent as the sand it lay on.

I ran to blast the thing out of my sight,
But the snake ran first (untouched) into the water
Fluid to fluid and so disappeared   10
And all I saw and heard was flowing water.

I dipped a foot in slowly and began
To saunter down the stream a little way
As I had done so many times before
That summer. Now I went more cautiously   15
Watching the water every step, but water
Had washed the thing away and washed it clean.

Over the stream I had a kind of bed
Built of an old smooth board and four large stones
And there between the sun and water I   20
Would often spend an early afternoon.
It was as near to Eden as I knew—
This alternating cool and warm, this blend
Of cool and warm, of water-song and silence.
No one could see me there and even insects   25
Left me alone.
                        I turned upon my face
And so had darkness for my eyes and fire
On my back. I felt my breathing slacken, deepen.
After a time I reached a hand over
And let the fingertips trail in the water.   30

From *Come Into the Sun: Poems New and Selected* by Robert Francis. Reprinted by permission of Robert Francis and the University of Massachusetts.

Strange, strange that in a world so old and rich
In good and evil, the death (or all but death)
Of one inconsequential squealing frog
Should have concerned me so, should for the moment
Have seemed the only evil in the world   35
And overcoming it the only good.

But they were symbols too, weren't they? the frog,
The snake? The frog of course being innocence
Sitting with golden and unwinking eyes
Hour after hour beside a waterweed   40
As rapt and meditative as a saint
Beneath a palm tree, and the snake being—well,
That's all been told before.
                        A pretty contrast,
Yet even under the indulgent sun
And half asleep I knew my picture false.   45
The frog was no more innocent than the snake
And if he looked the saint he was a fake.
He and the snake were all too closely kin,
First cousins once removed under the skin.
If snakes ate frogs, frogs in their turn ate flies   50
And both could look ridiculously wise.
But neither one knew how to feed on lies
As man could do—that is, philosophize.
And having reached that point I closed my eyes,
Rhyming myself and sunning myself to sleep.   55

And while I slept my body was a sundial
Casting its moving, slowly moving shadow
Across the moving, swiftly moving water.

When I awoke I had one clear desire:
The coolness of that swiftly moving water.   60
Yet still I waited, it was so near, so sure,
The superfluity of heat so good.

And then I sat straight up having heard a sound
I recognized too well. It was no bird.
Slipping and splashing as I went I ran   65
Upstream. I couldn't see, I didn't need

To see to know. So all the time I'd slept
And sunned myself and entertained myself
With symbolizing and unsymbolizing
Good and evil, *this* had been going on.   70

They were hidden now among the roots of a tree
The stream had washed the soil from. I found a stick
And jabbed it in as far as I could reach
Again and again until I broke the stick.
But still I kept it up until the snake   75
Having disgorged slipped out and got away.
And still I kept it up until the frog
Must have been pulp and ground into the sand.
The stick, all that was left, I threw as far
As I could throw.
                    Then I went home and dressed.   80
Eden was done for for one day at least.

WHEN EVE FIRST SAW
THE GLITTERING DAY

James Agee (1909–1955)

When Eve first saw the glittering day
Watch by the wan world side
She learned her worst and down she lay
In the streaming land, and cried.

When Adam saw the mastering night   5
First board the world's wan lifted breast
He climbed his bride with all his might
And sank to gentlest rest.

And night took both and day brought high
The children that must likewise die: 10
And all our grief and every joy
To time's deep end shall time destroy:
And weave us one, and waive us under
Where is neither faith nor wonder.

From *The Collected Poems of James Agee*, edited by Robert Fitzgerald. Reprinted
by permission of the publisher, Houghton Mifflin Company.

Halfway: A Delicate Balance

Keats's talent in *Ode to a Nightingale* and *Ode on a Grecian Urn* balances the idealized Edenic world of perfect, unself-conscious, spontaneous, natural joy against the fallen, rational, analytic, self-conscious forces of mind, which simultaneously destroy ease and beauty, and torment the poet with an awareness of what these mental forces have cost. The speaker in *Ode to a Nightingale*, admiring the nightingale for the "full throated ease" with which it can sing, attempts various modes of escape from his fallen self, strategies which he hopes will regain for him a lost innocence, a natural harmony with the unfallen world. Because the speaker recognizes the fact of Time and his own mortality, these strategies fail; but he concedes his failure and can therefore begin to accept his human lot, the fallen condition. Though he is not redeemed to a positive view of the value of knowledge, he seems able to face his human condition honestly, without evasion. The speaker admits that fancy is a cheater; the nightingale's suddenly plaintive song and the Garden it created fade, leaving the speaker in an ambiguous state midway between innocence and the realization of the Fall, but closer to a truly human awareness of self.

ODE TO A NIGHTINGALE

John Keats (1795–1821)

My heart aches, and a drowsy numbness pains
  My sense, as though of hemlock° I had drunk,
Or emptied some dull opiate to the drains
  One minute past, and Lethe-wards° had sunk:
'Tis not through envy of thy happy lot,   5
  But being too happy in thine happiness,—
    That thou, light-wingèd Dryad° of the trees,
      In some melodious plot
Of beechen green, and shadows numberless,
  Singest of summer in full-throated ease.   10

O for a draught of vintage! that hath been
  Cooled a long age in the deep-delvèd earth,
Tasting of Flora° and the country-green,
  Dance, and Provençal° song, and sunburnt mirth!

°*hemlock:* a poison, the kind Socrates drank   °*Lethe:* Hades's river of forgetfulness.   °*Dryad:* wood nymph   °*Flora:* spring; Flora was the goddess of flowers.   °*Provençal:* southern France, i.e., rural

O for a beaker full of the warm South, 15
    Full of the true, the blushful Hippocrene,°
    With beaded bubbles winking at the brim,
        And purple-stainèd mouth;
    That I might drink, and leave the world unseen,
        And with thee fade away into the forest dim: 20

Fade far away, dissolve, and quite forget
    What thou among the leaves hast never known,
The weariness, the fever, and the fret
    Here, where men sit and hear each other groan;
Where palsy shakes a few, sad, last gray hairs, 25
    Where youth grows pale, and specter-thin, and dies;
        Where but to think is to be full of sorrow
            And leaden-eyed despairs,
    Where Beauty cannot keep her lustrous eyes,
        Or new Love pine at them beyond tomorrow. 30

Away! away! for I will fly to thee,
    Not charioted by Bacchus and his pards,°
But on the viewless° wings of Poesy,
    Though the dull brain perplexes and retards:
Already with thee! tender is the night, 35
    And haply the Queen-moon is on her throne,
        Clustered around by all her starry Fays;°
            But here there is no light,
    Save what from heaven is with the breezes blown
        Through verdurous glooms and winding mossy ways. 40

I cannot see what flowers are at my feet,
    Nor what soft incense hangs upon the boughs,
But, in embalmèd° darkness, guess each sweet
    Wherewith the seasonable month endows
The grass, the thicket, and the fruit-tree wild; 45
    White hawthorn, and the pastoral eglantine;
        Fast-fading violets covered up in leaves;
            And mid-May's eldest child,
    The coming musk-rose, full of dewy wine,
        The murmurous haunt of flies on summer eves. 50

°*Hippocrene:* The Muses's fountain, source of poetic inspiration °*pards:* leopards °*viewless:* invisible °*Fays:* fairies °*embalmèd:* fragrant

Darkling° I listen; and, for many a time
I have been half in love with easeful Death,
Called him soft names in many a musèd rhyme,
To take into the air my quiet breath;
Now more than ever seems it rich to die,   55
To cease upon the midnight with no pain,
While thou are pouring forth thy soul abroad
In such an ecstasy!
Still wouldst thou sing, and I have ears in vain—
To thy high requiem become a sod.   60

Thou wast not born for death, immortal Bird!
No hungry generations tread thee down;
The voice I heard this passing night was heard
In ancient days by emperor and clown:
Perhaps the self-same song that found a path   65
Through the sad heart of Ruth,° when, sick for home,
She stood in tears amid the alien corn;°
The same that oft-times hath
Charmed magic casements, opening on the foam
Of perilous seas, in faery lands forlorn.   70

Forlorn! the very word is like a bell
To toll me back from thee to my sole self!
Adieu! the fancy° cannot cheat so well
As she is famed to do, deceiving elf.
Adieu! adieu! thy plaintive anthem fades   75
Past the near meadows, over the still stream,
Up the hill-side; and now 'tis buried deep
In the next valley-glades:
Was it a vision, or a waking dream?
Fled is that music:—Do I wake or sleep?   80

*   *   *

°*Darkling:* in the dark; perhaps also a term for the bird   °*Ruth:* Old Testament, Book of Ruth. She accompanied her mother-in-law into an alien land. °*corn:* grain   °*fancy:* imagination

The Redemptive Phase: Out of Eden and Beyond

The final group of Fall poems emphasizes a positive aspect of the Myth, the "Rising" part of the figure. They suggest in a variety of ways that, while knowledge that is worthwhile always has a price, the price may be worth paying, and the very paying or experiencing may provide dividends or benefits not considered in older interpretations of the story.

WORMS

Walter Kaufmann (1901–   )

Worms granted sight complain they were thrown into darkness,
children of angels, not dazzling thrusts from the slime;
conquerors of peaks see the sky and fable a fall,
stoutly denying their unseen climb.

TO THE GARDEN THE WORLD

Walt Whitman (1819–1892)

To the garden the world anew ascending,
Potent mates, daughters, sons, preluding,
The love, the life of their bodies, meaning and being,
Curious here behold my resurrection after slumber,
The revolving cycles in their wide sweep having brought   5
    me again,
Amorous, mature, all beautiful to me, all wondrous,
My limbs and the quivering fire that ever plays through
    them, for reasons, most wondrous,
Existing I peer and penetrate still,
Content with the present, content with the past,
By my side or back of me Eve following,   10
Or in front, and I following her just the same.

From *Cain and Other Poems* by Walter Kaufmann; reprinted by permission of Random House, Inc.

AS ADAM EARLY IN THE MORNING

Walt Whitman

As Adam early in the morning,
Walking forth from the bower refresh'd with sleep,
Behold me where I pass, hear my voice, approach,
Touch me, touch the palm of your hand to my body as I pass,
Be not afraid of my body.   5

WHEN THE RIPE FRUIT FALLS

D. H. Lawrence (1885–1930)

When the ripe fruit falls
its sweetness distils and trickles away into the veins of the earth.

When fulfilled people die
the essential oil of their experience enters
the veins of living space, and adds a glisten   5
to the atom, to the body of immortal chaos.

For space is alive
and it stirs like a swan
whose feathers glisten
silky with oil of distilled experience.   10

From SONGS FOR EVE

Archibald MacLeish (1892–   )

WHAT EVE SANG

Space-time
Is all there is of space and time
But is not all. There is a rhyme
For all of space and all of time.

I heard it on that Eden night   5
The branching tree stood dark alight

From *The Complete Poems of D. H. Lawrence* edited by Vivian de Sola Pinto and
F. Warren Roberts. Copyright © 1964, 1971, by Angelo Ravagli and C. M. Weekley.
Reprinted by permission of The Viking Press, Inc.

From *Collected Poems* 1917–1952. Copyright © 1962 by Archibald MacLeish. Reprinted by permission of the publisher, Houghton Mifflin Company.

Like willow in the wind, so white
Its unknown apples on the night:

I heard beyond that tree a tree
Stir in silence over me.   10
In space and time, eyes only see,
Ears only hear, the green-wood tree:

But Oh! I heard the whole of time
And all of space give ringing rhyme
And ring and ring and chime and chime   15
When I reached out to touch and climb
In spite of space, in spite of time.

EVE'S EXILE

Eden was an endless place,
Time enough for all of space
And space for all that time to pass.

We lived in time as fishes live
Within the lapsing of the wave   5
That with the water's moving move.

We lived in space as hawk in air:
The place we were was everywhere
And everywhere we were, we were.

Fish and hawk have eyes of glass   10
Wherein the skies and waters pass
As in a glass the images —

They mirror but they may not see.
When I had tasted fruit of tree
Fish and hawk, they fled from me: 15

"She has a watcher in her eyes,"
The hawk screamed from the steep of skies,
Fish from sea-deep where he lies.

Our exile is our eyes that see.
Hawk and fish have eyes but we   20
Behold what they can only be.

Space within its time revolves
But Eve must spin as Adam delves
Because our exile is ourselves.

ADAM'S RIDDLE

Raddle° me riddle,
I'll spell you the word:
Two are together
And still there's a third
Mingles to meddle   5
Beneath the green tree:
One is its father,
One is its mother . . . .

What's born of three?

EVE TO THE STORM OF THUNDER

Who teaches child that snivelling guilt
For space rejected and time spilt?
Tell me, how was Heaven built?

Space and time I disobeyed:
It was so that he was made,   5
Little man so fast afraid.

Had I not, in wonder's awe,
Disobeyed the lion's law,
Voice and hand were shriek and paw.

Had I not, for wonder's sake,   10
Broken law no leaf may break,
Lids were closed that now awake.

°*raddle:* twist together

Only when I disobeyed
Was the bliss of Eden stayed—
Bliss of sleep in that thick shade.   15

Was it shame or was it sin,
Shameful out and shameless in,
So in waking to begin?

How else can heavenly thunder shake
The heart but if the heart awake?   20

who were so dark of heart

E. E. Cummings (1894–1962)

who were so dark of heart they might not speak,
a little innocence will make them sing;
teach them to see who could not learn to look
—from the reality of all nothing

will actually lift a luminous whole;   5
turn sheer despairing to most perfect gay,
nowhere to here, never to beautiful:
a little innocence creates a day.

And something thought or done or wished without
a little innocence, although it were   10
as red as terror and as green as fate,
greyly shall fail and dully disappear—

but the proud power of himself death immense
is not so as a little innocence

"IN NATURE THERE IS NEITHER RIGHT NOR LEFT NOR WRONG"

Randall Jarrell (1914–1965)

Men are what they do, women are what they are.
These erect breasts, like marble coming up for air
Among the cataracts of my breathtaking hair,
Are goods in my bazaar, a door ajar
To the first paradise of whores and mothers.   5

Men buy their way back into me from the upright
Right-handed puzzle that men fit together
From their deeds, the pieces. Women shoot from
Or dive back into its interstices
As squirrels inhabit a geometry.   10

We women sell ourselves for sleep, for flesh,
To those wide-awake, successful spirits, men—
Who, lying each midnight with the sinister
Beings, their dark companions, women,
Suck childhood, beasthood, from a mother's breasts.   15

A fat bald rich man comes home at twilight
And lectures me about my parking tickets; gowned in gold
Lamé,° I look at him and think: "You're old,
I'm old." Husband, I sleep with you every night
And like it; but each morning when I wake   20
I've dreamed of my first love, the subtle serpent.

LIFE CYCLE OF COMMON MAN

Howard Nemerov (1920–   )

Roughly figured, this man of moderate habits,
This average consumer of the middle class,
Consumed in the course of his average life span
Just under half a million cigarettes,

°*Lamé:* a brocaded fabric

Four thousand fifths of gin and about   5
A quarter as much vermouth; he drank
Maybe a hundred thousand cups of coffee,
And counting his parents' share it cost
Something like half a million dollars
To put him through life. How many beasts   10
Died to provide him with meat, belts and shoes
Cannot be certainly said.
                              But anyhow,
It is in this way that a man travels through time,
Leaving behind him a lengthening trail
Of empty bottles and bones, of broken shoes,   15
Frayed collars and worn out or outgrown
Diapers and dinnerjackets, silk ties and slickers.

Given the energy and security thus achieved,
He did . . . ? What? The usual things, of course,
The eating, dreaming, drinking, and begetting,   20
And he worked for the money which was to pay
For the eating, et cetera, which were necessary
If he were to go on working for the money, et cetera,
But chiefly he talked. As the bottles and bones
Accumulated behind him, the words proceeded   25
Steadily from the front of his face as he
Advanced into silence and made it verbal.
Who can tally the tale of his words? A lifetime
Would barely suffice for their repetition;
If you merely printed all his commas the result   30
Would be a very large volume, and the number of times
He said "thank you" or "very little sugar, please,"
Would stagger the imagination. There were also
Witticisms, platitudes, and statements beginning
"It seems to me" or "As I always say."   35

Consider the courage in all that, and behold the man
Walking into deep silence, with the ectoplastic
Cartoon's balloon of speech proceeding
Steadily out of the front of his face, the words
Borne along on the breath which is his spirit   40
Telling the numberless tale of his untold Word
Which makes the world his apple, and forces him to eat.

PREFACE TO A TWENTY VOLUME
SUICIDE NOTE

LeRoi Jones (1934–   )

(for Kellie Jones, born 16 May 1959)

Lately, I've become accustomed to the way
The ground opens up and envelops me
Each time I go out to walk the dog.
Or the broad-edged silly music the wind
Makes when I run for a bus. . .   5

Things have come to that.

And now, each night I count the stars,
And each night I get the same number.
And when they will not come to be counted,
I count the holes they leave.   10

Nobody sings anymore.

And then last night, I tiptoed up
To my daughter's room and heard her
Talking to someone, and when I opened
The door, there was no one there. . .   15
Only she on her knees, peeking into

Her own clasped hands.

JAZZONIA

Langston Hughes (1902–1967)

Oh, silver tree!
Oh, shining rivers of the soul!

In a Harlem cabaret
Six long-headed jazzers play.
A dancing girl whose eyes are bold   5
Lifts high a dress of silken gold.

Oh, singing tree!
Oh, shining rivers of the soul!

Were Eve's eyes
In the first garden   10
Just a bit too bold?
Was Cleopatra gorgeous
In a gown of gold?

Oh, shining tree!
Oh, silver rivers of the soul!   15

In a whirling cabaret
Six long-headed jazzers play.

ADAM'S DREAM

Edwin Muir (1887–1959)

They say the first dream Adam our father had
After his agelong daydream in the Garden
When heaven and sun woke in his wakening mind,
The earth with all its hills and woods and waters,
The friendly tribes of trees and animals,   5
And earth's last wonder Eve (the first great dream
Which is the ground of every dream since then)—
They say he dreamt lying on the naked ground,
The gates shut fast behind him as he lay
Fallen in Eve's fallen arms, his terror drowned   10
In her engulfing terror, in the abyss
Whence there's no further fall, and comfort is—
That he was standing on a rocky ledge
High on the mountainside, bare crag behind,
In front a plain as far as eye could reach,   15
And on the plain a few small figures running
That were like men and women, yet were so far away
He could not see their faces. On they ran,
And fell, and rose again, and ran, and fell,
And rising were the same yet not the same,   20
Identical or interchangeable,
Different in indifference. As he looked

Still there were more of them, the plain was filling
As by an alien arithmetical magic
Unknown in Eden, a mechanical   25
Addition without meaning, joining only
Number to number in no mode or order,
Weaving no pattern. For these creatures moved
Towards no fixed mark even when in growing bands
They clashed against each other and clashing fell   30
In mounds of bodies. For they rose again,
Identical or interchangeable,
And went their way that was not like a way;
Some back and forward, back and forward, some
In a closed circle, wide or narrow, others   35
In zigzags on the sand. Yet all were busy,
And tense with purpose as they cut the air
Which seemed to press them back. Sometimes they paused
While one stopped one—fortuitous assignations
In the disorder, whereafter two by two   40
They ran awhile,
Then parted and again were single. Some
Ran straight against the frontier of the plain
Till the horizon drove them back. A few
Stood still and never moved. Then Adam cried   45
Out of his dream, 'What are you doing there?'
And the crag answered 'Are you doing there?'
'What are you doing there?'—'you doing there?'
The animals had withdrawn and from the caves
And woods stared out in fear or condemnation,   50
Like outlaws or like judges. All at once
Dreaming or half-remembering, 'This is time,'
Thought Adam in his dream, and time was strange
To one lately in Eden. 'I must see,'
He cried, 'the faces. Where are the faces? Who   55
Are you all out there?' Then in his changing dream
He was a little nearer, and he saw
They were about some business strange to him
That had a form and sequence past their knowledge:
And that was why they ran so frenziedly.   60
Yet all, it seemed, made up a story, illustrated
By these the living, the unknowing, cast
Each singly for his part. But Adam longed
For more, not this mere moving pattern, not
This illustrated storybook of mankind   65
Always a-making, improvised on nothing.

At that he was among them, and saw each face
Was like his face, so that he would have hailed them
As sons of God but that something restrained him.
And he remembered all, Eden, the Fall,   70
The Promise, and his place, and took their hands
That were his hands, his and his children's hands,
Cried out and was at peace, and turned again
In love and grief in Eve's encircling arms.

THE GATE

Edwin Muir

We sat, two children, arm against the wall
Outside the towering stronghold of our fathers
That frowned its stern security down upon us.
We could not enter there. The fortress life,
Our safe protection, was too gross and strong   5
For our unpractised palates. Yet our guardians
Cherished our innocence with gentle hands,
(They, who had long since lost their innocence,)
And in grave play put on a childish mask
Over their tell-tale faces, as in shame   10
For the fine food that plumped their lusty bodies
And made them strange as gods. We sat that day
As with that great parapet behind us, safe
As every day, yet outcast, safe and outcast
As castaways thrown upon an empty shore.   15
Before us lay our well-worn scene, a hillock
So small and smooth and green, it seemed intended
For us alone and childhood, a still pond
That opened upon no sight a quiet eye,
A little stream that tinkled down the slope.   20
But suddenly all seemed old
And dull and shrunken, shut within itself
In a sullen dream. We were outside, alone.
And then behind us the huge gate swung open.

THE CELEBRATION

James Dickey (1923–   )

All wheels; a man breathed fire,
Exhaling like a blowtorch down the road
And burnt the stripper's gown
Above her moving-barely feet.
A condemned train climbed from the earth   5
Up stilted nightlights zooming in a track.
I ambled along in that crowd

Between the gambling wheels
At carnival time with the others
Where the dodgem cars shuddered, sparking   10
On grillwire, each in his vehicle half
In control, half helplessly power-mad
As he was in the traffic that brought him.
No one blazed at me; then I saw

My mother and father, he leaning   15
On a dog-chewed cane, she wrapped to the nose
In the fur of exhausted weasels.
I believed them buried miles back
In the country, in the faint sleep
Of the old, and had not thought to be   20
On this of all nights compelled

To follow where they led, not losing
Sight, with my heart enlarging whenever
I saw his crippled Stetson bob, saw her
With the teddy bear won on the waning   25
Whip of his right arm. They laughed;
She clung to him; then suddenly
The Wheel of wheels was turning
The colored night around.
They climbed aboard. My God, they rose   30
Above me, stopped themselves and swayed
Fifty feet up; he pointed
With his toothed cane, and took in
The whole Midway till they dropped,
Came down, went from me, came and went   35

From *Buckdancer's Choice* by James Dickey. Copyright © 1965 by James Dickey.
Reprinted by permission of Wesleyan University Press.

Faster and faster, going up backward,
Cresting, out-topping, falling roundly.
From the crowd I watched them,
Their gold teeth flashing,
Until my eyes blurred with their riding   40
Lights, and I turned from the standing
To the moving mob, and went on:

Stepped upon sparking shocks
Of recognition when I saw my feet
Among the others, knowing them given,   45
Understanding the whirling impulse
From which I had been born,
The great gift of shaken lights,
The being wholly lifted with another,

All this having all and nothing   50
To do with me. Believers, I have seen
The wheel in the middle of the air
Where old age rises and laughs,
And on Lakewood Midway became
In five strides a kind of loving,   55
A mortal, a dutiful son.

ONE FOOT IN EDEN

Edwin Muir

One foot in Eden still, I stand
And look across the other land.
The world's great day is growing late,
Yet strange these fields that we have planted
So long with crops of love and hate.   5
Time's handiworks by time are haunted,
And nothing now can separate
The corn and tares compactly grown.
The armorial weed in stillness bound
About the stalk; these are our own.   10
Evil and good stand thick around
In the fields of charity and sin
Where we shall lead our harvest in.

Yet still from Eden springs the root
As clean as on the starting day.   15
Time takes the foliage and the fruit
And burns the archetypal leaf
To shapes of terror and of grief
Scattered along the winter way.
But famished field and blackened tree   20
Bear flowers in Eden never known.
Blossoms of grief and charity
Bloom in these darkened fields alone.
What had Eden ever to say
Of hope and faith and pity and love   25
Until was burned all its day
And memory found its treasure trove?
Strange blessings never in Paradise
Fall from these beclouded skies.

FIG LEAVES

George Garrett (1929–   )

At times sick of the dishonesty of men
to men, the lies that lie in the mouth
like tongues (O fluttering of tongues
like the snapping of flags in the wind!). . .
At times sick unto death of myself   5
and the lies I tell myself, waking, walking,
sleeping, dreaming, lies that must choke,
gag me like a drunk man's vomit
until I lie (indeed) on the ground,
face the color of a bruise, arms and legs   10
kicking vain signals like a roach on its back . . .
I could crack my pen in two like a bone,
a thin bone, wishbone, meatless, chewed
down to the slick and bitter surface.
Better my tongue were a dead leaf   15
(just so dry and crisp, to be bitten to powder).
Better my ears were stone, my pen
at least a hoe, a shovel, a plough,
any good servant of growing things.

From *Abraham's Knife* by George Garrett. Reprinted by permission of the publisher,
The University of North Carolina Press.

Better our sole flag were fig leaves 20
at least to salute the mercy of God
when in the cool of the evening. He came
(Adam and Eve on trembling shanks
squatted and hoped to be hidden)
and cursed us out of the garden. 25
But not before we learned
to wear our first costume
(seeing the truth was a naked shame),
to lie a little and live together.

FOR MY SONS

George Garrett

This world that you're just beginning
now to touch, taste, feel, smell, hear and see,
castled in enigma, and daily more and more
finding sounds in your throats, tremors on tongue
to play with, words (some like a ripe plum 5
or an orange to daze the whole mouth
with a sweetness, so that in speaking
you seem to kiss, some like a bitter phlegm
to be hawked up and spit out clean), the world
is all I would claim for you, save you from. 10

I'm a foolish father like all the rest,
would put my flesh, my shadow in between
you and the light that wounds and blesses.
I'd throw a cloak over your heads
and carry you home, warm and close, to keep 15
you from the dark that chills to the bone.
Foolish (I said), I'd teach you only words
that sing on the lips. Still, you have to learn
to spit in my face and save your souls.
Still you have to curse with fever and desire. 20

Nothing of earned wisdom I can give you,
nothing save the old words like rock candy
to kill the taste of dust on the tongue.
Nothing stings like the serpent, no pain greater.

From *Abraham's Knife* by George Garrett. Reprinted by permission of the publisher, The University of North Carolina Press.

Bear it. If a bush should burn and cry out,   25
bow down. If a stranger wrestles, learn his name.
And if after long tossing and sickness you find
a continent, plant your flags, send forth a dove.
Rarely the fruit you reach for returns your love.

JOYFUL PROPHECY

Vassar Miller (1924–   )

If he is held in love,
the thin reeds of my baby's bones
are pipes for it, it hums
and chuckles from the hollows
as a flower whispers,   5
it ripples off him, suave
honey of the sunlight
stored for his kin, his kind, such lovely
mirrors of it, he
is tempted to hoard it in   10
his well where he may gaze at it,
yet held in love and gracious
he shares it with his sister;
but, lest death waste it on the wind,
love measures him for the man   15
who can hold its heartiness
fermented to a man's delight,
if he is held in love.

From *Wage War on Silence* by Vassar Miller. Copyright © 1960 by Vassar Miller.
Reprinted by permission of Wesleyan University Press.

QUESTIONS

1a. What subject matter or experience represents the new knowledge after the Fall in each of the poems in the first group? Do these poems contain sources of bitterness which have not been encountered before? Which poems are responses to similar kinds of knowledge?

b. Describe the tone or attitude taken by the poems toward the unpleasant kind of knowledge that has been acquired. Which poems are the most intense, which the least? Which are most restrained? Are there any poems where the tone seems out of keeping with the subject matter? If so, which are they and why?

c. Which poem is closest to the Old Testament or traditional view of the Fall and the traditional definition of Sin? Explain your choice.

d. Without reading ahead, suggest some possible responses to, refutations of, or improvements on the attitudes suggested here. What views of experience would you offer to these poets that they seem to need?

2a. In *Ode to a Nightingale,* what does the speaker admire about the nightingale? What contrasts are established between its condition and his?

b. What different strategies does the speaker attempt in order to achieve the state of mind suggested by the bird's song? Why don't these attempts succeed? What have they in common?

c. This is a poem of experience—that is, it enacts what is says. Trace the evolution of the speaker's state of mind, of the way his consciousness of the song and of himself changes as the poem unfolds.

d. How do alien influences enter the speaker's mind? What is their content, and what makes him think of them? What causes the bird's song to be ineffective when opposed to Knowledge. Why, for example, do the flowers in stanza V lead to the thoughts of death in stanza VI?

e. What is the speaker's state of mind in the last stanza? What is the effect on the reader of the final questions? What shifts in imagery and diction support the movement of the speaker's mind?

f. Compare this poem with Keats's *Ode on a Grecian Urn.* In which poem does the speaker advance further toward a positive view of the fallen human condition?

3a. Describe the view of the Fall and its positive affirmative uses given by the poems in the final group. What does each poet think redeems experience? Which redemption seems most convincing, most honest, most realistic?

b. Many of these poems have to do with the relationship between parents and children (Dickey, Garrett, Miller). Explain why. Compare those poems which take the child's view with those which take the parents'.

c. How would the world be different if we agreed to call the "Fall" the "Rise"?

PART IX

Reading, Writing, and Projects

Reading

There are many other works of literature that can be usefully read in the light of topics and themes suggested in this volume. Many of them will have already occurred to the thoughtful reader. We will endeavor to present only a few of the more obvious ways in which the study of this text may be extended to other works.

The Encounter

Almost any work with a clearly defined villain, a stalwart enough Satanic figure, will give a good illustration of the dynamics of the confrontation of Good or Innocence, and Evil. Henry James's short novel, *Daisy Miller*, presents a conflict between Daisy's Innocence and New World charm, and the Old World traditions and Calvinism of Mrs. Walker and Mrs. Costello, with Winterbourne somewhere in the middle. James's *The Turn of the Screw* offers a more complex confrontation between the governess and Miles and Flora, with the question of who is Innocent and who is not somewhat more ambiguously presented.

Melville's *Billy Budd, Sailor* places the problem within a more social framework, and contains a number of interesting speculations about the origin and nature of Innocence (Billy) and the Satanic character (John Claggart). In this novel, socialized man (Vere) must choose between the two sides. Finally, the confrontation is perhaps as deftly portrayed by Shakespeare in *Othello* as anywhere. The play can be seen as the attempt by the cynical and corrupt, and therefore Satanic, Iago to destroy the Innocence of Othello by converting his belief in love (faith in Desdemona's fidelity) to doubt, thereby destroying his entire sense of the moral order of the universe.

Childhood and Growth

Any number of novels about young men coming of age can be used to trace the process through which the accumulation of experience affects growth.

Charles Dickens's *David Copperfield* and *Great Expectations* both give a moving view of how youth gathers experience, and William Golding's novels, particularly *Lord of the Flies, The Inheritors, The Spire,* and *Free Fall,* trace the same theme with Golding's characteristic intelligence and inventiveness. Although the novels are different in setting and circumstances, each is concerned with disillusionment and its cost.

The Fall is very important in the work of Robert Penn Warren, as has already been noted. Perhaps his best work, and one of the best novels specifically modeled on this myth, is *All the King's Men,* which is full of precipitous descents by Ann Stanton, Jack Burden, Willie Stark, and others. The problem of how one lives with knowledge is solved by Willie Stark in an instant, but leads to a four-year struggle for Jack Burden. *The Cave, Flood,* and *World Enough and Time* also deal with the theme of the Fall.

The themes of Time, Love, Change, and Death generate almost all of the emotional energy of Dylan Thomas's verse. Consider, for example, *A Refusal to Mourn the Death by Fire of a Child in London, Poem in October, In the White Giant's Thigh, Ballad of the Long-Legged Bait,* and *Poem on His Birthday.*

Innocence and Experience are also reflected in the novels of John Fowles: *The Collector, The Magus,* and *The French Lieutenant's Woman.* Similarly, J. D. Salinger's small body of writing has been narrowly concerned with the perils of sensitivity and talent in a world of harshness and hostility: *Catcher in the Rye, Franny and Zooey, Nine Stories,* and *Seymour: An Introduction.*

An interesting study in contemporary autobiographies can be made by comparing Frank Conroy's *Stop-Time,* Willie Morris's *North Toward Home,* Norman Podhoretz's *Making It,* James Baldwin's *Go Tell It on the Mountain, The Autobiography of Malcolm X,* and Ralph Ellison's *The Invisible Man.*

Mythology

One consequence of the 18th century's elegant literary sophistication was a very cultivated interest in simplicity, rusticity, and primitivism. The most devastating confrontation of innocence and the cruel world is perhaps Voltaire's *Candide;* but Samuel Johnson's *Rasselas* is nearly its equal and is perhaps more sensible. A variety of 18th century poets who lived in the city wrote poems about how much they admired the simple country—the most famous example being Thomas Gray's *Elegy in a Country Churchyard.* Gray's *Ode on the Death of a Favourite Cat, Drowned in a Tub of Gold Fishes* is another Fall poem. For a modern version of pre-18th century innocence abroad, see John Barth's novel *The Sot Weed Factor.*

The spiritual crisis, or dark night of the soul, when all values come in question, is a favorite topic of 19th century writers. One can begin with Coleridge's *The Rime of the Ancient Mariner,* and follow that with Goethe's *The Sorrows of Young Werther,* John Stuart Mill's *Autobiography,* Thomas Carlyle's *Sartor Resartus,* and in a more difficult vein, Matthew Arnold's *Empedocles on Etna* and Tennyson's *In Memoriam.*

American fiction of the 19th century seems at times to deal with little else but the Adam figure trudging into the wilderness, or the New England Puritan struggling with the burden of his Old World sense of Sin. James Fenimore Cooper's frontier represents the American sense of a new Eden discovered, as do the historical accounts of Francis Parkman (*The Oregon Trail, History of the Conspiracy of Pontiac*); Henry David Thoreau found a kind of Edenic frontier a few miles west of Concord at Walden Pond. A number of excellent critical works cover this ground in interesting detail: R. W. B. Lewis's *The American Adam*, Leslie Fiedler's, *Love and Death in the American Novel*, Ihab Hassan's *Radical Innocence: Studies in the Contemporary American Novel*, Leo Marx's *The Machine in the Garden*, and Henry Nash Smith's *Virgin Land*.

The Faust story, too, can be studied in connection with the Myth of the Fall. See Christopher Marlowe's *Dr. Faustus*, Goethe's *Faust*, John Hersey's *Too Far to Walk*, and Thomas Mann's *Dr. Faustus*.

Sociology and Psychology: Modern Theories of the Fall

A great body of writing that is derived from Freud and the psycho-analytic movement, and, like the passages from Erikson and Fraiberg above, is concerned with questions of growth and change. Erikson's books *Childhood and Society, Youth: Identity and Crisis*, and *Young Man Luther* are extensions of his ideas that stages of growth are vital determinants of adult conditions. Robert Coles's *Childhood in Crisis*, Herbert Kohl's *Teaching the Unteachable*, Jonathan Kozol's *Death at an Early Age*, Paul Goodman's *Growing Up Absurd*, and most of the work of Edgar Friedenberg, particularly *The Vanishing Adolescent*, have to do with the difficulties of growing up in contemporary America.

Writing and Projects

1. Can one protect oneself from the injurious effects of the Fall? Can one protect others? Can parents protect a child? How? Should they do so? Does a child need to be protected from Innocence as well? Describe a home or an educational system (a school or college) that offers the young proper Fall Experiences.
2. Construct your own mythology, story, or autobiography, giving a dramatic setting and illustration to the psychological forces in the encounter between Innocence and Experience.
3. Recount an illustrative myth from your own life of your own encounter between Innocence and Experience. Remember that it need not be true in the historical sense, only in the mythical sense.
4. Why is nudity no problem to the Innocent, while the Fallen Adam and Eve require fig leaves? What is the difference between innocent and non-innocent forms of self-display? and forms of display which lack innocence? Divide costumes and styles of dress into those that are innocent and those that are not. What does nudity have to do with innocence anyway?
5. Discuss aspects of the behavior of small children which you would consider innocent. What makes the same behavior innocent in a child and not so in an adult? If there is such a thing as childish innocence, is there also such a thing as adult innocence? Are all children innocent? Are some never so? When does a child lose his innocence? Can you tell whether he has or not? What are the indicators of the presence or absence of Innocence? Do the same indicators apply in the case of an adult? Make a list of test questions which would serve as an Innocence Index.
6. Construct a situation in which Innocence is safe and impervious to Evil, and temptations are perfectly resisted. Under what circumstances is Innocence safe and untouchable?
7. What are some of the stereotypical appearances, forms, habits, or types of Innocence and Evil in popular fiction, folklore, films, and television?
8. Consider the question of Taking Advantage of the Innocent. Why is such a situation especially evil? Describe the state of mind of someone who was been taken advantage of. What happens in the mind of the Advantage Taker? Discuss practical jokes, tricks, and teasing. What sort of person likes practical jokes? On whom are they best played? Under what circumstances? Play a practical joke on someone and ask him to explain how it felt. Then explain how it felt to play the joke.

9. Work out a series of dramas in which participants take roles illustrating the Fall Experience. Suggested situations: the seat of a parked car on a date; a used car dealer; a drug pusher and his friends; a politician and his backers; a policeman and a traffic violator.

10. Consider the feeling of Guilt. Is it a desirable, constructive condition, or is it destructive and bad? Is it solely one or the other? What circumstances affect this quality? What sort of person is most liable to Guilt? Under what circumstances does one feel it most severely? What should one do to avoid Guilt? Does Guilt always involve a relationship with a parent or with an authority figure, or can one feel guilty all by oneself?

11. Think up a way of exerting authority over others without implying that disobedience is either suspected or possible.

12. Give some beneficial and some destructive ways a parent can deal with Evil ideas in a child.